Under the Tropic

UNDER
THE TROPIC

Tom Hopkinson

Hutchinson

London Melbourne Sydney Auckland Johannesburg

To Dorothy
Mirror of Truth

Hutchinson & Co. (Publishers) Ltd

An imprint of the Hutchinson Publishing Group

17–21 Conway Street, London W1P 6JD

Hutchinson Publishing Group (Australia) Pty Ltd
P.O. Box 496, 16–22 Church Street, Hawthorne, Melbourne,
Victoria 3122

Hutchinson Group (NZ) Ltd
32–34 View Road, PO Box 40-086, Glenfield, Auckland 10

Hutchinson Group (SA) Pty Ltd
PO Box 337, Bergvlei 2012, South Africa

First published 1984
© Tom Hopkinson 1984

Set in Linotron Bembo by Input Typesetting Ltd, London

Printed and bound in Great Britain by Anchor Brendon Ltd,
Tiptree, Essex

British Library Cataloguing in Publication Data
Hopkinson, Sir Tom
 Under the Tropic.
 1. Hopkinson, Sir Tom   2. Journalists—
 Great Britain—Biography
 I. Title
 070'.92'4   PN5123.H6

ISBN 0 09 156190 6

'Under the tropic is our language spoke'

Edmund Waller 1606–87

Contents

Foreword

In *Of This Our Time*, published in 1982, I set down some impressions of my life from my birth in 1905 to the peak of whatever success I have enjoyed, which was principally during the ten years from 1940 to 1950 when I was editing *Picture Post*. From this job I was removed in October 1950, at about which time the present book begins. Its title relates to the nine years my wife and I spent in Africa, at a moment when the giant was breaking free from his colonial chains, and countries were becoming independent almost as fast as the blooms of the night-flowering cactus opened out in our garden outside Nairobi when darkness fell.

To supplement memory I have relied mainly on the note-books I have kept ever since I grew up – not, unfortunately, by including everything I should wish to recall half a century later, but on the principle of recording whatever impressed me at the moment. This I did regardless of its apparent unimportance or lack of news value. The result is capricious, seemingly trivial events being set out in detail, while upheavals which made headlines across the world receive scanty mention or slide by unnoticed.

This highly personal record has been supplemented by newspaper cuttings I had sense enough to keep or have been able to refer to since; by articles I wrote, during our time in Africa, for various publications, British and American; and from my book *In the Fiery Continent*, published by Gollancz in 1962, from which they have kindly permitted me to quote.

13

That was a lengthy book, and in the interests of brevity two or three incidents have been shortened or brought closer together in time.

Some fraction of all I owe to Dorothy, my wife, will be evident from the following chapters. Once again I thank Phyllis Jones for her prompt and accurate typing.

1
Settling Down

In the early summer of 1952 I settled down with Dorothy
Kingsmill, whose husband Hugh Kingsmill, the author, had
died three years earlier. Our home was the upper part of a
Georgian house in Stanhope Place, a backwater in the angle
made by the Edgware and Bayswater Roads. Though only
a stone's throw from the hubbub of Marble Arch, the little
street was blessedly quiet. Hyde Park, where I took a daily
walk, was at the lower end, visible from the curved windows
of our living room, and the garden of Connaught Square
was at the other. From our back windows we looked out
on to an enclosed convent garden, where the nuns came out
each day for a brief spell of chatter and recreation and to
play with a white cat. We knew when it was twelve o'clock
by the babel of shrill voices, dying suddenly away into
silence when their time was up. In Stanhope Place we were
close enough to theatres and cinemas to be able to walk
home after the show. In Connaught Street and some of the
little streets on the far side of the Edgware Road, a few shops
remained that were old-fashioned both in appearance and in
courtesy: a family butcher, a chemist, a picture framer in
whose folders of unframed prints and watercolours I could
rummage for treasures, finding, amongst others, a Row-
landson drawing entitled *Two Ladies in a Tavern*.

During our first year together, encouraged by Dorothy, I
wrote two books. The first was a short book or pamphlet
on George Orwell, commissioned by the British Council for

their series *Writers and their Work*. This came out in the summer of 1953 and received, according to the British Council report, 'more critical notice than any in the series, the overwhelming majority being favourable'.

The second book, which appeared at almost the same time, was called *Love's Apprentice*, a far longer work in which I had invested much time and effort, and for which I had correspondingly high hopes. Its theme, the sex war, was one I had been turning over in my mind since early in the Second World War when, living on my own in London throughout the week and wishing to read something not connected with the troubles of our time, I started on Samuel Richardson. Determined to find out what it was in *Clarissa* that had so impressed his contemporaries, I set myself to read its four volumes through without missing a sentence. Having swallowed my fill of Richardson's slipshod moralizing and armchair religiosity, I put the last volume down thanking God there was no fifth or sixth – only to find my mind continually returning to its theme almost against my wish. Finally, having tried unsuccessfully to become involved in other novels, I came back to *Clarissa* with the intention of reading it through again, marking passages and making notes in order to understand why a book which contains so much that is silly and ill contrived had once exercised so powerful a hold.

The result was a long article, 'Robert Lovelace; the Romantic Cad', which Cyril Connolly published in *Horizon*.* From Richardson I had been led on to read again Choderlos de Laclos's *Les Liaisons Dangereuses*, Maupassant's *Bel Ami*, Meredith's *The Egoist* and a string of other works in which different aspects of the sex conflict are exposed or exploited. Ideas buzzed in my head. I made notes, extracted passages and flung together a first draft. The draft – with the *Horizon* essay, which had attracted some attention – was sufficient to interest a publisher and I began to write.

For a time I was elated and all seemed to be going well.

*Horizon, August 1944., pp. 80–104

But part way through my task I lost the thread of ideas which alone could carry such a mélange of material, and realized, after painful self-examination, that I had not the erudition, the command of languages, nor the variety of experience for what I was attempting. But too much had already been invested in the project, so that, instead of putting it aside or leaving it to someone better qualified, I ploughed on like an alligator in a pit of wet cement.

When it appeared, the attitude of the critics ranged over a wide spectrum. Peter Quennell in the *Daily Mail* called it 'a gallant failure', which was generous. Jill Craigie in *Tribune* described it as 'a psychological frolic', adding that 'its gaiety belies the seriousness of its message'. Maurice Richardson in the *Observer* said it was an 'eminently moral and most instructive treatise'. And the Irish government, through its Censorship of Publications Board, placed it on the banned list. At the time I was deeply disappointed by this reception, but consider now that it was perfectly just. Most authors regret the books they never wrote. For myself I regret no unwritten books, though a few unwritten stories. But two or three which *were* written I should be happy to recall, paying if necessary the appropriate fine.

For my Orwell book I had been paid an outright fee of fifty pounds and, though it would continue to be republished over the next decades, it brought in no royalties. For *Love's Apprentice* I probably received two or three times as much. I had also written three or four short stories which appeared in various magazines, and in addition during 1953 made a series of five programmes for the BBC on 'The Life of a Riverside Borough'. All in all, I could feel that I had done a full year's work. However, when Dorothy and I looked at the amount it brought in compared to how much was going out, it was evident that we were still travelling back-wards. I had heavy responsibilities, having been married twice before, so that when in the late summer of 1954 a regular job was offered for the first time since I was sacked from *Picture Post*, I was happy to take it up. A voice from the management side of the *News Chronicle* had invited me to lunch and its owner proved to be Frank Waters, a man of about the same age as myself, but tall, handsome and a Scottish rugby international. A reconstruction of the paper was on foot, he explained; a new editor, Michael Curtis, a former leader writer, was about to take over and a great effort was going to be made to recover the paper's position and prestige. He asked if I would take on the job of features editor.

From the first I felt doubtful about the offer. The *News Chronicle* had been going downhill for too long; successive efforts to arrest its decline had met with no success, and privately I considered the paper more likely to go under during the next five years than to sail through into calm weather. However, I liked Waters and, when I met Curtis, liked him too. He had youth, energy, confidence and, I thought, the evenness of temper he was certainly going to need. I was also tired of the hazardous nature of a freelance life, and so, having talked the suggestion over with Dorothy, agreed to take the job on for two years. But before I could join the paper in early autumn, Waters was killed in a car accident. Besides being a tragedy for his family and friends, I could not help regarding this as ominous for my own association with the *News Chronicle*, and possibly for the paper itself to which he had devoted his energy and interest.

Over the next two years I did my best in the job and, working for the first time in my life on the staff of a daily, learned a lot about newspaper routine which would prove useful later. But I had joined the *News Chronicle* too late in its career. Many of my colleagues had worked on it most of their active life and some had never worked anywhere else. Though I liked almost all, I never became one of them, inhibited by the fact that, not only had I not shared their past but felt very doubtful whether there was going to be a future.

Essentially the *News Chronicle* was trying to be a paper of similar type to the *Daily Express* and *Daily Mail*, but with far fewer staff and smaller resources. Though differing from its rivals in political and social opinions, it did not differ

18

from them in its basic idea of what a newspaper should be, and it lacked a certain professional flair which gave those papers liveliness, dash and the element of surprise. As a result we were like a destroyer fighting a battleship, constantly outmanoeuvred and outgunned. At home and abroad our competitors covered events more thoroughly and more entertainingly than we did. The only salvation I could imagine for the paper would lie in its becoming something totally different – not a destroyer but a submarine. However to effect such a transformation would have demanded an imaginative gamble on the part of the management for which they were, I thought, far from being either ready or equipped. So I resolved to see my time out and resign.

From my two years on the paper I made in my notebooks only one brief entry referring to the office. This referred to our news editor telling us in conference: 'Leslie Henson has had two heart attacks, and is flying back from abroad. He says he's quite well and will be starting work immediately. . . . I've had his "obit" rewritten and brought up to date.'

Ian Low, a colleague in the features department, was the only one to whom I ever spoke about what, I thought, might be done to give the *News Chronicle* a fresh lease of life, and for years after leaving the paper I would receive an occasional postcard from him, couched in nautical terms.

The *NC* is now driving along under bare poles – the barest of which is X [a senior colleague]. All hands are at the pumps, but most are pumping water in instead of out.

Or:

The *NC* has now entered the Iceberg Zone. Officers and passengers (of which we have many) are feasting in the saloon, undeterred by an occasional white-faced stoker rushing up from the engine room to fling himself into the sea.

But long before receiving these messages I had gone overboard myself, thinking it better to take my chance in the ocean of Fleet Street on my own rather than wait till it was full of other desperate strugglers. In the event the *News*

Chronicle kept afloat rather longer than I had expected and did not finally go under until 1960, four years after I had left it in the autumn of 1956. During 1957 which would be – though I did not know it – my last year of freelancing, Dorothy and I were supported by my writing an unsigned book on an industrial subject and by a stint of reviewing novels for the *Observer*, at which I worked far too slowly for it to be profitable. In the course of that year, however, several events took place, seemingly quite disconnected, which changed altogether the pattern and direction of our life.

The chief of these was my father's death. He was now about eighty and for the past seven or eight years, ever since he had retired from his post as curate to my brother Stephan at his parish in Battersea, he and my mother had been living in a small house on the outskirts of Kendal found for them by my eldest brother Jack, head of a firm of solicitors in the town. Early that year, in reply to some letter of mine proposing to put off a visit which was already long overdue, Jack had written: 'If you want to see father as you have always known him, you had better come at once.' Jack was not given to exaggeration, and I took his advice.

After supper with my father and mother, the three of us sat by the fire in the little room that had become my father's study and contained those few treasured pieces of his which had been familiar to me all my life – a sepia reproduction of a Raphael *Madonna and Child*; two photographs of the Parthenon, in one of which, when small, we had detected what we took to be a ghost lurking in the shadows; one or two porcelain lustre jars given him by the Pilkington firm when he had helped them over some problem of classical design half a century before; his earthenware tobacco jar with the screw lid; and the china rhinoceros whose horn had been smashed off in some nursery accident in our infancy and never successfully restored. The walls were lined with books, but the room was too small to contain his library of classical and religious works and many I had known were missing. I looked in vain for the handsome texts in half calf with TOM. I, TOM. II, and TOM. III on the spines, containing, I had imagined when I first learned to read, a record of my own behaviour.

As we sat there, my mother was attempting to knit as she had done almost every evening since I could remember, but successive operations for cataract had now made this nearly impossible and before long she put down her work and went into the kitchen to wash up. My father, who was wearing a vague, distracted look and sitting idly – something I could scarcely remember ever having witnessed – now rose and went over to a bookshelf. He drew out a large volume of photographs brought back from his two-year stay in Athens at the turn of the century, and began showing me the pictures as he had done when I was eight or nine years old. 'This is the old paved road leading down from Athens to the Piraeus. . . . That's the approach to Delphi through the olive groves. As you come round this corner you get your first glimpse of the temple. . . . Oh, and that, of course, is the Hermes of Praxiteles with the baby on his arm. . . . And this, and this. . . .' His voice faltered and died away.

He was showing me a landscape with a road in the foreground and a distant view over the plains towards the sea. It may have been Marathon, but my father was seeing something that was not in the picture. . . . 'Here is the head,' he said, pointing to some trees, 'and that's the torso,' and he put his finger on the road. A shadow crossed his face. He saw, or half saw, that the photograph and his description did not tally. Shutting the book with childish anger, he pushed it away and we sat on in silence.

Next morning I returned to London. Some weeks later my brothers Jack and Stephan drove father to a large hospital outside Manchester, and when I came back to Kendal again it was for his memorial service. Afterwards my mother, who was now going to live in London at the headquarters of the religious order in which my sister was a nun, told me to take any books of father's that I wanted. I took Gibbon's seven-volume *Decline and Fall of the Roman Empire* and two or three others, but when she urged me to take some clothes

21

and shoes of his, I refused. I knew I ought to take them, since she was giving up their home and wanted to dispose of everything she could. I should indeed have taken them – if only to dump them or hand them to the Salvation Army – but I could not bring myself to do so.

Other, lesser ties were cut for me in May when *Picture Post*, which had been for twelve years part of my life, came to an end. In recent years it had staggered on despite falling circulation, loss of advertising and a succession of editorial crises, but this was now the finish. Its rival, *Illustrated*, had been struggling too, but it was generally expected that, revitalized by absorbing some of the readership and advertising its rival had enjoyed, it would take on a fresh lease of life. Instead, like a dray-horse lost without its old companion, *Illustrated* too gave up the ghost. The age of the picture magazine, in Britain as in most of Europe and before long in America, was at an end.

Since leaving *Picture Post* seven years earlier, in 1950, I had now tried my hand at writing books, reviewing, and working on the staff of a daily newspaper. I had also made radio programmes, and acquired some months of television experience as one of two 'journalistic advisers' to the Independent Television programme *This Week*, the other being Bill Hardcastle, a former *Daily Mail* editor, who was always a great deal sharper and more 'clued up' than I was. But out of all this variety of experience I had been unable to find any satisfying niche or purpose in life. Inwardly restless and dissatisfied, I was far from being an agreeable companion for Dorothy. Even on our holidays – spent usually in Normandy or Brittany, parts of France which we both particularly liked – I was always thinking about work or involved in some writing project. If these projects had involved writing for its own sake, as with the few short stories I produced, Dorothy could have been happy and felt the time well spent, but too often they were intended to retrieve our fortunes or secure some toehold of literary reputation. Introvert by nature and tending to be morose, I was brought out of myself by what I looked on as success, whereas failure

– and lack of visible success for me amounted to failure – drove me inwards. Having little capacity to share, I kept even my disappointments to myself. I did not sound off or complain; I just disappeared from sight, so that Dorothy must often have wondered who or what it was that she had married, and whether he still existed somewhere inside that shell.

My father's death and the collapse of *Picture Post* had severed two links with my past life, but a link of great importance to me in the present was also now temporarily broken. In settling down with Dorothy I had put an end to my marriage with Gerti Deutsch, a Viennese musician and photographer to whom I had been married since 1938. Our relationship had been a hollow one for some years before its formal ending, and the focus of my emotional life had been my two young daughters, Nicolette and Amanda. Since settling down with Dorothy I had struggled, with her support and cooperation, to preserve normal contact with the children. Six years, however, had now passed, and still all kinds of difficulties and objections were being made to any except brief, almost official, meetings with them. Finally I concluded that if after all this time my former wife and I were still engaged in a tug-of-war over our daughters, it would be better for them if I let go the rope, kept in touch by letter, and remained in the background till times were easier or they became old enough to make decisions for themselves. My daughter Lyndall, whose mother was Antonia White, my first wife, was already grown up and living on her own in Rome, and Dorothy's daughter, 'young Dorothy', who had been living with us at Stanhope Place, was now almost ready to embark on her career.

Taken together, these various happenings might seem to indicate approaching change, and a fourth indication – which was not an event but a dream – could have been seen as pointing out the direction this change would take. The dream, which came in August, impressed me so much that I wrote it down fully when I woke. I did not feel as if I had been dreaming nor as though I had experienced any kind of

23

vision; what I saw was as clear and sharp as though I had been looking through a window at the scene before me, except that it carried an impression of immense antiquity, belonging to an age before windows were invented.

What I am looking at is a rocky tower, a colossal pile shaping up from a broad base into a cone, round whose rough flanks, spiralling down, runs a road or track. The tower is of a sandy colour, dark against the brightness of the sky and lighter where it nears the base, and the track is pale with dust. Descending this track is a horde of crocodiles, those at the base enormous and those at the top seemingly small as toys. Many have their jaws open and are snapping around as they slither down the incline. What they are snapping at are the vultures which hover in clouds to swoop and perch upon their backs. The crocodiles and the vultures are at war. The crocodiles, when they reach the end of the sloping track, disappear as though falling into an enormous pit and attempt to carry some of the vultures with them to destruction. I have the sense, though I do not actually see it happen, that a few of the crocodiles even try to fling themselves off the tower so as to catch and destroy the enemies swooping in or clinging to them.

The whole scene is in movement and reminds me, when I wake up, of some medieval woodcut or engraving come to life, depicting an imagined war in the heart of Africa, such as that described by Herodotus as taking place every year on the southern borders of Egypt between the defending storks and invading hordes of serpents. Oddly enough I had had no thoughts, nor read any books about such creatures throughout the weeks before I experienced this dream, but in the few days following it I received for review two novels, in one of which vultures,* and in the other crocodiles,† played an important role.

It was 3 November when I got back to London from my father's memorial service in Kendal, and the next morning

---

*The Animal Game, by Frank Tuohy, Macmillan, 1957.
†Equator, by John Lodwick, Heinemann, 1957.

I had to go down by an early train to Bristol where I had promised to give a talk. As I ran out of the house to find a taxi, I crammed into my pocket the few letters addressed to me, but later, reading them in the train, found nothing of much interest. The same evening, on arriving home, I passed them over to Dorothy. Among them was an airmail letter.

> *Drum*, 'Africa's Leading Magazine'
> 176 Main Street
> Johannesburg
> 30 October 1957

Dear Tom,

Thank you for your letter of 12.10.57 which I have just received on my return from East Africa. I regret you have not been able to find an editor for me.

We are building here a really very fine and important instrument in *Drum* and the result of it is that it becomes very difficult to find a man of sufficient expertise to play it.

If we can play it right, and that demands of us considerable knowledge and discretion, we can do a great deal by the inhabitants of this continent. I know that you, Tom, possess eight* children and innumerable ties in London town. Would you not, however, consider seriously taking on this venture of ours for several years and see what you can do with it. For a great deal can be done once there is skill and understanding here.

Best wishes,
    Yours sincerely,
      Jim

This was not quite my first contact with Jim Bailey, whom I had met a couple of times in London, and following our meeting someone on the staff of *Drum* had taken to sending me each monthly issue for criticism and comment. I would do the best I could, hampered by having no idea of the conditions under which *Drum* was produced, what sort of staff it had, and whether my recommendations were possible with its resources. Though sympathetic to the idea of a black man's magazine in a country dominated by whites, I had no

---

*This was an overstatement. However, the combined families of Dorothy and myself did amount to eight, or almost.

25

more idea of going to live and work there than I had of walking across the Sahara barefoot. But here was my wife reading the letter as though she took its contents seriously, and, having read it, looking across at me.

'Well, what are you going to do about it?'

'Nothing at all, of course,' I replied, still confident the proposal would somehow go away.

But Dorothy acted as though she had not heard. 'What are you going to do about this one?'

'You don't mean that you'd consider giving up our home . . . and everything . . . and going out to South Africa? To live in that bloody country where everybody hates each other?'

'I will if you will,' Dorothy replied, and so the matter was decided.

Before readers find themselves in Africa, there is one other figure who must be brought into the picture. His name is Meher Baba. Persian by origin, he had been born and brought up in India but paid a number of visits to the West, and we had met him for the first time in August 1952, shortly after Dorothy and I settled down together. Unlike myself, Dorothy had from childhood been a conscious seeker after truth, and during the latter part of the war a strange sequence of events had brought her into touch with the one known to his followers in India and the West as 'Baba'. Though remaining in contact ever since, she had never met him, and his visit was her first opportunity to see him in the flesh. Baba and his little group of attendants were staying at the Rubens Hotel in Victoria, but personal interviews with those wishing to meet him were to be held in – of all improbable places – the Charing Cross Hotel.

We had to be there by eight o'clock, and it was a fine blowy morning as the bus carried us through the still half-empty streets – Dorothy, young Dorothy, aged eleven, and myself all sitting on top of the bus. Dorothy's concern over the coming meeting had communicated itself to us too, and we sat silent. In the corridor outside Baba's room a small crowd had already gathered, and, attempting as a journalist to form an impression of the followers this master had attracted, I remarked to myself that we seemed a pretty weird bunch. However there was little time for forming judgements before the door opened and someone called us in.

At the far corner of a large room, in the angle between wall and window, sat a man in white clothes, and from the moment I entered the room I had eyes only for him and for Dorothy. Two or three months earlier, while travelling across the United States, Baba had been involved in a severe car accident which he had foretold, it seemed, as far back as 1928. Besides facial injuries, he had suffered a broken arm and leg, and was now seated in an easy chair with his leg, either bandaged or in plaster, stretched out upon a stool. There were seven or eight Indians in the room standing against the wall in shadow, and two more immediately behind Baba whom I guessed must be his interpreters or 'voices' since almost the only thing I knew about him at this time was that he never spoke and had kept silence since 1925. Baba gave a hand to each of us and we sat down, Dorothy in a chair a little distance away on his right, myself close to his outstretched foot, and young Dorothy facing him.

Baba looked at Dorothy with an encouraging smile, but she – struck dumb at finding herself after so long in his presence – could not bring out a single word. Resting on Baba's arm was a small black alphabet board with white letters. He did not point to individual letters – his fingers flickered across the board and one of the interpreters at his elbow inquired in a low voice, 'Why do you not speak?'

With an enormous effort Dorothy managed to bring out the words . . . 'I c–c–can't speak, Baba.'

Baba smiled. His hand flickered over the board again and the voice remarked, 'Neither do I speak.'

This put Dorothy more at ease and she managed to get out, 'But Baba, *you* don't speak because you don't want to speak. . . . I don't speak because I *can't* speak.'

During this exchange and the talk which followed I was

watching Baba closely. I had the impression that the words he used were less important than the contact established by his presence. He looked at Dorothy and young Dorothy too with deep intensity, and twice said, 'I will help you.'

Physically Baba was of medium height, looking frail after his accident and slow recovery. A mass of black hair stood out around a face paler than I had anticipated. A thick moustache obscured his mouth of which I could see little more than a thin, wavy line. All his movements were made with elegance, grace and absolute authority. As he 'talked' and listened, his face lit up or darkened with a continual change of expression which made every other face look wooden. Most striking were his eyes which were dark and clear with what seemed like many different focuses. . . . He seems able, I was thinking, to hood them, unhood them, veil them again, open them wide in order to see deeper. . . . 'A benevolent and infinitely wise snake,' I was mentally recording in my notebook, 'the serpent of old Nile, or at any rate old Ganges.'

But my reflections were cut short. Baba had turned to me and the voice was asking, 'Well, why have *you* come here?'

Shaken out of my journalist's detachment, I replied with the first thought that entered my head: 'I only wanted to see you.'

The words were feeble and sounded so. But Baba's hand shot up as though to welcome some profound response. Then he looked into my eyes and asked as a child might have done, 'And do you *like* me?'

This apparently naive inquiry went into my heart like an arrow, and I found myself struggling to bring out the words, 'I love you, Baba.' But after tense seconds, the inhibitions of fifty years gained the day and I said only, 'Yes, Baba, I like you.'

'And I like you,' he answered, and put a hand up to my face.

After we got outside – for Baba spent longer talking to young Dorothy than to either of us – Dorothy asked me, 'Well, and what do you think of Baba?'

'For fifteen years,' I said, 'I've been meeting so-called important people – politicians, heads of state, scientists, writers, painters . . . and I never came away from seeing one without asking myself, "Is *that* all there is to being great and famous?" '

'Well – and this time?'

'This time was beyond my reach. Nothing at all like that has ever happened to me in my life.'

We had met Baba once again, in July 1956, and again he was staying with his small group in the Rubens Hotel. I was working all day at the *News Chronicle*, but Dorothy spent most of her time in his company and listening to him. On the day he was leaving I worked till the last moment in my office. The traffic was heavy between Fleet Street and the airport and I arrived only shortly before the plane was due to leave. The airport was still under construction and I drove wildly round seeking a parking place, but the only empty spaces were marked 'General Manager', 'Traffic Manager', and so on. Instead of seizing one of these and arguing after- wards, I weakly continued to search for a permitted slot. By the time I had parked the car and dashed over to the temporary buildings, Baba and his men were already cros- sing from the departure lounge to join their plane. Stepping over the barrier I started to run towards them, but security men – fearful of the packet of drugs or diamonds I might hand over to the AVATAR – quickly prevented me. All I got was a glance from Baba. It was the last time I should see him in that form, and the last time he would ever visit Britain.

2

First Days at *Drum*

Once I had agreed to take on the job at *Drum*, Jim Bailey was anxious to get me out to Johannesburg at once. Dorothy and I decided therefore that I should fly out as soon as possible, which was late January 1958, and that she would follow later by sea. This left her with all the work of disposing of our flat and winding up our home. Young Dorothy, who had been at a theatre school for a year or two, went to live for a time with my brother Stephan, his wife Anne and their large family in St Andrew Street, almost under the shadow of St Paul's where he was now a canon. We planned to take with us the furniture and pictures we particularly liked, and to sell or give away what we could not take. True, the furniture would get knocked about and my favourite watercolours would fade, however carefully I might try to protect them from the African sunlight, but at least we should have them with us to enjoy. Also, if we took our treasures along we would be more likely to settle down and make the best of what we found, whereas if we retained the nucleus of a home in England we might find ourselves looking over our shoulders and wondering whether, after all, we would not be better off where we came from.

I flew out by way of Rome and Tripoli, Kano and Lagos to Accra, where I spent my first week in Africa. Then I returned to Lagos, trying in Ghana and Nigeria to get to know *Drum*'s staff, form some idea of their needs and capacities, and begin to reorganize our chaotic West African edition. But my true destination was Johannesburg, where I arrived early one morning after a long and tedious flight.

Johannesburg is a city of well over a million people, but spread over a wide area so that the million includes whites living in the rich suburbs to the north, where almost every house has a large garden, tennis court, swimming pool – or pools – and staff of black servants and gardeners. But it also takes in the locations to the south and east, roughly covered by the name Soweto, where the African families swarm in endless rows of two- and three-room boxes. The actual heart of the city was at this time tiny and one could walk across it either way in a quarter of an hour.

The gaunt building which housed the *Drum* offices stood at the extreme edge of this central part of the city, in a district where the skyscrapers dwindled down into a shambles of small factories, arid waste patches, and the half bare, half built-over lots of second-hand car dealers, displaying their unconvincing clichés in both Afrikaans and English – '*Uitge-soekte Gevruikte Karre*', 'Quality Used Cars'. Southwards, across a couple of streets and a dusty stretch used as a car park, was the Native Affairs Department for the City of Johannesburg, its name changed by a masterpiece of official tact to the Non-European Affairs Department. Outside this building there was always a queue of Africans hoping for passes, permits to remain, houses to live in; and it was hardly possible to walk from the car park to the office without being asked: 'Any job for a boy, baas? Any job for a good boy, my baas?'

The *Drum* offices, on the first floor, consisted of about a dozen glass-partitioned rooms. Blue-painted pillars carried a low whitewashed ceiling. The linoleum on the floors was new, but so thin that it showed heelmarks the first time one walked across it. Ours was not much of a place, but in one respect it was, in that city, almost unique, for within these walls there was no apartheid – no separate entrances for blacks and no separate lifts (this was easy because there was no lift at all). Blacks and whites sat side by side, made use of the same washbasins and lavatories and drank out of the same teacups – whereas elsewhere the teacups for whites and blacks were kept rigorously separate. How extraordinary our communal living truly was I did not yet realize, for this was my first morning in the office and I was spending it trying to get to know and memorize my staff. It should not be too difficult, I thought. There were after all very few of them, and I had been reading and re-reading their work in old issues of *Drum* ever since I had known I would be coming out here.

Daniel Canadoce Themba, my assistant editor, known as 'Can', was a tall, lightly built African in his early thirties. He walked with a jaunty step and wore a bright red shirt. A small knitted cap, perched to one side of a cannonball head, gave him a knowing look. Between his lips was a pin which he switched from side to side with his tongue as we talked, and the flow of words poured out of him in a torrent.

'Cripes, chief! Am I glad to meet you! I remember all the letters you used to write us from England. I never thought we should see you out here. Welcome to South Africa, chief! What d'you want us to do now?'

I suggested he should call the journalists together and get the day's work started while I went round to talk to the photographers, look in on the darkroom and have a word with our proprietor, Jim Bailey. Later we could all have a conference together.

'Okay, chief. But what do you want us to get working on?'

'Whatever stories you have in hand. I suppose you make out a list each month, don't you? You've got various ideas half finished, and others you're planning to do later. Just pick the ones it's easiest to complete, and get everyone started on something.'

Can mopped his forehead thoughtfully. When at all agitated, sweat poured down his face as though he were under a shower.

'What system are you working on now?' I asked. 'How d'you get the month's work organized?'

'Well. . . .' Can answered, switching his pin. 'We've really been waiting for you to come out, to see what system you prefer. At present we all just go out from day to day according to the news.'

'What were you going to do this morning?'

'Have a look through the papers, chief, and see what's cooking.'

'Good,' I said. 'And let me know by lunchtime what everyone is working on.'

Casey Motsisi, a frail figure with the face of a worldly-wise choirboy, was in charge of our library, but since almost no library existed and Casey evidently did, I had already resolved to move him somewhere else where his talents would be more effective. That he had talent was plain, since he wrote as he saw and not in some made-up journalistic language. I had marked his account of a children's party: 'It starts an hour late and there are so many kids around I can't even count them. Only they are on the outside goggling in. Inside the house there are only adults making merry and long-winded speeches. The only kid around is Teaspoon in whose honour the party is being held. Teaspoon is crying his little head off and I don't blame him. . . .' And his glimpse into a police station – which I had not yet seen but with which I would soon become all too familiar – included these words: 'A few more guys, including the old geezer who's wearing an outfit that looks like a hand-me-down from Noah, were then charged.' No magazine, I thought, can afford to leave someone who writes like that in the library, especially a library as bare as ours.

Our second reporter, Butch, had not been with *Drum* long. Big and burly, he was a friend of Can and, like him, had been a student at the University College of Fort Hare and later, also like Can, a schoolmaster – schoolteaching being about the only occupation open at this time to an educated African.

Our junior reporter, Nat Nakasa, was nearly as short and slight as Casey. He had a lively look and quick response and, though he could hardly be more than twenty-one, had already gathered some years' experience as a newsman.

33

Though the others tended to shut Nat up as being too young to know anything of life, he was, I would discover, a patient investigator who could press his inquiries uncomfortably close to the one being interviewed, whether African gangster or white official. He also had a sense of balance, and I soon learned that when he told me something I could depend on what he said. The key to Nat's lifestyle, which was a lot quieter than that of his colleagues, lay in his being the eldest of his family, so that every month a large part of his slender salary, instead of being spent in the normal way on girls, booze, and the high life of the townships, went to educate and clothe his young brothers and sisters.

In the darkroom I found our only African photographer, Peter Magubane. Peter was sturdy and thickset with an open face and determination in every line. He had a habit of wrinkling up his brows when talking, as if all speech were a matter demanding concentration. At twenty-six he was one of the older ones, having made his way up by way of being, first, a driver, then a darkroom assistant. Peter was fond of good clothes, and always drove an old American convertible. African cameramen were not popular with the South African police, and his big car marked him out for the attentions of gangsters in the townships, so that in his three years as a *Drum* photographer Peter had already survived more rough handling than many professional fighters take in a career. He would no doubt have met with much more trouble, but for the fact that he did not drink; just how rare and precious a quality this was among African journalists I did not yet know, but I would find out before long.

Apart from a few freelances and hangers-on, the last of the African staff was our office boy, Sidney Andrews, an office boy approaching middle age with a family dependent on him. Very different from the others in appearance, he had a jet black skin, protruding lips, and that timid fearfulness of manner which invites the tiger's claws or the policeman's club. Sidney's life and mine would be mixed up far more closely than either of us guessed when I told him that he was to forsake his desk for an hour or two later on and attend the office conference with the rest.

That 'rest' took in the whites, Jurgen Schadeberg and Joe Blumberg. Jurgen was a fresh-faced young man with a friendly manner. He had not yet quite lost his German accent but had acquired a wide knowledge of cameras, photographic processes and equipment. He had also an eye for a good picture, and was ready to spend hours helping Peter and the occasional African freelance who would drift in from time to time with sets of pictures. Joe Blumberg was our chief – indeed at this time our only – sub-editor, and it was his patience, even temper, and knowledge of what it was possible or not possible to print under South African conditions which provided much of the cement that had so far held the magazine together.

Also present, but soon to vanish, was a likable young South African journalist, Humphrey Tyler, who had served as editor for the past six months and with whom I now had a somewhat foreboding chat.

'Had you had much to do with picture magazines before?' I asked.

'Not a single ruddy thing,' Tyler replied cheerfully, 'though I'd worked for a bit in the *Drum* office in Durban. I guess they just couldn't find anyone else.'

'I think you've kept it going very well.'

'Thanks. All the same, it's been hell. Pure bloody HELL! Thank God you've come out. It'll be your baby now,' he added with satisfaction.

'What's been the trouble?'

'*Trouble*? The lot! Printing. The staff. The bloody West African edition – don't know what they want and always complaining when they get it. And of course the management. I could have coped all right if I were left alone – though just to keep things ticking over with the staff we've got is one hell of a job. Trying to do it with one hand and fend off proprietors with the other is too much. However, it shouldn't be so bad for you,' he added reassuringly. 'You know photography. I suppose you know what you want, and you'll have the authority to get your own way.'

'Maybe,' I said doubtfully. 'My worry is not knowing the country. Being new, I won't know which way I want to go – or whether it's possible or safe to go that way. Thank God you're here! I shall rely on you a lot.'

'For a while,' Humphrey hedged uncomfortably, 'for as long as I'm around.'

'How d'you mean "for a while"? You're not *leaving*, are you?'

'Yes. I pack up at the end of this month. I'm going to the *Rand Daily Mail*.'

'In a fortnight? But how do I pick up the routine, get to know the staff and so on?'

'There's a couple of weeks yet,' said Humphrey philo-sophically. 'You'll get the hang of things all right in that time. At least I hope you will.'

Though I had an office to myself, its 'walls' were glass partitions and the door always open, so that we lived a communal life which allowed few secrets.

It was now half past nine on a Monday morning a week or two after my arrival, and Can had just come in. He still had on his red shirt but must have lost his knitted cap because what he was wearing on his head was an old brown sock. Can's morning entries were dramatic. He would come in with his sliding, catlike walk, head forward, eyes sparkling with excitement. He addressed himself to Casey, but in a minute or two everyone had stopped work to listen; clerks and drivers from the circulation department were leaning across the barrier which separated their office from ours, and one or two of the reporters from our sister publication *Golden City Post* would have drifted over to join them.

'Jeefies, Casey,' Can began, his high-pitched voice half lost in an explosion of laughter. 'Jeefies, man! You ought to have been there last night. What a night, man! What a night! Everyone was shouting for their little Casey. You remember that big girl we met the other night in Orlando? She was jumping mad, ready to swallow you up alive. "Where's that Casey-man?" she kept saying. "Where's that honey-man Casey? What you all done with my man Casey?" And what were *you* doing while the girls were all hungering after you? Prowling around at home, feeling married!'

Casey smiled. 'Some of you boys never grow up. But where was this party anyway?'

'The nurses' home. That new nurses' home the other side of Diepkloof. We were christening it, man, *christening* it. I've never seen so much hooch in any one nurses' home – even the matron was pughead. Oh what a time for the evil-doer! Half those patients must have perished by this morning, man. I swear they have! Rows of patients all passed out in their beds – one lot will have died because the nurses never attended to them, and the other lot because they did. Jeepers! I could do with a bit of attending to myself this morning. . . . I think I shall just . . . very quietly. . . .'

Through the open door I called out, 'Can!'

He danced in, beaming. 'Morning, chief. What can I do for you?'

He leaned over me and it was like the opening of a furnace door. That must indeed have been a party.

'How's the work going, Can? What stories are you all on for the next issue?'

'Hang on a sec, chief. . . . I'll just make one or two inquiries and then rough you out a list.'

By the evening the only ones still in the office were Joe Blumberg patiently subbing some half completed pages, Nat Nakasa writing up an interview, and myself going through all the pictures Peter had been taking during the past week. I would have liked to believe that the others were hard at work on the stories assigned to them at our morning conference, but by now I knew it was much more likely that they were in one or other of the shebeens,* such as the Tall Trees

---

*A shebeen was an illegal drinking den for Africans, who were at this time only allowed to drink so called 'Kaffir beer' in official compounds provided for them in the townships.

or the Classic. The Classic was the favourite with our staff, it was tucked away, almost invisible, behind a dry cleaner's and most of them kept a package that looked like dry cleaning always on hand. This they would hand in at the front of the shop and slip through to the back where they would alternate bottles of beer with shots of a sweetish South African brandy, known from its colour as 'mahog', while their credit lasted. As they left they would pick up their dry cleaning package, and bring it back again the next day. Everyone in South Africa was paid monthly and everyone lived on credit and settled up, or tried to, at the month's end.

Nat had finished his work, but before leaving paused at Joe's desk for a word. I knew what the subject was likely to be, for the passion of Joe's life was jazz. Mysterious figures were to be seen hanging around his desk, bringing furtive packets out from beneath their coats – the latest pressings, straight from the factory back door. Either he must have a special warehouse for his record collection, I thought, or else he just drops them down a grating on his way home, for he was always too good-natured to refuse to buy. Joe's long, sad face concealed a sharp sense of humour. He would not be put upon by management but was endlessly patient with the rest of us, by whom his good nature was constantly exploited.

'What about coming to a jazz party this weekend, Joe?' Nat was asking.

'Good! Where at?' Joe answered eagerly.

'Your place,' answered Nat. 'We're always well looked after there.'

I too before long had finished my work. Until Dorothy came out and we could look for a home I was living in a hotel not far away run by Indians, which – after trying two or three white hotels – I found comfortable and cheap. It was dark when I left the office and I had to pick my way carefully. Most of the paving stones were broken and a couple of manhole covers were missing – stolen for some purpose or other and never replaced.

'Won't someone fall into that after dark and break a leg?' I had asked naively when I first came out.

'If you stick around here after dark you'll get worse than broken legs,' was the reply. I had already stuck around for a few evenings, however, and met little except the dark and silence. Coming out now on to the patch of waste ground, which at lunchtime had been packed with cars, I could dimly make out the shape of a solitary car, the ancient Ford lent me by Jim Bailey 'till you can get transport of your own'. As I came closer I could see that the bonnet had been prised up and two Africans were just taking out the battery. When I shouted at them they ran off, leaving an old jacket and the tools with which they had been unfastening the connections.

I threw the jacket on the ground for them to pick up later, but kept the tools for my trouble – and in the general interest of the motoring community.

3

Demon Alcohol

It was again a Monday morning and I came into the office in good spirits at 8.30, the hour we were all due to begin work. My first edition of *Drum* had been safely put to bed, and the editions for Ghana and Nigeria – we were bringing out a separate edition for each territory for the first time – were with the printer.

All our editions were printed in Johannesburg and those for West Africa went down by train to Cape Town and then on up the coast to Lagos and Accra. This was a slow process since there were no longer regular sailings and the copies had to be put on to whatever ship would take them. Sometimes a ship would be held up outside the port for days or weeks, and after the copies landed it took several days to distribute them round the country by 'mammy-wagon' – the name given to lorries in West Africa where most of the transport was in the hands of wealthy women traders or 'market mammies'. Since the magazine took so long to reach its destination, the issue we had just put to press in February had been dated May. But at least, I told myself, the first month's work had been done on time and we should start next month with a clean sheet. We should also reap the benefit of the system I had agreed with Can – a number of stories completed by the reporters under his direction during the last two weeks, while Joe and I had been hammering out our West African editions. However, there was no one around as I walked through the main office, and still no one around at nine o'clock.

I called to the secretary, 'Where are the letters?'

'I don't know.' She looked up despondently from her knitting. 'They haven't been brought round yet.'

'Well, go and look for them! We can get them answered before the rest turn up.'

Wearily she laid her knitting on her typewriter and went off, but was back in a minute or two, triumphant. 'There *isn't* any post this morning.'

'But there must be *some*.'

'No, there isn't. They haven't been to fetch it from the post office.'

'Whyever not?'

'Patrick's away ill.'

'But if Patrick is sick, does that mean that the whole office gets no post?'

'Yes.'

By ten o'clock there was still no one in the office except myself, Jurgen Schadeberg and Joe Blumberg. Jurgen was reading the paper with his feet up on the desk, a casual attitude which always drew a critical glance from Jim Bailey on his way through to the lavatory. Joe, incapable of idling, was sorting out readers' letters, 'pen pals' photographs, inquiries from the lovesick and the other bits and pieces which filled up odd corners in the magazine.

At half past ten Butch rolled up, red-eyed, bleary and unshaven.

'Where the hell *is* everyone, Butch?' I asked irritably. 'We've got to get started today on the new issue.'

Butch knuckled his bloodshot eyes and looked round as though expecting that one or two members of the staff, invisible at the moment, might reveal themselves.

'Casey's not in,' he observed, 'and Nat's not in. Can's not in either, Mr Hopkinson.' Butch always used my name each time he spoke to me. 'Perhaps they'll all be turning up just a little bit late this morning, Mr Hopkinson.'

'All out on the piss,' Jurgen suggested, turning the page

41

of his *Rand Daily Mail.* 'Probably won't see any of them at all today. Nor tomorrow either.'

'But I fixed with Can on Saturday to have a meeting first thing this morning to get everything moving for the next issue.'

Jurgen smiled and turned over to the sports page, and Joe went on busily sorting letters.

'Butch,' I asked, 'd'you know where everybody lives? Can, Bob, Casey – and the rest?'

'Yes, Mr Hopkinson. I think I know.'

'Okay then, we're going out to bring them in. And you come too, Jurgen. Joe – if anyone rings, say I'll be back at lunchtime.'

'All right,' said Joe. 'I'll tell them you've passed out in a shebeen. What about Bailey? Supposing the big boss wants you?'

'Tell him I'm seeking his lost sheep.'

We drove first to Sophiatown, then the African 'Latin Quarter' where most of our staff were still managing to find some corner to live, though the district was in process of being turned into a 'white' area. We sat, all three of us, side by side on the front seat of my car. It puzzled me that, as we drove through the battered streets, avoiding potholes, swerving past lumps of concrete, straying children and skinny dogs, Butch kept leaning out of his window, smiling at passers by as if we were on a royal tour, and bellowing 'Hi, Samson!', 'Hi there, Wilson!' or 'Hey, man!' to anyone he knew.

Jurgen noticed my surprise and whispered, 'Butch is afraid his buddies'll think he's with two cops. He's shouting to show he's just driving around with friends.'

'Do we look like cops?'

'In the townships all white men look like cops.'

We went first to Can's house – round to the back where we hammered on the door. At last a face appeared at the window and a girl let us in. Can, lying across rather than in bed, was in a sleep from which no shakings or shoutings could recall him. Once his eyes rolled up, and it seemed that the dying man might recover consciousness, but a second later he had slid back into the pit.

'It's no good,' said Jurgen. 'You could pull the house down round him and he wouldn't wake.'

We left word with the girl to say who we were, and that Can should be told to come into the office as soon as he could be told anything at all. We called next at the house of Bob Gosani, a photographer who worked for us as a free-lance. His young wife and baby helped our efforts, and before long he was apologetically on his feet – but it was clear he would not look through any viewfinders or click any shutters today. His wife began making him some tea.

'What about Casey?' I asked.

'Oh, Casey lives a long way off, Mr Hopkinson. A *very* long way off. D'you want to go and look for Casey too?'

But it was already half past one and I'd had enough of trying to collect my staff.

Butch saw my hesitation. 'Would you like a drink, Mr Hopkinson, before we go back?' he suggested. When I agreed heartily, he took us to the home of a girlfriend who, he said, was a 'part-time amateur shebeen queen'. The part-time queen proved to be a large, good-natured brown girl, with a pleasant voice and dignified manner. The room into which she led us was neat and well-furnished; she pulled a curtain over the bed alcove, and drew chairs for us to a table in the window. Leaning out over the sill, she called to a child playing in the road, whom she sent to bring a half bottle of gin and some beers. As fast as we drank Butch kept filling up the glasses, and our hostess, mellowing, turned her attention to Jurgen. His youth and good looks obviously interested her but, being thoroughly married, Jurgen was unresponsive and the hot afternoon sun had in any case made him drowsy – which annoyed her. After half an hour of chat I looked across at Butch to say it was time to move, but Butch's face was no longer where I had last seen it. He was lying full-length along the window seat, out cold.

Our hostess looked at him with disgust. 'That *Butch*!'

To my surprise, however, I found I was looking at Butch

43

with a new sympathy. He lay there in the window, legs apart and mouth wide open, at peace with himself and all mankind. His habitual nervous, guilty expression was all smoothed away; the doubts about his competence which forced him to say 'Mr Hopkinson' appealingly with every sentence had all vanished. Butch drunk was clearly a lot happier – and for himself at least much better company – than Butch in possession of his senses.

'You can leave him here if you want,' said the part-time queen, but she didn't seem anxious to keep him so we agreed to take the body along to Bob's house and drop it there. Bob's gentle, kindly wife would make him tea when he woke up, and most of our staff – I had begun to realize – could stay indiscriminately in one another's homes in times of need. Before carrying Butch out, Jurgen and I shook hands with our hostess, thanked her for entertaining us and asked to be allowed to pay for the drink. She waved our offer aside, saying we were her guests and could certainly not be allowed to pay. By the time Jurgen and I got back to the office and sent out for sandwiches and tea, the day was gone and the place almost empty. The sole achievement of my ill-tempered expedition was that the one member of our staff who had been partly sober when we started out was now more drunk than the rest.

Thinking all this over in the evening, I had what I thought was a good idea for coping with our staff's drink problem. I put it to them at our next conference.

'Look,' I said, 'what you do in your own time is your concern. But what you do when you're on the job concerns us all. I'm determined that between us we're going to make a first-rate magazine, but we can only make a good magazine with a staff that stays sober while at work. From now on we're going to have new regulations about drink. From today, anyone who gets drunk on a job or in office hours will be sent home for one week without pay. Anyone who's drunk on a job or in office hours a second time gets sent home without pay for a month. Anyone who does it a third time has had it. He's out! . . . There's no discrimination about this!' I added. 'It applies to whites as much as to blacks. If anything, it's milder than you'd find in Fleet Street or the States. I hope none of us is going to be sent home – even for one week. But from now on those are the rules.'

Everyone nodded and looked solemn as though forming resolutions of sobriety. But within a couple of weeks Butch was found incapable in the office one night after the rest of us had gone home. The white who found him reported the matter to the management, adding that Butch had pissed all down the corridor, a point I thought the informer might have kept to himself.

'What a bloody fool you are, Butch,' I said to him next morning. 'Why can't you keep clear of the office when you're drunk? If you hadn't come back here, nobody need have known anything about this. Is it true that you pissed outside Mr Pierce's room?' I was tempted to add that if he were going to piss anywhere, that was a good place to have chosen. But the matter was too serious for fooling.

Butch hung his head and looked downcast. 'I can't *remember* doing anything bad, Mr Hopkinson.'

'Were you sober enough to remember if you *did* do anything bad?'

'No, Mr Hopkinson.'

Before any worse fate could befall him I ordered Butch to go home payless for a week, warning him that his journalistic life now hung by a thread. Then I told the general manager – a new man named Weatherstone recently appointed by Jim Bailey – what I had done. To my surprise, instead of calling for worse punishment on Butch, he said; 'But you can't sack Molotse in any case.' (Molotse was Butch's official name.)

'I certainly don't want to sack him, but why can't I, if he keeps on getting drunk?'

'He owes the firm thirty pounds. He's paying back five pounds a month. You mustn't sack him till he's paid his debt off.'

'God Almighty!' I objected. 'If a chap causes trouble or is inefficient, surely it's better to get rid of him and lose thirty quid than have him hanging about the place when he isn't wanted and receiving far more than thirty quid in pay?'

'I must keep order in the books,' Weatherstone explained severely. 'Jim Bailey has instructed me that there are to be no more office loans – except in the most special circumstances. And if there *are* loans, they've got to be repaid in full by the due time. Molotse had this loan before I took over – how am I going to explain to Jim Bailey, if he clears off owing thirty quid? No – if you want to sack the man, sack him – but *not* till he's settled up his loan.'

I went out relieved so far as Butch was concerned, but also scratching my head. The way to survive, I thought, was to get the largest possible loan out of the firm and fix the slowest possible rate of repayment. Then, when any part of the loan got worked off, you should think up a powerful excuse for borrowing more.

If drink was part of my staff's problem, they had others, in particular the insecurity and harassment to which they were continually subjected, and the fact that they lived on the edge of penury, with little or no provision against the common setbacks of daily life. Joe Blumberg happened to be away for a couple of days, and I was busy trying to make up a page of readers' letters one Saturday. I enjoyed doing this, but would become so absorbed trying to visualize the writers and their circumstances that I would forget to make up the page.

Magalie St
Lady Selborne
Pretoria

Greeting to you Mr *Drum*

I am one of the girls who read *Drum* every month and I am not satisfied to see other girls on the covers. And please Mr *Drum* help me to be a cover girl too and I will pray God to help me be a cover girl and one thing is this Mr *Drum* I am the Kit who does not have Father and Mother and I am suffering about Mr Wrong. I can't get Mr Right. I wish one of our readers could help me to get Mr Right because I don't want to be Miss Monareng for ever no marriage.

Christine Monareng, Amen

Letters from West Africa were always recognizable by their high-flown language and lofty tone.

from Mr Clement Adeboh Jones
12 Ajayi St
Ebute Metta
Lagos

The Editor
African Drum Publications Ltd
Johannesburg City
Southern Rhodesia [sic]

Sir,

Though I have got it in mind to be contributing to the editions of your monthly Journal some important and interesting stories, but circumstances has seized the gateway of that during the past period.

Now, I wish to be doing so, and I hope you will assist me as per my request. The first one for trial, I enclose herein for you to treat as necessitated.

I remain to be, Yours sincerely
Clement Adeboh Jones

While busy on letters and some layouts, I became irritably aware of a slight figure hovering by the door. I avoided looking up, hoping he would go away, but he stayed on, and I now saw that it was the office boy, Sidney, holding out some kind of printed form.

'Well? What is it?'

'This was my trouble, sir.'

The odd phrase struck me. However, I knew Sidney had come in late that morning and supposed what he was holding was a doctor's certificate. I was just going to say, 'Oh, hell – don't bother me with that now,' when I saw there were tears in his eyes. I took the form from him. It was a death certificate. I went over and closed the door, and pulled a chair up for him.

'It's another one, sir. Another child dead.'

'How did this happen, Sidney? Had she been ill for long?'

The certificate showed that the child was a girl just under two years old.

'No, sir. It was only since last Wednesday. On Wednesday she brought up a small worm, so I took her to the doctor. He told me to bring her back again on Monday – the day after tomorrow. Only she died, sir, in the night. Last night. He was very surprised himself to hear that she was dead.'

'Had the doctor seen the child since Wednesday?'

'No. I wasn't told to bring her back till Monday.'

I looked at the certificate again. Cause of death was given as 'bronchial pneumonia'. No one would ask in the case of Sidney's daughter when the doctor had last seen her, what treatment – if any – he had prescribed, nor indeed anything about the matter.

'I've had so much trouble,' Sidney burst out, the tears now pouring down his cheeks. 'It's been *so* hard. Five deaths in my family, one after the other, and three I've had to pay for. . . . I don't like troubling you, sir, but I'll have to ask can the firm lend me some money?'

'How much d'you need?'

'Seven pounds, sir. I've been to the undertaker, and now I'll have to go to the office that gives burial certificates.'

'We'll send you in the car.'

'It's too late, sir. The office closes at eleven on Saturdays' – I looked at my watch: it was eleven already – 'that means I can't get a certificate till Monday. . . . And now there's this hot weather come,' he added distractedly.

I must have looked uncomprehending because he added, 'We can't have the funeral now till Tuesday. . . . Because of the hot weather we must find somewhere to put the body.'

'Can't the undertaker fix that? Hasn't he a special place?'

'Yes he has, sir. Only they charge for it. . . .'

I arranged with the firm about the money and told Sidney to take Monday and Tuesday off. Three days later he was back at work, but fate, it seemed, had not finished with him.

It was again a Saturday morning, some three or four weeks after the earlier one. We were all just preparing to go home when we heard sudden shouting in the street and we ran to the windows.

'It's a pass raid,' someone shouted.

'No it isn't, it's a shebeen raid. They've been raiding Tree Tops.'

The photographers snatched their cameras and we dashed down into the street. A mixed selection of humanity was already bundled into two police vehicles, squat metal cages on low wheels. Eight or ten 'flat boys' – household cleaners recognizable by their undignified uniform of dark blue vests and sloppy, knee-length shorts; a dozen labourers in ragged clothing; three or four well-dressed Africans in suits and ties; and a couple of hard-case whites.

These last were known as 'mailers', purveyors of liquor which at this time the Africans were not allowed to buy themselves. Mailers would buy drink, chiefly brandy and beer, at liquor stores and turn it over to the shebeen queens who would either pay them or give them free drinks in return. After a few years all mailers looked alike – red-faced, sandy-haired, filthy. They trembled, their eyes refused to focus. They kept shaking their heads and blinking as though somewhere below the surface they were still hoping to understand what was happening to them. Degraded, some-times brutal but more often childish, there was about them something deeply touching, as though they were uttering through inflamed and broken lips: 'Don't hate us. We're human too – if only we could get at it.'

Directing the raid were two white plain-clothes cops, a tall thin one and another little more than a boy with the face of a debauched cherub. Under the strain of heckling from the bystanders they were getting rattled. I nodded to Peter and another cameraman to clear off. Shebeen raids were nothing new, and if the cops started pulling in bystanders the photographers would be the first they'd pick on.

At this moment I caught sight of Sidney. He had been helping in the darkroom and now, conspicuous in a long white coat, was rashly jeering at the raiders. I was about to order him indoors when he was seized by another cop – one we hadn't spotted because he was an Indian – who twisted his white coat and shirt into a tight knot so that there seemed nothing left of Sidney's narrow chest and skinny neck. From

49

his wild eye and splutter of protest I saw what was going to happen.

'Keep quiet, Sidney!' I called out, trying to get to him through the crowd.

Too late. With a push and a twist he tried feebly to escape. In a flash the Indian pinned Sidney's arms behind his back and he was thrust into the cage with the rest.

'What's this for? Where are you taking him?' I called. None of the cops took the least notice. The Indian made a further captive, and the thin white ordered the driver to get going. Running to the front, I put my hand on the arm of one of the cops.

'That boy in the white coat works for me. Where are you taking him?'

'Police headquarters.'

'On what charge?'

'Assault.'

Inside the crowded cage men were clinging to each other for support as the vehicle lurched off, but I managed to catch Sidney's eye.

'See you in five minutes.'

Back in the office I found Nat. 'Let Sidney's wife know he's pinched. It may take me a bit of time to hook him out.' I ran to get my car and go down to police headquarters where I drove straight in behind the police vans and parked. Inside the place the prisoners were disappearing down a corridor, so I followed and stood near a doorway. Before long someone would be sure to ask what I was doing there and I'd enlist his help. So it happened; another plain-clothes cop in a sports coat and suede shoes approached me and I told my story.

'That's okay. That lot was drinking in a shebeen. Only names and addresses taken, and a fine.'

'No,' said the thin cop, who saw me talking to the other. '*His* boy's booked for assault.'

'Pity,' said the first one, walking off. 'Or you could have taken him back right away.'

'We've got to sort 'em out,' the thin one told me. 'It'll take us an hour. Come back then.'

'How shall I find you?'

'Ask in the charge office. They'll know.'

I was back again after an hour. A sergeant ran his eye down the book. No Sidney Andrews. I must be mistaken. As a last resort he told me to call in at the CID, Room X.

Packed into Room X were the occupants of the vans, in attitudes of apathy and dejection. At a table facing them were the two cops who had carried out the raid.

'We're just coming to your case,' said the thin one, beckoning me over. He told the Indian to bring a chair for me, and I sat down as though making a third at the tribunal. The baby-faced cop was laboriously filling in a long official form, asking Sidney questions in Afrikaans to which he replied in the same language. I sat silent till we came to 'Charge'. This I guessed was the crucial moment, since once the charge was filled in the case must go forward to the magistrate.

The thin cop described the assault, adding that Sidney was carrying no reference book or 'pass'.

'That's true,' I broke in. 'But he had it in his jacket, and could have got it in a moment. He just happened to run out in his white coat. As for the assault – well, he *did* start to wriggle about when he was seized, but. . . .'

'Is this your native?' the short cop cut in sharply.

I nodded.

At once he began to shout at Sidney, bellowing as if on a parade ground, trying to make Sidney admit that he'd fought back and hit out at his arrester. I thought, 'I've got to let him shout a bit, but if he shouts too much Sidney will shout back. Then it's all up.'

Under the storm Sidney began to tremble and his eye slewed round like a horse that's about to kick.

I leaned across. 'May I just say a word or two?' I asked.

The shouter grunted and hesitated, but let me speak.

'Look,' I said. 'It's true this chap ought to have had his pass, but he left it in his coat when he ran into the street. And it's true he wriggled around when your man seized hold

51

of him. But he *didn't hit the detective*. I was there all the time
– so were a dozen people from my office. If there's a charge
of assault my firm will defend it and I shall go and see the
lawyer straight away. But does there *have* to be a charge?
The fact is he's a nervous chap – quickly gets excited and
upset. Especially if he's frightened.'

I could feel Sidney flash me an angry look.

'He was trying to show off,' asserted the short cop. 'That's
his trouble – trying to show off in front of other Kaffirs. I
know his type – make a row to show how brave he is when
he feels safe among a crowd.'

'No doubt that happens,' I agreed. 'But there's something
else as well. Sidney's had a lot of trouble lately. Only last
month he had his pay packet pinched by gangsters. He's had
other troubles too. I know he shouldn't have struggled, but
it was a natural thing to do.' I caught a sympathetic glance
from the thin detective.

'Look,' I said, 'I don't know if it's in your power to show
leniency. But if it *is* in your power to be lenient, I think this
is a case for it.'

The two policemen looked at one another. The first passed
the grey form over to the second and they studied it for a
while. At last the thin one spoke.

'It's up to the detective who pulled him in. He's the only
one can withdraw the charge. If he likes to withdraw, it's
withdrawn. Otherwise it goes on.'

He called the Indian detective over, and after a moment's
talk, declared, 'If he' – nodding at Sidney – 'will apologize
to the detective, the detective will withdraw his charge.'

I conferred for a moment with Sidney.

'Apologize?' he muttered angrily. 'What *for*?'

'Look,' I said, getting exasperated myself. 'Either you
apologize or you spend the weekend inside. Take your
choice.'

'But why?'

Time was running away fast. I turned to the detective.
'He says he is very sorry.'

'He has to say so himself.'

52

For a moment it all hung in the balance, then Sidney swallowed and brought it out, not looking at the Indian. His two words – 'I'm sorry' – sounded more like defiance than regret. However, I didn't wait. Thanking the two detectives and the Indian, I led Sidney off. The crowd from the shebeen looked enviously at us as we walked rapidly through. I couldn't wait to get safely outside.

In the car I could feel Sidney's troubled eye on me, his lip once more a-tremble: 'Sir, I *wasn't* really sorry. You shouldn't have said I was.'

I switched the engine off and started to climb out. 'Okay, then, back we go!'

Sidney paused for a second in bewilderment, then his face relaxed into a huge smile. 'I'm not sorry I tried to hit that cop. But I'm not sorry I'm outside either,' he admitted.

When I asked Sidney where he wanted to be dropped he said he must go back to the office to pick up his pass – 'Otherwise I may get pinched on the way home, and then you'll have to do this all over again.'

Sidney ran off to collect his pass, but at the top of the office stairs I stopped. Over to the right, on a table used for sorting out entries for competitions and letters from the lovelorn, someone was lying. I thought it could be one of the office staff, passed out, and had just time to hope it was someone from *Golden City Post*, not *Drum*, when I saw he was half naked.

I went over to the table. A youth was lying there face downwards. There was blood on his head and arms, blood on the table, smears on the blotting paper and the wall, blood dripping to the floor. His shirt had been removed and a dirty face flannel laid over the knife wounds in his back from which most of the blood was flowing. The back of his khaki shorts was also soaked in blood as though he had been stabbed in the behind as well. I remembered that at the big hospital at Baragwanath there is a special ward with more than eighty cases of Africans paralysed from the waist down, victims of gangsters who have planted their knives or sharpened knitting needles with delicate skill between the vertebrae. But this didn't look like delicate skill, more like amateur bungling. Being Saturday afternoon there was no one around the offices, but I hung about until after a while two reporters from *Golden City Post* drifted in.

'Who is he?' I asked.

'No idea! We found him staggering about outside the office.'

'How'd he get like this?'

'Been to bioscope,' (cinema), they told me.

'The bioscope?'

Patiently they explained. There were always stabbings in the bioscope. This kid was probably a *tsotsi*.★ He'd gone there with someone else's girl and then either the chap himself or others in his gang had caught sight of the couple – so naturally they stabbed him. 'After all,' they ended up, 'it *is* Saturday afternoon.'

'So what's going to happen to him now? Can't we take him along to hospital? I've got my car here.'

'That's all right,' they assured me. 'We've phoned the ambulance. It's on its rounds, but when it comes down this way they say they'll pick him up.'

★Small-time gangster or tearaway.

4

Christmas in the Golden City

Towards the end of April I went down to Cape Town – a beautiful and dignified city with an atmosphere more relaxed and tolerant than that of the Transvaal. Dorothy was coming out by sea, and I had arranged to meet her and bring her back by train to Johannesburg. She arrived at a misty daybreak at the quayside where, in my eagerness to catch the first sight of her after our three months' separation, I had been waiting since four in the morning.

After our few days' holiday, we rented furnished rooms in a block of so called 'mansions', while Dorothy got to know the town and decide where she would like to make our home. We planned to take a flat and not a house because, with visits to West Africa and elsewhere, I might often be away for two weeks or more at a time. Houses in Johannesburg are continually being broken into – burglary insurance is many times what it is in most parts of the world – and I could not go away contentedly and leave her on her own. We needed a place big enough to house our furniture when it came out from England, and it had to be somewhere where we could entertain *Drum* staff without too many confrontations with our neighbours. Finally we found a flat on the seventh floor of a new block in Hillbrow, a suburb with a commanding view over the city. From here I could be at the *Drum* office in a quarter of an hour, and there was quick access to the main road leading out to the African suburbs for contact with my staff. Our neighbours too proved tolerant of the sight of Africans going in and out of our flat – at least to the extent of not sending for the police.

The law at this time was peculiar. Despite the provisions of apartheid, it was not illegal to entertain Africans in one's home, but it *was* illegal to offer them drink. In the whole of Johannesburg there were said to be no more than some fifteen homes in which the races were entertained on equal terms; my own impression was that there were actually a good many more, but even so the number was extremely small. And though in course of time we came to have a number of 'liberal' white friends, there were not more than two or three we could invite to our flat when black guests were present. Since the offer of drink brought risk to the hosts, this was the test by which African guests judged whether they were being treated equally or not, and the more they were given to drink, the more equally they felt they were being treated. This, of course, set problems when it came to getting our black guests – mainly members of *Drum* staff and their wives – safely out of the building in which they were not supposed to make use of the 'white' lifts. Most of our fellow tenants would say nothing provided guests left quietly, so that I would take them down two or three at a time, see them safely off the premises and go up for more.

At night the street door was guarded by a Zulu, a formidable figure with sergeant major moustaches and an armful of clubs and knobkerries. If burglars should break in, I used to think, it would take him so long to select the most suitable weapon that they would have been in and out again before he could make up his mind. Though ferocious in appearance he was mild enough in nature and – since I took care to slip him a few shillings every month – not anxious to make trouble. But if white tenants were around he felt it necessary to threaten any black man entering the building, shout at him and drive him off. In that case our visitor would usually walk round the block and then return, hoping the Zulu would by now be out of the way.

Once, when Can had been driven off in this way, he showed his enterprise by dodging round the back of the building and going up the fire escape, making for the seventh floor. But the doorman was suspicious, dodged round to the back too, saw Can and started to bawl him out. Can came down slowly a floor or two, put his finger to his lips and pointed to the top floor where the black house girls had their quarters.

'Hush, man! Don't spoil sport! The girls have asked me up' – and he made signs of his intentions.

The doorman laughed. 'My frien', you take any girl you wantin' – 'cept Charity. Charity *my* girl. Don' you go touchin' Charity.'

Can drew his finger across his throat in promise and came on up to the seventh floor.

By the time midwinter came – roughly the time of midsummer in England – we were beginning to feel truly settled in. Just at this moment came a cable telling me of my mother's death. Within a few months of going to live in the London convent which was the headquarters of the Community of the Resurrection, the order to which my sister Esther belonged, she had suffered a severe stroke, from which in the last months of her life she emerged only rarely for brief moments. In these she seemed always to be trying to utter the same words – an apology for the trouble she was causing. More than once I had heard my father say, as though it were a matter already decided, that he would be the first to go, implying that my mother would outlive him by a considerable time. He had indeed been the first to die, but when it came to living on her own, a few months were as long as she found bearable. By my father's instructions they were both to be buried in the graveyard at Burneside, the Westmorland village where he had been vicar during the 1920s when we children were growing up. No stone or marble gravestone was to be erected, only wooden crosses bearing their initials and dates with the words 'Per Ignem' (through the fire). Even the crosses were to be allowed to decay without being replaced. This provision we decided to disregard when the time came for replacement, and I imagine each of his five children must have pondered long and often over my father's choice of an inscription.

During the second half of the year I paid a visit to Ghana and Nigeria, where sales of the magazine in its new form were going well, and then before long came Christmas – our first Christmas in Africa. Early in the month we were given a hint of what this was going to mean.

'Mart,' Dorothy said to our servant Martha, 'I want you to take this skirt to the cleaners.'

'But you mustn't send nothing to the cleaners before Christmas, madam,' Martha answered with astonishment.

'Why ever not, Mart?'

'It'll only get stole.'

It was true that Christmas in South Africa, so far from being a season of peace and goodwill, released an annual wave of crime and accident in which hospitals made ready to receive a flood of casualties. Dry cleaners and bottle stores barricaded themselves against raids, and the police became even quicker than usual to hit first and ask questions afterwards. On *Drum* our staff also responded to Christmas in their own way. Dorothy and I were asleep one night when the phone rang.

'Is that Mr Hopkinson?'

'Yes. Who's that?' I answer angrily.

'It's me,' says a thin faraway voice. 'Me – Can.'

'Where are you, Can?'

'In the office.'

'God Almighty – what are you doing there?'

'I'm locked in. I must have gone to sleep.'

It isn't hard to guess what has happened. Can has gone out for a few drinks at Whitey's, Under the Heavens, or one of the other shebeens nearby. He's had a few drinks and not felt up to going home. So he has come back to the office, sat down automatically at his desk and fallen asleep. In locking up the place, the attendants haven't noticed him and now he can't get out.

I go downstairs and get the car. The streets are empty; it's been raining and a fresh breeze is blowing. It's only blowing off wet asphalt and puddles, but I feel as if it were blowing off a lake. Near the office the town is deserted. I run the car up on to the pavement so that the headlights shine against the gates. The outer gates open without difficulty, being fastened with a combination lock whose formula I happen to remember. But our *Drum* offices are on the first floor, up a separate staircase secured with plate glass doors for which I have no key. I can see Can's shadowy form gesticulating on the other side.

'Can't you get it open?' His moan comes faintly through the panes as though he were drowning in a glassy pool.

'The hell I can – I haven't any key!'

'Can't you go and get one?'

'Where from?'

'I don't know,' he says despairingly.

'Would Weatherstone have it?'

'He might.'

'D'you know where he lives?'

'No.'

We are stuck. I go outside and take a look up at the windows. Suddenly I notice that from the general manager's office one could jump out on to the flat porch which overhangs the main doorway. I go back and slowly shout the plan through the closed door to Can, and in a minute he's capering about on the porch above my head.

'Now – lower yourself down! Hang on by your hands, and then let go. I'll catch you.'

Can starts to lower himself over, but the distance evidently looks more frightening from above. 'Hell no, man! I'll never make it. It's too far. Can't you get a ladder or something?'

Round at the back of the building, up a narrow yard, I find the night watchman. He is roasting potatoes on a bucket full of holes, quite unaware that his building is being broken into by the main entrance. He is a Zulu, like ours at the flat, with a similar fierce moustache, pierced lobes into which bits of wood the size of dollars are inserted, and the usual collection of warlike sticks. I tell him the problem, and after searching about the yard he finds a ladder and brings it round to the front door. When he sees Can hopping about up on the porch he nearly falls into the road with laughing, but we get the ladder up and Can down, and Can manages to pick up a late-running taxi which saves me the run out to his home.

However we are not through Christmas yet, and a few days later my phone rings again. This time it's around midnight.

'Is that Mr Hopkinson?'

'Yes.'

'Who is that speaking?'

'It's me – Hopkinson.'

'Then why can't you say so when I ask?'

'Who's that?'

'I'm trying to tell you. . . .' A long pause. Then, faintly, 'It's me – Casey.'

'Where are you, Casey?'

'In Marshall Square.'*

'Good God! Are you in trouble?'

'Trouble? Who's talking about trouble? The thing is this, Mr Hopkinson – ' another long pause, then – 'they won't put me in the cells. This cop here won't put me in the cells. He just keeps telling me to go away.'

'Casey – you're pissed!'

'No – no! It's like this, Mr Hopkinson, I've had a drink. I will say I've had a drink. Not a lot – just a drink or two. . . . Are you *there*? I'm *talking* to you.'

'Yes. I'm listening, Casey. You've had a drink.'

'Just one or two little drinks. I don't want to go home when I'm like this – only cause trouble. Cause trouble . . . with my wife. So I've come along to Marshall Square. I said to the cops here – "Put me in the cells." That's what they're

---

*The police headquarters.

supposed to be for, isn't it? And these cops won't put me in
the cells – I've argued with them, but they won't.'

'What d'you want, Casey?'

'To go home,' irritably. 'That's what I want – to go *home*.'

'Okay. With you in twenty minutes.'

When I arrive at Marshall Square and go in by the 'Non-
European' entrance I find Casey sitting on a bench in a dimly
lit corridor. Never large, Casey, when cold, miserable and
in a bad temper, huddles into himself and looks like a sick
child. A white cop is watching him from his desk in a
bewildered way, as though knowing he ought to fling Casey
out on his ear but lacking the heart to do his obvious duty.
Not for the first time I ponder over a strange fact, that,
whoever gets knocked about or beaten up, it's never Casey
– though he often asks for it. I've been with him when he's
cheeked, even ridiculed a white cop to his face, but always
in so bland and innocent a manner, interspersing his sarcasms
with, 'Yes, baas', 'As you say, baas', that the cop has no
chance to lose his temper.

'Come on, Casey – let's go.' And to the cop I ask, 'It's
okay for him to come with me, isn't it?'

The cop shrugs and turns away. 'Do what you like. We
didn't pull him in. I don't know what in hell he's up to.'

Casey climbs into the front seat beside me. The drive out
to the township is a long one and I'm in no mood for light
chat. Casey appears to have fallen asleep, which is about the
best thing he can do, but after half an hour's driving I can
feel one eye fixed on me in the darkness. I take no notice,
hoping it will close.

'Mr Hopkinson.'

'Yes.'

'D'you know what that cop said to me? That cop you
were speaking to in Marshall Square?'

'No, of course I don't. How the hell should I know?'

'Well, he said, "If your boss comes out here at this time
of night and drives you home, then he's a bigger bloody
fool than I think he is!" '

I know what Casey is up to – he's preparing the story to

tell everyone tomorrow in the office. I know what I should do – stop the car and push him out, leaving him to walk the last five or six miles to his angry wife. But I can no more shove him into the road at this hour of the night than the cop in Marshall Square could lay into him with his truncheon. . . .

Christmas drinking goes on at all levels. Dorothy keeps a bottle of methylated spirits in the cleaning cupboard, but now she finds it disappearing.

'Mart, what are you doing with the methylated spirits?'

'*Me*, madam? Nothing,' she replies defensively.

'Well, it's going.'

'Tisn't me takes it, madam. It's Abraham. He carries it away in his little tin.'

Abraham is our flat boy. Blocks of flats provide certain services for tenants, such as polishing the parquet floors which are universal in Johannesburg, washing out the bathrooms, emptying rubbish and cleaning the *stoeps*, or balconies. Abraham – a lean, bearded African of about thirty, with a handsome face, humorous eye and an agreeably deep voice – is the flat boy for our own and three or four other flats on the same floor. We had often noticed his little boot polish tin, but had foolishly supposed it to hold some special cleaning preparation of which we – or our floors – were being given the benefit.

Now Abraham is missing for two days, so I go up on to the roof where the Africans have their quarters and inquire. Abraham, I learn, has been taken to hospital with bad pains in his stomach. If he isn't at work by Saturday, we decide, I shall go and visit him in hospital. On Friday morning, however, he is back again, his face a mauvish grey. Dorothy gives him some warm milk and a good talking to. At first he denies everything, but when she tells him not be so silly, that she knows all about it and that he must have suffered agonies with his stomach, Abraham hangs his head and says he is sorry. Dorothy says that she doesn't mind about the methylated, but has he learned his lesson and will he lay off drinking poison in the future? Otherwise he'll rot his insides and suffer very much worse. Abraham says he *thinks* he'll know better in future, and the methylated stops disappearing.

A day or two later Martha says, 'Madam, the boys upstairs is different now.'

'How are they different, Mart?'

'Abraham's told them what madam said. They don't drink that methylated no more. They know it isn't good for their insides.'

'Oh,' says Dorothy, *'that's* a good thing.'

'What they're drinking now,' Martha informs her, 'is benzine, and they always mix that with a little milk.'

Christmas is over, but there's still the New Year to face. On New Year's Eve, feeling tired, Dorothy and I agree to go to bed early and forget about seeing New Year in. But towards midnight we are woken by a deep vibrating hum. We go out on the balcony. It's a brilliant starry night, with the moon lighting up the silvery and brassy edges of the clouds, though out of sight itself behind the towering blocks of flats. All the lights are on in all the blocks and many people are either on their balconies or at their windows. The whole city seems to be one gigantic party.

From our seventh floor we look down into the street. Up and down it range bands of Africans, many of them flat boys and girls, but also others who have come in from the townships. Many wear fancy dress and some of the men are dressed as women. They roam up and down, shouting, forming into groups and separating aimlessly. They are in a special African state, neither drunk nor drugged but far from sober, a state of trance-like elation in which each one is lost in a private world but yet, like fishes, they are impelled to shoal together.

At crossroads and street corners they are jiving, but each has his or her own rhythm and the musicians who wander in and out of the crowd are playing for themselves without coordination. A few guitarists lean, strumming, against lamp

standards or doorways; squeeze-box players thread a determined way in stride with their own music. But the deafening
noise, which deepens as midnight nears, comes from more
primitive instruments. Dozens of small boys dodge in and
out, rattling cans filled with pebbles, blowing piercingly on
whistles. One youth scrapes the surface of the road with a
piece of metal the size of a large book, sending showers of
sparks and producing a penetrating screech like the death cry
of a tormented tram.

The whites, no soberer than the Africans, are all in cars.
With horns blaring they force their way through the throng,
some trying to avoid the jiving groups, others pressing close
to make them leap out of the way. Immediately beneath us
a car slews to a stop in a wild skid. An African gazes up
astonished, scrambles to his feet from almost underneath the
bumper, and vanishes into the crowd.

And now suddenly from a piece of vacant ground are fired
three maroons to signal midnight and the start of a new
year, and at this an uproar bursts out which makes everything hitherto seem like a whisper. Its undercurrent is a
tremendous drumming which rises up out of the ground and
roars through the streets above the people's heads. It carries
echoes of the drums of Congo and Nigeria, but this is harsh
and clanging instead of threatening and sullen, a noise of
metal, not of wood and skin. It is made by the women.
They have gathered round the lamp standards and are
hammering on them with stones and bits of iron.

The hammering rises to a throbbing peak, the youth with
the scraper scours the road madly, the children rattle their
tins and whistle, voices scream 'Happy! Happy! Ha-Ha-
Happy!', and the cars all sound their horns in one uplifted
wail as though the city were simultaneously being sacked
and celebrating some stupendous victory.

At last the noise weakens and dies down. And now as
rapidly as it poured in, the tide flows out. The whites on
the balconies vanish indoors to drink champagne and brandy
and hope for still more prosperity next year. The streets
begin to thin. The hooting cars have disappeared or lost their

voices. A police van drives up, and half a dozen African cops come spilling out. They take their stand on the corner of the crossroads, leaving their van – it's a *kwela-kwela* or pick-up cage – unattended in mid-street, its heavy metal doors swung loosely open. The cops make no arrests. On the contrary, one of them is soon drinking brandy from a bottle somebody has passed him. Another scrambles up into the back of the *kwela-kwela* with a house girl. But the mere presence of the hated van conveys a warning, and the crowd melts rapidly away. After ten minutes the cop lowers the giggling woman to the ground and his fellow cops climb in. Following noisy attempts to start the engine it coughs suddenly to life and the *kwela-kwela* rocks up the street, the doors, still open, clashing as it rounds the corner. The deserted streets are strewn with bottles, newspapers and rubbish, and the whole uneasy city hums and seethes as if fiery lava might burst up out of the ground at any moment.

Next morning among the letters on my desk is one from an African author who has asked me to read and criticize his work.

Dear Sir,
Please give bearer my MS. Thanks for having had a look at it.
I was hit with a hammer behind the ear Christmas Eve, that's why I can't come personally.
Yours,
Dugmore Boetie

5

A Little Peace and Quiet

The season of Christmas goodwill – at least in its drinking aspect – lasted a long time, and by the end of February the staff of *Drum* had taken on a new look. Can Themba, the assistant editor and a writer of talent, had run through his week and his month off without pay, and then gone absent for five days on a spree just when his help was needed most. I had been obliged to sack him as well as the hapless but likable Butch, and in their places had taken on two new reporters very different in character from their predecessors and from one another. Matthew Nkoana – tall, with a frail body, concave face and double-thick glasses – was full of expository fervour. From his manner of sitting with legs crossed, ceaseless cigarette smoking and high-pitched splutter when excited, he might have been an intellectual, probably a university lecturer, of any country. His driving force was political passion and later, having fled the country, he would become a leading light overseas of the banned South African political organization, the African National Congress.

Benson Dyantyi was less easily placed. Short, thickset and tough, he was in with the big township gangs and at once became our crime reporter – no writer but an excellent news gatherer. It was evident to me that he must get his 'exposures' approved by the gang bosses before *Drum* published them, otherwise he would not have remained in business long. He could not be telling us all he knew, but what he did pass on stood up to criticism, and his pieces were highly popular in the townships along the Reef. How did he get away with it? Gangsters, I learned – for one or two came into the office – are extremely vain, even vainer than us well-behaved citizens. They love to see themselves in print. Moreover gangsters in Johannesburg are, or were, popular heroes – that is, the big-time gangsters who robbed banks and warehouses or broke into the homes of wealthy whites. *Tsotsis*, the small-time thugs who preyed on their own people, stealing wage packets at knife point on the desperately overcrowded trains, were dreaded and despised. Benson's stories dealt with the 'Robin Hood' gangsters, and often took the form, familiar to British Sunday newspaper readers, of a detailed retelling from the inside of a crime which had hit the headlines a few years previously. Besides their journalistic abilities, both Matthew and Benson had another invaluable quality – neither of them was a drunk.

In addition to trying to get a staff together, my chief task during the past year had been to straighten out the picture side of *Drum*. Photographs were even more important as a means of communication in the African context than elsewhere. English was a second language for most of our readers, whose first language varied according to the part of the country from which they came. English, fortunately, was popular among South African blacks, partly because it was not Afrikaans, language of Afrikaners, the inventors and enforcers of apartheid; partly also because it opened the door on to the outside world. English was the language of the bioscope, of films, newspapers, books, the language also of jazz. It was important for those who planned to progress, within the limits allowed by the apartheid system, as foremen or overseers. But above all it was vital for those enterprising spirits who cherished the hope of one day breaking out of the enormous racial prison of South Africa. So on the whole our readers liked English and were proud to be seen reading an English magazine, but in general their knowledge of the language was still slight. Communication would be much easier and fuller if we could transform the haphazard nature of *Drum*'s layout into something more like the modern picture magazine of the fifties and sixties, which told their stories through photographs, using text mainly to explain and amplify, and in staff discussions we had together worked out a way of doing this appropriate to our audience.

So far as possible we would build up our stories through a sequence of photographs used almost in the manner of strip cartoons, so that a reader could get a clear impression simply from the pictures. To help readers having only a small command of English, we would put the headings and captions into simple words. But the main text, which might be several thousand words long, we would write as well as we could even though the language might at times be difficult, since no one without a fair knowledge of English would embark on it at all. This technique, of course, involved using photographers who were more than snap-shoters or picture stealers, and who understood exactly what the technique demanded, and in this I had been fortunate.

Shortly after I had joined the magazine, Peter Magubane, our one and only African photographer, had consulted me about entering for a photographic competition, with a request that I help him select his best photographs. We spent some time on this and Peter – in a competition open to both black and white press photographers throughout the country – had carried off one of the top prizes, proving that not quite everything in South Africa was decided by racial bias. We began to work closely together and on one or two picture stories I went out with him as a reporter. Already an excellent single-shot photographer, he soon began to acquire the technique of building up stories into a sequence. One of the stories on which we worked together was 'A Night with the Ambulance Men', the weekend round-up of beatings up and stabbings which kept the non-white ambulances on the go from Friday night until Monday morning. We used my car and trailed along behind the ambulance, stopping whenever it pulled up.

Most of the casualties were routine – an elderly cyclist riding home from the city to his township had been jumped on by two men from behind a tree. One cracked him on the head with an iron bar, and the other went rapidly through his pockets. Though his head was badly split, he was still conscious and didn't at all want to come to hospital. He thought he had recognized one of his attackers and wanted to go first to the police station in the hope of recovering his money. The ambulance men, however, thought he might be suffering from delayed concussion and insisted on taking him along to be patched up first.

Our next victim was a drunk who had run out of a beer hall, got involved in a fight, been stabbed and flung into a doorway. Distressed by the thought of his sufferings, or more probably irritated by his groans, the shopkeeper had rung for the ambulance. Once again I was astonished at how much the African can take; when I looked at this man he seemed to be a moaning mass of blood and injury. Rushed back to the hospital, he was carried inside on a stretcher. Doctors worked for an hour or more, cleaning, disinfecting, stitching. He was then given a sedative and put to lie down under a blanket, where it was assumed he would remain all night and be re-examined in the morning. But when, our night's work ended, I came back to learn how he was getting on, the victim was nowhere to be seen. I asked a nurse what could have happened. After a couple of minutes she came back. 'He's gone,' she said. 'One of the other patients saw him. He just got up and walked home – they're always doing that. If his head doesn't get better, he may come back in a day or two – but it's ten to one we'll see no more of him. Till next time, that is!'

In between handing the drunk over for treatment and calling back later, an incident happened which increased my already high esteem for Peter. We had been summoned urgently to one of the compounds in which the mineworkers – imported from many parts of southern Africa – live their lives of hard work, rough play and compulsory celibacy. As soon as I saw the casualty, I doubted if we should get this one to the hospital alive. While the ambulance men argued over how to stretcher him out of the compound, the mine-workers were telling us what had happened.

Half a dozen of them, they said, had been quietly playing cards out in the open, when suddenly they heard a shout. Someone was scrambling over the high fence – a thin wall of corrugated iron – which surrounded the compound. They heard the sound of a fall, then this stranger came rushing into the middle of them, and collapsed. When they picked him up, they saw he had a bullet hole over his right eye and so at once phoned for an ambulance. That was all they knew. Had any of them heard a shot? No. From which direction had the man come? From up the hill. Had any of them any idea who this man could be? They shook their heads; he was a stranger. Had they sent for the police? No. The management did not like their bringing police into the compound.

As we were getting back into the car to follow the ambulance to the hospital, Peter said to me, 'Sir, the story these men are telling us is not true.'

The moment he said this, I knew he was right. No man could have scrambled over the high compound wall and arrived running with a wound like that. It was doubtful if he could even have stood upright.

'What d'you think happened, Peter?'

'I tell you, sir, what happened. This is the end of the month. All these men have just been paid. They have been having drinks together, and they have been gambling.'

'Well? What then?'

'This man they call a stranger, he is not one of themselves. But certainly they know who he is. Very likely he comes from another compound. Tonight they are all gambling together and this man wins. It's midnight now – let's say he was shot nearly one hour ago – so they have been gambling all evening and this man has won all their pay from them. Then one of the men who has lost his pay says, "We've sweated a whole month to earn six quid – why should this stranger take it all away? He hasn't sweated for it. He is not even one of us." So either by agreement or just suddenly in a rage, one of them pulls a gun and shoots him. I think he has shot him sitting down, just putting the gun up against his head. You can't shoot a man over the eye like that unless he's lower down than you are. This man who has been shot can't speak, or perhaps they would have shot him some more times. They will not fire more shots than they need because the sound might bring the overseer. Then every man takes back the money he has lost, and they make this story up together.'

'Will the police find out what happened?'

'I don't think so, sir. The gun will be no longer in the compound. It is now buried somewhere outside. The men will all keep to their story – there is only *one* way the police can know what was done here tonight.'

'What's that?'

'If one of those men has a grudge against the one who fired the shot and tells the police the whole story. But even if a man wished to tell the police, he would be afraid of what would happen to him if he did.'

Peter was shrewd, but he was also fearless, and I was continually anxious for his safety. Twice already I had had to go and take him back out of the hands of the police when he had been, not 'arrested', which would involve the formulation of a charge, but picked up and taken inside for a going over. Usually, if I could find an officer, it was not too difficult to secure his release, but this was not always possible. Once four young policemen had got hold of him when he was taking pictures in the street and hauled him inside the magistrates' court, a huge building on several floors, with long corridors and dozens of smaller rooms in addition to the courts. While I was asking and searching for him everywhere, the four had taken Peter into a small room and locked the door. Fortunately, before anything could happen, a major I had spoken to earlier and who noticed what was going on hammered on the door, pushed his way in, and ordered them to let Peter go.

But to operate successfully under South African conditions we needed a good white photographer as well as a good black one. There were many situations in which a white

71

man could get by unchallenged but a black would be thrown out, or worse. Here too I had been extremely lucky. On my very first morning at the *Drum* offices I had been standing in Jim Bailey's room, looking with growing despondency through a pile of so-called stories – articles and photographs put together for future use. Both Bailey and Jurgen Schadeberg were in the room and I was trying to avoid saying just what I felt. Better, I thought, not to complain but to try in the next week or two to assemble some few pages that would be worth using. Suddenly my eye was caught by a handful of prints. At a place along the Reef called Benoni there had been a strike of clothing workers. Someone who really understood photography had evidently been present; clearly, too, he also understood how to make good prints. Black cops, well clad and helmeted, were laying into the strikers with long wooden clubs. One old man on his knees raised a hand appealingly to the cop about to strike him and you could see that seconds from now the old man would be dangling a broken arm.

'Thank God!' I said.

Both Jim and Jurgen looked at me with astonishment.

'Are these yours?' I asked Jurgen.

'No. They're from a freelance – Ian Berry. He does odd jobs for us now and then.'

'Okay,' I said, 'we'll buy them,' and made a mental note of Ian Berry's name.

Ever since that day I had been hoping to get Berry on the staff, but on *Drum* it was no easy matter even to get a cracked camera lens repaired, and to take on a cameraman at twenty pounds a week meant a major battle. Now, however, in the general atmosphere of change following Can's departure, Jurgen Schadeberg was also going and it was possible to get Ian Berry appointed in his place. This brought us not only a photographer of world class, though at that time still unrecognized; Ian would also, I knew, be a help and inspiration to Peter and to anyone else who might work for us in the future.

At this moment, late in February 1959, something altogether unexpected happened. A few months previously I had been asked to write an article on 'The African as Journalist' for the American magazine *Holiday*. It was to form part of a special issue about Africa. Now out of the blue came a cable from *Holiday* asking whether I would fly over to Washington late in March at their expense, and take part in a seminar on Africa to be held at the University of George-town. From the office I rang Dorothy, who said immediately, 'Of course you'll go.' When I called in at the United States offices in Johannesburg to see about a visa, a friendly official said: 'And we hope you'll stay on an extra week or two as guest of the State Department. We can work out a programme for you later on.'

If I was going to the United States in six weeks' time, it was essential to secure an assistant editor before I left, and I was happy when I found I could persuade Humphrey Tyler, my predecessor, to come back and take on the job. He would give notice to the *Rand Daily Mail* straightaway, and so could work with me for a couple of weeks before I left.

'We've been here a little over a year,' I said to Dorothy when I got home, 'and for the first time, I begin to feel we are settled in and that *Drum* is really getting on its feet. All we need now is about six months' peace and quiet.'

6

'The Cops Have Got Sidney!'

I was due to leave Johannesburg for the United States on a Saturday. On the Friday evening I had got my things sorted out for packing, and we had finished dinner. I was just saying to Dorothy that I would be glad to go to bed early, seeing I should have to spend the next two nights in the plane, when the phone went. It was Casey.

'Sidney Andrews has been pinched. The cops have got him.'

'Where are you speaking from?'

'A call box not far from Marshall Square. Sidney's inside. I've seen him. He's been beaten up.'

'What happened?'

'Sidney and I and Matthew Nkoana – he's here in the box with me now – were walking across town towards the bus terminus. It must have been around half past seven. There was another fellow from the office with us – Johnson, his name is. We had some trouble with a cop out of uniform, and while Matthew was trying to calm him down a squad car came along, the cops all seized Sidney and bundled him inside. I don't know why they picked on Sidney and not us. We guessed they'd be taking him to Marshall Square, so Matthew and I decided to follow along and see what we could do.'

'Good! And then what?'

'Well, we couldn't see or hear anything of Sidney, so after a while I managed to slip in through a side doorway, wandered around a bit, and then saw Sidney. His head was bleeding and his face all swelled up. He's still inside there now.'

'Okay, Casey, I'll be with you right away. Where are you exactly?'

'Marshall Square, the Marshall Street side, round near the "Non-Europeans" entrance.'

'Can you hang on there with Matthew till I come?'

'Yes, sir, we'll stick here. They came out and tried to chase us away once, but if we have to move we'll hide in a doorway. We know your car and we'll be on the lookout.'

'In ten minutes then.'

I told Dorothy and got the car out. When I reached Marshall Square the two were standing on the pavement in the darkness. I made them go over the whole story quickly so that I could get it clear in case any argument arose over getting Sidney out.

Casey, Sidney and Matthew had been walking along the pavement in Commissioner Street. Johnson, the fourth man with them, I hardly knew; he worked in the circulation department. They were making for the bus terminus, from which, if they couldn't get a bus, they would share a taxi out to the locations. As they got near the centre of the town, they saw a tall white man coming towards them on the inside of the pavement. As they passed him, he swerved and elbowed into Johnson. Johnson, they thought, had not realized till after this chap knocked into him that he was a cop; but Matthew spotted he was a cop because, though he had no tunic, he was wearing uniform trousers and a khaki shirt. Johnson then said something like, 'That fellow must be drunk.' He had not meant the cop to hear him, but obviously he did, because he swung round and made a grab at Johnson, tearing off the pocket of his jacket. Johnson dodged, slipped away – and ran out into the traffic.

'He was hopping in and out among the cars,' Matthew explained. 'It was just before theatre time and the streets

75

were full. I shouted to him, "Come back! Come back!" and waved my arms. But Johnson just ran dodging off – and that's the last we saw of him. So then the big cop turned on Sidney.'

'And then what?'

'He slammed at Sidney once or twice, but he couldn't do him much harm because Sidney kept twisting and turning and covering his head with his arms. I saw this cop was getting mad, and I kept trying to catch hold of his arm and saying "*Don't* do that! *Don't* do that!" I still thought we could calm things down.'

'But while Matthew was trying to pacify this cop,' Casey broke in, 'a squad car drew into the side of the road just by us. There were a couple of white cops in the front – they didn't look much more than boys. This big fellow shouted to them in Afrikaans, and they all three grabbed Sidney by his arms and legs and flung him down into the back. This cop we'd been arguing with jumped in beside Sidney or on top of him – and off they all went.'

'We knew they'd take him to Marshall Square,' said Matthew, 'so Casey and I came along here – we hoped they'd allow us to pay a fine and take him home. But after a while when we saw nothing, and the cops had chased us away from the office where we were trying to find out what was going on, Casey slipped in through a side door. An African cop spotted him but he didn't give him away, so Casey went on down a passage – and there suddenly he caught sight of Sidney sitting on a bench. . . .'

'I didn't *know* it was Sidney,' Casey took up the story. 'I just thought "Who the hell's this poor bugger they've been beating up?" Then he looked up at me, and I looked back at him – and then I saw from his eyes that it was Sidney.'

'How long ago was this?'

'P'raps three quarters of an hour now, sir. Just a little while before we rang you.'

'And as far as you know they've still got Sidney inside there?'

'He *must* still be inside there. They certainly haven't brought him out.'

All the time we were standing talking on the broad pavement, pick-up vans were driving up to the kerb with engines racing. White policemen, chatting and shouting, were leading files of handcuffed blacks into the building. Then the whites would come out without the blacks, pile into the cars and go roaring off again into the night. Once a door in the wall just beside us was flung open and a white-faced policeman, wild-eyed and handsome in a heavy way, stared out at us. He had no tunic and no shirt; just khaki trousers and a vest. He stared at me and at the others, seemed about to speak, then suddenly drew back and slammed the door.

'That's *him*! That's the one! Now he'll have gone back to report.'

'Let him report!' I said, feeling myself growing angrier with every minute. 'You two stick around here. If you're chased away, stay where you can see my car. I'll try not to be long.'

Inside the charge office there were a number of police behind a grille. Some were entering up particulars in books; two or three were chatting in the background. There was a general sense of bustle. The only one who appeared not to be occupied was a pale, uncertain looking youth.

'I want to find a boy called Sidney Andrews who was picked up and brought in here about an hour and a half ago. Can you tell me anything about him?'

The youth I was speaking to said nothing, but the one beside him, who was filling in a form, held the form up: 'Sidney Andrews? This is him.'

'Where is he?'

'Gone to hospital.'

'Gone to hospital? What's he gone to hospital for? There was nothing wrong with him two hours ago.'

'It's his mouth.'

'His *mouth*? What's happened to his mouth? I want to see him.'

At this a sergeant, a short man with red moustache and

77

reddish hair who had been listening to the talk, stepped in: 'He's not in hospital. He's in the cells.'

'Can I see him?'

'Who are you? Are you a lawyer?'

'No – I'm his employer. I can give you all particulars if you want.'

He looked me up and down. 'No – you can go in and see him if you want to.'

The sergeant lifted a big key down off a hook and led me across the office and down a short passage to a heavy metal door, which he unlocked. Beyond this door was a small office or guard room in which a young policeman was leaning back with his feet on a desk, reading a coloured comic. There were empty Coca-Cola bottles on the floor, and grape stalks and a screwed-up paper bag on the desk in front of him. The policeman's golden hair and chubby face gave him a sort of schoolboy jollity. I said nothing to him, as I thought he might have had a hand in what had been happening to Sidney.

Meantime the sergeant had unlocked an iron grille to one side, and disappeared. After perhaps a minute he came back, leading a shambling figure by the arm, and I wondered why he was bringing this with him. Then, looking closer, I saw it was a kind of fearful parody of Sidney, who seemed to have become nothing but an enormous mouth. His lips always protruded; now they stuck out like those of a plate-lipped woman in a circus sideshow. They were so swollen and heavy that the facial muscles could no longer hold them up. His whole jaw sagged loosely down – there seemed to be teeth missing – and blood was soaking down his shirt and dripping directly out of his mouth on to the floor. I could see the trail running away behind him. His eyes were full of blood, and his head rolled loosely on his neck. He was barefoot.

'Good God! Sidney – what's happened?'

He didn't speak. He mewed. For a minute I couldn't make out what he was trying to say. 'Go away, sir. Go away. Don't stay here. Leave me alone' – and then, as he made a pitiful attempt to threaten his captors, I caught the words 'in court'.

I wanted to stop Sidney threatening. I wanted to register my horror in a way that might be remembered. I wanted above all to get Sidney out of here. I turned to the sergeant. 'This is a shameful and disgraceful sight.'

'I quite agree, sir.'

I remember putting my hand over my eyes. 'What's been done to this man makes me sick.'

'I quite agree, sir,' the sergeant said again.

I put a hand on Sidney's shoulder; it was damp and trembling. 'I'll be back before long, Sidney. We shall get you out of here.'

We went out, and Sidney was taken back into a large cell, on the floor of which I caught sight of what appeared to be half a dozen or more black bundles lying.

'What d'you intend doing with this man?' I asked.

'We are sending him to hospital.'

'How soon?'

'As soon as we can obtain an ambulance.'

'Can I go with him?'

'I'm afraid not, sir.'

'What *can* I do? How shall I be sure he really *gets* to hospital?'

'You can ring me at ten o'clock.'

I looked at my watch. 'All right. I shall do that. But how do I get hold of you? What's your name?'

'Just ask for the charge office sergeant. Oh – and the case against Andrews will come on in Court B at 9.30 tomorrow morning.'

'Case *against* him? Good God – whatever for?'

'He is being charged with assault.'

'Assault? But you couldn't even bring him into court in this condition.' At the same moment the thought flashed through my mind that perhaps the best thing for Sidney would be to be brought into court in that condition, and charged with 'assaulting' his powerfully built captor. 'He's going to be in bed for days.'

'Possibly,' said the sergeant. 'In that case there will have to be a remand.'

In the street Casey and Matthew were waiting for me. I had hardly begun talking to them when a thought struck me, and I went back to the sergeant.

'Look,' I demanded, 'do you know the name of the man responsible for bringing Sidney Andrews in here tonight?'

'I do.'

'I'm not asking you to give me his name now. I'm asking you to be sure you can identify the man concerned when you are required to do so.'

'I know the man.'

Back again with Casey and Matthew, I told them the position. I was sorry I couldn't drive them home to the townships, but there was a lot to do and I must be around to make sure Sidney really got to hospital. That was okay, they said, they would make their own way home. I asked if they had money for a taxi, and they said they had. We shook hands, and I told them to be sure and be in the office by half past eight next morning in case the lawyers wanted statements from them.

As soon as I got home I rang the firm's attorney, Kelsey Stuart, whose home number I had taken the precaution of learning some time back. Unfortunately he was out, and our general manager proved to be out as well. Around ten I rang the charge office sergeant, but was told he was 'going round the cells', and I must ring back in half an hour. At 10.30 I rang again, and he told me Sidney Andrews was now in the General Hospital.

A moment later the attorney for whom I had left a message rang through, and I told him briefly what had happened. He was a young man whom I had got to know well during previous difficulties in the harassed lives of *Drum* staff, and I knew him to be shrewd as well as sympathetic.

Now, after listening carefully to the whole story, he said, 'You've got your three witnesses, and you've seen Sidney in the cells, but it's terribly important to get the fullest record of the case you can. There's sure to be a remand tomorrow

– they won't dare bring Sidney into the box in the condition he's in. But these sort of surface wounds can heal up very quickly. . . . See the doctor at the hospital and warn him to keep all particulars. Say you'll be needing them in court. Is there anything else you can do?'

'What about a photograph? Would that help?'

'That's the *very thing*! If you can get one of your photographers to go along to the hospital and take a picture of him as he is now – can you do that?'

'Yes. I'll fix it right away. Is there anything else?'

'No – I don't think so. You'll want Sidney defended on this assault charge?'

'Certainly. I can't get through to the general manager, but I'll answer for that myself.'

'Then I'll be down at the court first thing in the morning. Even if the magistrate remands the case, it's just as well to put in an appearance. And, by the way. . . .'

'What?'

'If this proves to be what it looks like – an absolutely clear case of beating up with no justification – it could be just what you need to stop this happening to your fellows in the future. We've had them taken inside and threatened, and we've had them knocked around and their cameras pinched and so on, but there's never been an actual assault as clear as this one. If we can pull it off, it might be a turning point for all of them.'

I thanked Kelsey, and said I would get my own record of the night's events typed out and handed in at his office next day before I left. I also told him I had arranged with Casey and Matthew to be available in the office from half past eight so that their affidavits could be taken. I then went off to get hold of Ian Berry. Peter, I knew, would be out in the locations and it would be hard to find him and bring him back into town at this hour of the night, but Ian had a flat not far away. He was not at home, but I guessed he would be coming back before long so pushed a note under his door, telling him to go round and photograph Sidney in the casualty ward of the General Hospital, either when he got back tonight or first thing in the morning.

At the Casualty Ward for Non-Europeans a clerk greeted me immediately. 'You're from *Drum*? He said you would be coming.' He took me over to the nurse in charge, who led me through to Sidney. He was lying in an alcove on a bunk with a blanket over him. He had been given sedatives, but the doctor had decided it would be wiser to wait a few hours for some of the swelling to subside before bandaging his face. I noticed now for the first time that he had a wound also on the top of his head. A heavy smell of sweat came from the bunk and from Sidney's soaking shirt; I knew it was not the sweat of heat or of exertion but the bitter, acrid sweat of pain and terror. I chatted to Sidney for a minute or two, assuring him he was now safe, that nobody could pull him out of here, that I would come and see him in the morning and that the firm would back him in any case that might come on. I said that Casey and Matthew would explain things to his wife and say that he was being taken care of. Then I went to find the doctor. She proved to be a friendly, competent, white-haired woman who – when I spoke about keeping a record – replied at once: 'I *always* keep careful notes of these police assault cases. You can be sure I shall keep a record of this one.'

Everyone about the place already knew, I found, that Sidney had been beaten up, first in the squad car and then again in the cell at the police station. The reception clerk to whom I spoke gave me his name without hesitation and said he was perfectly willing to be called into court to testify to Sidney's condition when brought in. On leaving the hospital I had a second thought and drove to Ian Berry's flat, where I pushed a further note under his door: 'Don't leave it till tomorrow. Make sure you get round there tonight.'

After that I went home and started to tell Dorothy what had happened.

'You look green, Hoppy,' she said, and went to fetch a drink. I was too disturbed to go to bed, and kept going over the events of the last three or four hours, fearing I might have failed to take some step which could make all the difference when we came to court.

'There's nothing else you can do tonight,' Dorothy assured me. 'Go and see Sidney in the morning. If you want your notes typed out for the lawyers, I'll do them for you. . . . What else is there you could possibly have done?' she asked, seeing me still undecided.

'I'm wondering if Ian will get back to his flat tonight. Supposing he stays with his family and only comes into the office in the morning. Perhaps I should try to dig out Jurgen or Peter, if I can find either of them so late.'

However, at one o'clock, just as we got up to go to bed, I noticed a piece of loose paper on the hall floor. I picked it up and read, 'Picture taken. Ian.'

I was away in the United States for two to three weeks, and while I was away Sidney was brought to court by the police on a charge of assault. In the course of the hearing it came out under Kelsey Stuart's questioning that the policeman who claimed to have been 'assaulted' was six feet tall and weighed 175 lb. He had learned boxing and wrestling at the police training college. Sidney – known as 'Baby' to his colleagues – weighed 124 lb and was only five feet four inches tall. Finally, after a two-day hearing, the case against Sidney was dismissed. The photograph Ian had taken was handed into court as evidence of Sidney's condition when he reached hospital, and it was as well it *had* been taken, since by now – more than a fortnight later – the only outward sign of Sidney's night of pain and terror was a missing tooth.

Now that Sidney had been acquitted of assaulting the powerfully built constable, the way was open for him to bring an action for damages. However, while the matter was still under discussion with our attorney, we were informed that the Crown intended to bring its own case against Sidney's attacker, thus taking the matter out of our hands. After a number of postponements, this came on towards the end of May, by which time I was able to attend the hearing. Sidney was the first person on our side to be called, and, though cross-examined by a persistent attorney with a high local reputation, he had all his wits about him and answered for himself with spirit.

The Star, Johannesburg's evening newspaper in the English language, reported the case, and the following excerpt is taken from that account.

Andrews said under cross-examination that he knew his attacker was a policeman.

[Attorney] Even though you knew he was a policeman, you still interfered? – Yes.

Did it occur to you that he might have been doing his duty and that he was arresting Johnson? – No.

Did he appear drunk? – Yes.

Did it occur to you that here was a European interfering with a Native purely on racial grounds, and that therefore you should go to your friend's aid? – I am sorry but I am not a racialist, and that did not occur to me.*

Two points new to me came up in the course of Sidney's evidence, giving an even grimmer aspect to the case. According to his statement, after he had been bundled into the squad car the car continued to drive around the city for something more than an hour instead of taking him directly to be charged. ('It is possible that it took forty-five minutes,' the constable who attacked Sidney had admitted at the earlier hearing, though the distance could easily have been covered in five.) Throughout the journey the constable in the back, Sidney said, kept hitting him – among other things he kicked off both Sidney's shoes, which were lost and not seen again. When they finally reached the police station, his assailant and several other policemen rushed him straight through to the cells without stopping at the charge office, and then fell on him and knocked him about once more. Later when he was taken into the charge office – Sidney declared – all doors were closed so that no one could see the condition he was in.

The second point was that, after I had left the police

The Star, 22 May 1959.

station and while Sidney was on his way to hospital, he was assaulted again *inside the ambulance.* There were two white police in front, and Sidney and an African cop were sitting in the back. Halfway there one of the white police stopped the van, came round to the back and started laying into Sidney all over again – though he was in a condition in which even an animal might have refrained from touching him out of pity. The cop who was doing this noticed the expression on the African policeman's face, and said, 'You've seen nothing! Remember that – *nothing!*'

After Ian Berry and I had given our evidence, Casey was called into the witness box. Casey happened at this time to have his head almost completely swathed in bandages, from which, however, his eyes peered out sharp as ever, though distinctly bloodshot. The defence attorney, who had made little headway hitherto, looked up with obvious interest.

'Hello, Casey – what's been happening to you?'

Casey, who resented being called 'Casey' as much as any European in the box whould have resented being called 'Billy' or 'Jimmy', replied, 'How d'you mean – what's been happening to me?'

'What's been happening to your head? How have you got that injury?'

'I walked into the wall,' said Casey blankly. Then, feeling perhaps that this sounded lame (as God knows it did!), he added, 'I was out walking with a friend. I missed my step and knocked my head against the wall.'

After a few similar exchanges, the attorney suddenly burst out, 'Come on now, Casey! Don't trifle with me! We're not children in this court.'

Threats, however, were not the way to deal with Casey. They both stimulated his intelligence and made him bloody-minded. A tiny figure, with not much more than his heavily bandaged head visible above the witness box, he replied wearily, 'I'm not *saying* you are children in this court.' He paused and looked round for the implication to sink in. 'I'm simply explaining to you how I got my head injuries. I knocked it against the wall.'

As Casey said this, I caught his eye. He knew, and I knew, the shebeen wall against which he had knocked his head and the circumstances under which he had knocked it – however he was under no obligation to answer questions he had not been asked. The attorney then turned to details in the affidavits, and amongst other things picked on the distance between the four Africans involved as they walked along the pavement in two couples. How far apart had they really been? Three out of four, it appeared, had used the phrase that they were 'within shouting distance'. A very odd phrase, the attorney thought; very surprising they should all have picked on this unusual phrase; how had it come about?

'Have you four been talking this case over between yourselves?' he demanded sternly.

'Yes,' said Casey – to which the attorney could only answer that it was 'at least honest', and now pressed Casey to explain exactly what he meant by this admittedly curious phrase 'within shouting distance'. Casey, by now thoroughly at home, replied that in using the phrase he had meant to convey 'rather more than speaking distance'. It could in fact be understood to mean 'about as far as a man can shout and still be heard'. When the attorney remarked that the phrase still had a very unusual ring, Casey offered 'screaming distance' as an alternative. Nothing else the attorney started led to more practical results. Casey simply stood there, bowed, bloody, but in full possession of his faculties, deploying a kind of unapprehendable defiance through which all inquiries and demands petered out to nothing.

If Casey's was a negative and subtle insolence, that of Matthew Nkoana was direct and positive. He had not been in the witness box three minutes before he was protesting, 'Your worship, I *object* to that question!' He never got the slightest change out of his worship, who simply told him to answer what he was asked. Once, when ordered to 'answer properly', Matthew replied in an aggrieved tone, 'But I did answer the question' – and then repeated the involved explanation with which he had just evaded it. The attorney pressed his questions, but Matthew – with his frayed collar floating around his ears, his double-thickness spectacles, his long angular figure, and his high-pitched intellectual's voice – dominated the scene. Whenever the attorney tried to draw conclusions or base any argument on anything he said, Matthew immediately interrupted him, always addressing himself to the magistrate.

'But, your worship, I did *not* say that while we were at the restaurant none of us had a meal. I said that while we were at the restaurant I did not *see* any of us having a meal.'

'And how long were you in the restaurant?'

'That would be very difficult to say – very difficult. Time, you see, passes at different speeds on different occasions.'

'Was it more than ten minutes?'

'Oh yes – it would have been more than ten minutes.'

'And less than an hour?'

Well – yes – it was probably less than an hour.'

'So it was between one hour and ten minutes?'

'Possibly . . . but then, as I explained just now' – and so on.

Often he asked questions back, so that at last the attorney cut him short. 'When you, Matthew, are standing here where I am standing, and I am standing there in your place, you may put questions to me – but till that happy day comes, *be good enough to answer my questions!*'

For three quarters of an hour, unaffected by rebuke or sarcasms and quite unawed by authority, Matthew talked on, adding nothing to anyone's knowledge on any point at issue, exasperating everyone in court – including myself – but giving an astonishing display of voluble evasiveness. 'I think', said Kelsey Stuart when we got outside, 'the cross-examiner this morning went through a lot more cross-examination than he got the opportunity to do himself.'

The most telling point made during our attorney's cross-examination of Sidney's attacker had been to inquire whether he had not been taught at training college that the most effective way to bring a man under control was to handcuff

87

him, and to suggest, 'It would have been quite easy for you to get handcuffs?'

'Yes – but I did not think it would be necessary.'

He had not, he admitted, asked the two policemen in the front of the car for assistance in subduing his prisoner nor to lend him their handcuffs. He could 'not remember' how many times he had hit Andrews.

The magistrate then wished to hear evidence from the two policemen who had been in charge of the squad car – but they could not be found. They could not be found next morning either when the case came on again. They could not be found until the afternoon, when they testified that all Sidney's attacker had given him were 'five or six slaps' which were necessary to bring him under control.

The magistrate, summing up, said that although an assault definitely took place, he could not say how bad the assault was. Addressing the prisoner, he observed, 'It is probable that you were not completely responsible for the injuries to Andrews' face, since Andrews himself has said that another policeman had struck him a tremendous blow across the lips before he was taken to hospital. But I am satisfied that the five or six blows which you struck him in the back of the squad car constituted common assault. It was not necessary for you to hit him. There is no evidence that you asked your colleagues for assistance. . . .'

'The photograph shows that Andrews could have been badly injured, but it is not entirely reliable. It is not clear whether the marks on the face are bruises or merely made by blood.'*

Passing sentence, the magistrate said that the constable would be penalized, not for the violence with which he hit or did not hit Sidney Andrews, but for having hit him at all.

He sentenced him to a twenty-five-pound fine, or two months' imprisonment.

*From accounts in *The Star*, 26 May 1959, and the *Rand Daily Mail*, 27 May 1959.

The fine was paid.

Sidney's attacker had now been convicted. His sentence, in my opinion, was a remarkably light one – amounting perhaps to a fortnight's pay. But at least he had not been acquitted, and his conviction meant that it would now be possible for Sidney to bring a civil action for damages against the constable. For a prosperous client the natural way of proceeding would have been in the Supreme Court; but there, though the damages to be obtained would be much higher, the costs would also be much heavier – far more than Sidney could afford to risk. It was decided therefore to proceed by way of the magistrates' court. Here the maximum jurisdiction would be limited to £200; but our advisers considered that, by claiming £200 for wrongful arrest, £200 for malicious prosecution, plus £200 for assault and injuries suffered, a maximum of £600 might be obtainable.

Accordingly a summons was issued on Sidney's behalf against the constable concerned and against the Minister of Justice. Before long approaches were made from the other side with a view to settling the case out of court, and after some negotiation a figure of £250 was arrived at, which Sidney, on advice, agreed to accept. Notification of acceptance was sent on 1 September, but it was only after letters, telephone calls and, finally, the threat of a further summons unless the agreed sum was immediately paid over, that it was received towards mid-November, and Kelsey Stuart rang me at the office to let me know that the long battle had been won.

At this point, however, a further difficulty arose. I had been to see Jim Bailey at various times to report progress. I now told him that the cheque had reached our lawyers, and suggested that he himself should hand it over to Sidney at an informal presentation in the office.

'But I don't think the money *should* be given to Sidney,' Jim objected. 'It's not his. Some part might be given him later on – we should need to think that over – but the money itself isn't his at all. It belongs to this firm.'

'How is that?' I asked.

'Because we are paying for his legal proceedings – Sidney wasn't. As a matter of fact I think the best way to use the money is to set up a fund for defending cases of this kind in future. They're constantly cropping up, and it will give our chaps encouragement to know that the fund is there to help them.'

I was so taken aback by this view of the matter that I could think of nothing to reply. I could only repeat that I thought Sidney had earned the money, and went out, worried and upset. As soon as I got home, I told Dorothy of the discussion.

'*What?* Not give Sidney the money for which he was bashed around, had his teeth knocked out, and has now had to endure weeks of worry over the case? Over your dead body, Hoppy. I *mean* that! Over your dead body! Sidney earned that money with blood and terror. Two hundred and fifty pounds could make all the difference to his life – what's an odd couple of hundred to the firm? A couple of pages of advertising, more or less. . . . Of *course* there ought to be a fund to support people who get beaten up or land in trouble. That's obvious! But it's not going to be founded at Sidney's expense.'

Dorothy, as many times before, had made a situation over which I was hesitating and confused as clear as day. But also while she was talking, something else came back into my mind. It was a memorandum shown to me weeks before, but which in the rush of later events I had entirely forgotten. Next day therefore I brought the matter up afresh, saying I felt Sidney should be given the money he had paid for so heavily, which was after all an award of damages for injuries which he and nobody else had suffered, and that I hoped Jim would reconsider the matter and present him with the cheque.

'No – that would be wrong,' Jim said. 'I've thought this

over thoroughly. The right thing to do is to start an office fund for defending our people when they need it.'

'If Sidney *wants* to use the money in that way,' I replied, 'then of course he can. But if he doesn't choose to, the firm can't make him. It was Sidney who instructed the lawyers to bring a case for damages, not "*Drum* Publications".'

'That's a mere technicality. The firm was paying for it all – how could Sidney possibly have paid for his own case?'

'I don't know how he could,' I said, 'but he was going to have to. I was shown a memorandum from the general manager to the accounts department, giving instructions that the costs of defending Sidney were to be deducted from his pay at so much a month. That will still be on the files. Sidney wasn't only bringing the case, he was going to have to find the costs of it out of his own pocket.'

'If that's true,' said Jim after a moment's thought, 'then there's no more to be said. All the legal expenses must be deducted. You can get a cheque from the accounts department and hand it over to Sidney yourself.'

The lawyers had kept their charges all through down to a minimum, but there had been a lot of work involved, and in the end Sidney received a little over £170. It was hardly a fortune, but it would be enough to buy a small house in one of the locations or, invested, would make something to fall back on in the many hazards of African life. I thought it some of the hardest earned money I had ever heard of, but I think several members of our staff would have accepted a night of beating-up if they could be guaranteed to come out of it with no lasting injury and the same financial return.

Sidney grinned a gap-toothed and grateful smile when I passed his money over, and – calling in Casey and Matthew – said he ought to thank them for having stood by him that evening eight months earlier, instead of melting away safely into the crowd.

7
Light in the East?

From the long drawn out struggle to obtain justice for Sidney
Andrews there were several consequences apart from those
for Sidney himself. First, police treatment of *Drum* staff
became more cautious and they harassed them much less.
Some kind of official warning had evidently been circulated,
and I no longer need feel that if a photographer or reporter
were missing I should drop other work and start looking for
him. Secondly, the staff's confidence in me, badly shaken
by the sacking of Can, had been restored. Can, who had
been longer on *Drum* than almost any of them, had become
a kind of elder brother to the African staff. He was a talented
writer; his humour and vivacity made him popular; and the
thought that a journalist could lose his job for so slight a
cause as being regularly drunk and absent just when he was
needed most, ran contrary to their idea of how a black
journalist should live and act.

For a black man to be a journalist at all in the South
African conditions of that time was an offence against
convention and official attitudes, and as I mentioned earlier,
for any African to drink – except the offensively named
'Kaffir beer' in officially approved drinking halls – was then
actually illegal. So it had become a point of honour for
journalists to drink heavily as a gesture of defiance, and my
refusal to tolerate an assistant editor who was too often
drunk to be dependable had given everyone a shock. Whose
side was I on, if I allowed a little thing like that to count

against him? With the staff my position had now been restored, but I was puzzled to find that with the proprietor, Jim Bailey, it had actually worsened.

Since my earliest days on the paper I had got used to receiving critical memoranda, mostly following the same line.

1. *Drum* is quite out of touch with its public. The reason is obvious – you are failing to identify yourself wholeheartedly with the people for whom you are working.

2. Our presentation is not tough enough. Since we cannot improve the printing, and shall be handicapped for several years by semi-visible pictures, you must find ways to overcome this difficulty by bold display and editorial ingenuity.

3. *Drum*'s staff of reporters are not doing their job. They collect third-rate stories, miss all the important facts and angles and write them in a soggy manner. *Drum* must have personality and guts. It must go all out for the tough stories.

To be constructive may I suggest:

1. You mix round the town with your readers here and in Cape Town and Durban. They will give you contacts, angles, and the feel of public opinion.

2. You invite highly critical outsiders to a monthly post-mortem, telling you exactly what is wrong with every issue. There must be no holds barred.

I think you know me well enough by now to realize that these comments are made with the best of goodwill and with full appreciation for all you have done for the magazine since you came out here.

Such instructions – of which the above is a much abbreviated sample – now started to flow in regularly, and they were supported by others from the general manager, Weatherstone, complaining over almost every item of expenditure, and in a particularly pompous manner.

MEMORANDUM 24/B

TO: T. HOPKINSON   FROM: G. WEATHERSTONE

1. I notice that you have paid the sum of £12 12*s* for a story illustration. This in my opinion is too high.

2. I must point out that I also think that £16 16*s* per issue for such material as that used on p. 57 is inexcusable.

3. If you continue at the present rate you will have spent your full budget for the year in a few months.

This is not a situation which either the Proprietor or myself can contemplate without anxiety.

MEMORANDUM 24/C

TO: T. HOPKINSON   FROM: G. WEATHERSTONE

STAFF SALARY INCREMENTS

1. In regard to your recommendations for staff salary increments I am obliged to reject those in favour of XX and YY, because as I told you the Proprietor has directed me to inform you that in his opinion these members of your staff are not necessary and should be retrenched.

2. Since we discussed this position, it has again been raised by the Proprietor who reaffirms his view.

3. Kindly inform me what action you intend to take on the above, as the salary costs for your paper are threatening to be grossly in excess of the amount budgeted.

Towards the end of 1959, having been in the country for over eighteen months, I had begun to get some idea of the problems *Drum* was facing, but it puzzled me that, with all the improvements we had made, the sale of the magazine rose only slowly. This was in contrast to the position in West Africa where sales had shot up by about 50,000 a month; there we were selling all the copies we sent up and had even negotiated a successful price increase, so that the whole West African operation was now for the first time on a paying basis. Why was it taking so long to achieve the same results down here?

As I stared at Jim Bailey's memo advising me to 'mix round the town with readers here and in Cape Town and in Durban', part of the answer seemed to come through. There was, of course, a certain physical difficulty about 'mixing round the town with readers' in these various centres. Cape Town is over 900 miles from Johannesburg, almost as far as Vienna from London; and though Durban lay much closer to our headquarters, it was still about as far as Edinburgh is from Ludgate Hill, so that I could not just walk out of the office and start to mix on the way home. The real problem, however, was not the distance in miles but the totally different nature of our readers in each area. Along the Reef *Drum* was read by black Africans, but in Durban our readers were largely Indian, as was our local editor, G. R. Naidoo. Down in the Cape, however, there were almost no Indians, and the comparatively small number of Africans was continually being reduced by mass deportations to the so-called 'homelands' such as the Transkei. In the Cape our readers were mainly Coloureds – that is, people of mixed race. No simple blend of black and white, their varying origins lay among Afrikaner and English-speaking whites, Indians, Malayans, West Africans, people from Madagascar and Ceylon, mixed in with Africans from all over South Africa and those now almost extinct Hottentots and Bushmen who had been in the country when the first white settlement was made in 1652.

The interests and tastes of our Coloured and Indian readers were not just different from those of the Africans, in some ways they were in direct conflict with them and, after a few visits to each area, I was coming to the conclusion that they could hardly be combined within a single edition. But to start producing three separate editions of *Drum* was going to involve heavy restaffing and expense at a time when it was proving impossible to arrange small increases in salary or much-needed camera repairs. Was there some other area where we could press ahead meantime to achieve the sort of quick success we had found already in West Africa?

One of the talents Jim Bailey had shown was for picking young men of little or no journalistic experience and putting them in positions they were soon filling with more success than someone possessing journalistic capacity but set ideas. His outstanding success had been Anthony Sampson. Taking over *Drum* when it was only six months old, he had transformed it rapidly from what he called 'a noble expression of the black soul' into the vivid product and portrait of a Black Bohemia. Sampson's early *Drum* was indeed shapeless and chaotic, but pulsating with energy and life, and the book* he wrote after returning to London in 1955 made the lifestyle of one corner of black South Africa familiar to the English-speaking readers. His later career on the *Observer* and as a writer on economic issues showed that he could be equally at home in the fierce competition of Fleet Street or of the literary world.

Another of Bailey's discoveries, Anthony Smith, had opened up *Drum*'s operations in West Africa, where he had made his home in one corner of a two-room office which lacked not only any pretence of comfort but even the most primitive facilities. Later, after a short stay in Johannesburg, Smith made his way back to England by motorcycle, having managed to borrow an overcoat from Jim Bailey which served as sleeping quarters, garage for the motorbike, and protective clothing against both cold and heat. He, too, having survived such a journalistic start, had established himself in Fleet Street, first as science correspondent for the *Daily Telegraph*, and later as the author of books based mainly on his own adventures as balloonist and naturalist in Africa and South America.

These two had moved on along the road to success, but there was a third of Jim's discoveries still around, Alan Rake. He was now existing in Nairobi on a modest salary which frequently did not reach him, selling copies of *Drum* which, through muddle or carelessness in our circulation department, too often never arrived. Rake, like Sampson and Smith, had been an enthusiastic young Oxford graduate whose journalistic experience consisted of a few months on the *Oxford Mail*. But once arrived in East Africa he had flung himself into his task with courage and enthusiasm, and on taking over at *Drum* I had found my desk filled with articles he had supplied and with letters pleading for them to be used.

The theory was, I found, that four pages of the normal

Drum, a Venture into the New Africa, by Anthony Sampson, London, 1956. Republished with additions as *Drum: An African Adventure – and Afterwards*, Hodder and Stoughton, 1983.

South African edition should be changed in each issue after supplies for South Africa had been run off, material from East Africa replacing whatever in the South African edition might be supposed to have least appeal for the Eastern territories – Kenya, Uganda and Tanganyika. In the rush of work, however, this had often not been done, and, impressed by Rake's obvious eagerness and competence, I at once arranged to change eight pages for him every month. We also had the covers overprinted with the words EAST AFRICA EDITION and the price marked in local currency.

The arrangement worked, and as sales moved ahead, Alan – who had begun by doing everything himself, from writing articles and taking photographs to typing the correspondence, checking the accounts, persuading shops to sell the magazine and putting up posters in their windows – acquired an office boy, some furniture, a few unreliable contributors, and finally a full-time cameraman.

Too often, however, our Johannesburg accounts department, in their anxiety to produce what they called a 'good figure' at the month's end for Jim Bailey, would omit to send any money to East Africa. When I protested angrily, they would assure me that the matter had 'already been dealt with', and I had once as many as three telegrams from Alan on my desk, imploring me to get the staff's salaries and petty cash sent up before they all starved or were arrested for debt. Despite these failures, our East African sales had been stepped up recently from ten to twenty thousand – so might *this* not be the basis for our next step forward? What I had in mind was that, instead of altering a mere eight pages, we should produce a completely separate East African edition. For the present we would print it in Johannesburg, but Alan would have his own small editorial staff in Nairobi and his own advertising manager to pull in local advertisements.

By the end of 1959 the East Africa project had been discussed over and over again between Alan and myself and also between Alan and Jim Bailey. It had been threshed out in Johannesburg in discussions with Bailey and the general manager; argued out and finally accepted, over the board-room table. Bailey had also been up to Nairobi to see the position for himself; and an advertising representative had been sent out from *Drum*'s London office to sound out interest among the big firms and advertising agencies. So when I finally flew up to Nairobi to meet Alan Rake for the first time, it was not to make plans for the new edition of *Drum* but to arrange the details of their execution.

Alan Rake, when he met me at the Nairobi airport, proved to be an unusually tall young man in his twenties with a mop of dark hair, a slight hesitation in his voice – caused, I later realized, not by uncertainty but by the rate at which words were trying to come out – and a devouring interest in Africa. Though he had only been out here for a couple of years, he knew and had gained the confidence of the African and Asian leaders in his territory. He took me to see Tom Mboya – with whom he shared a flat in a quarter of the town where no whites lived – and Dr Kiano, Mboya's close associate, both of whom would become ministers and leading figures in the first Kenyan government following independence. Both were enthusiastic over the idea of an East African *Drum*. So too was Julius Nyerere when we flew down to see him in Dar-es-Salaam. He was not yet head of state, but as leader of TANU (Tanganyika African National Union) was already the country's most important politician.

Having met him first at a party gathering, we called on him next day in his office. Nyerere was a slight, dapper man in his middle thirties with a cheerful, unlined face, a toothbrush moustache and curly hair which was already withdrawing far back on his domed forehead. He wore sandals, a freshly ironed dark green shirt (the TANU uniform) and carried an ebony stick with an ivory handle. A number of African leaders, such as Jomo Kenyatta and Joshua Nkomo, also always carried sticks, but Nyerere's was particularly elegant and had for him the significance of being both black and white.

Nyerere sat at a big desk on which in a glass of water

stood a head of frangipani blossom, a cluster of five-petalled white trumpets unfolding into stars to release a delicious scent, and from time to time he sniffed the blossom as we talked. He came directly to the point: 'It is essential for us to be given independence quickly. Instead of the present government – one of civil servants with a few elected ministers – we must have an elected government in which a few civil servants still participate. It is essential we have this soon, since we want to maintain goodwill and a harmonious relationship with Britain. I want the people of Tanganyika to understand that the British are their friends, not their oppressors, and I want to demonstrate to the people of Britain that the white man who comes here in the right spirit will be *more* welcome when we have our independence than he was before. We must demonstrate the true position to both sides. The frightened Europeans must be shown they can stay and work with us on proper terms. And those Africans who want to sit on the heads of the white man – because their own black heads have been sat on so long – must give up ideas of "getting their own back". Both sides, you see, have to give up something. We want to make this country an example of races working together. We want the world to say, "Look at Tanganyika! If *they* can do it, why can't we?" ' He turned to me. 'You,' he said, 'come from South Africa; a white minority dominates your country. They do this because they believe their only security lies in domination. They equate domination with safety and cling to power like limpets because they dare not share, dare not relax. But we mean to show that in Tanganyika lives a white minority which is *more* secure – as well as happier and more free – than the white minority in South Africa, Kenya or elsewhere.

'Here in Tanganyika we Africans are the more powerful. We hope independence is coming next year or at latest in 1961, but we know for a fact that it is coming. There are nine million of us and the power is already in our hands, so it is for us to reassure the white man and the Asian – and that is just what we are doing. Any white man or Asian

99

who accepts loyalty to Tanganyika can come and live among us and get on with his lawful business. Your Dr Verwoerd can come here, if he likes! Provided he accepts loyalty to Tanganyika, and doesn't expect to boss people around because they're black, he can come and live here just like anybody else.'

After he had been talking for a while I told him of our plans to make a new *Drum* solely for East Africa. He was delighted. 'You can do first-rate work with it,' he said. 'You can help to explain the races to each other. You can make people understand what we are trying to do, and why we can't always go as fast as they would like. You can inform our people what's happening in other parts of Africa, and in your other editions you can tell them what we're doing here. And then with your pictures – which attract people's eyes and minds – you can make people *want* to read, and in this way you help us to spread literacy. Make your paper in two languages, English and Swahili, using both languages together in the same paper – then those who speak only one of our languages will get to know the other. Your magazine can be of *real value* in what we are trying to do here, and I shall see that you are given all the help we can.'

I returned to South Africa convinced that our proposed East African edition could not only become a big publishing success, but achieve something of importance for the three territories, Kenya, Tanganyika and Uganda, at a critical moment in their development. *Drum* could become more than just a magazine. It could be part of, and an influence on, the whole African independence movement. The opportunity was dazzling.

On the Monday after my return I went into the office full of excitement, eager to hand on the good news. Our new edition was due to come out in February 1960; we had only a couple more issues before then, and I had worked out how to use them to the best advantage. We must change more pages, print more copies, and use the two issues to announce and advertise our plans. Jim Bailey was not in yet, so I called

100

on the general manager, Weatherstone, to secure agreement for the extra printing.

He laughed sardonically. 'You haven't a hope in hell! I can tell you that right away. It's *out!*'

'Why?'

'He won't want it.'

'But you haven't even heard what the prospects are up there.'

'No – and I don't need to hear. I know what I'm talking about. I tell you Jim Bailey doesn't want it. . . . Oh, and by the way, there's to be an all-round reduction in expenses. I'll see you about that later.'

'God damn it!' I said. 'What the hell was the point of sending me up to East Africa for three weeks if the whole matter's settled before I get back?'

'Don't ask me!' Weatherstone replied. 'But I'm through with all these arguments anyway. I've arranged to leave in a few days' time.'

It was a couple of days before I could see Jim to report on the prospects for our new edition. Both Nyerere and Mboya had promised support and agreed to write for it. Alan Rake was convinced we could sell many extra copies in the next two months, giving us a platform of 25,000 readers on which to launch the new edition.

'I'm afraid that's out of the question.'

'Why?'

'Postage is far too high. We're losing money on every copy we send up there. We can't possibly send all those extra copies over these next two months – it's simply giving circulation away.'

'But we have to aim a bit high to be sure of having our guaranteed 25,000 readers by February. If we're only selling 20,000 copies in December and January, we may not get the 25,000 in February when we need them.'

'In that case we shall have to build more slowly,' Jim replied. 'With printing and postage costs so high, we can't throw money around. I've had to tell Weatherstone that pretty sharply and I'm having to call for economy right through the firm. So far we've only got eight pages of extra advertising booked for East Africa and we need at least twenty to break even. The whole project has to be put off.'

I paused, then said, 'I'm really puzzled', seeing the whole picture falling to pieces for no reason.

'Puzzled? What about?'

'If things are so difficult and every penny has to be counted twice, why have I been up to East Africa at all? The last thing you gave me before leaving was a memo saying that an edition partly in Swahili could sell 30,000 copies in Tanganyika, plus another 30,000 in Kenya "provided Rake and I play it properly". And one of the things you asked me to do was to organize putting part of the text into Swahili. But if we aren't going to print more than the usual 20,000 copies, that's a waste of time and money. We can sell far more than 20,000 as we are.'

Jim put his head in his hands like a schoolmaster faced with an impossibly dense pupil. 'It's simply a matter of finance! Since you haven't got the South African edition on to a paying basis yet, we just haven't the money to push ahead in East Africa as fast as we might like.'

'But the financial position has been with us all along,' I argued. 'We've been planning this undertaking now for a good six months. We've had board meetings on it and you've been up there. How is it, after all this, we now suddenly find we can't afford what we all agreed on doing?'

Jim turned away. 'You can see the facts and figures if you want to, Tom. There's not much point in your doing so because you never really pay any attention to the business side of the magazine.'

'I realize,' I said, 'that you've got a small potential gold-mine in East Africa – but you have to put down the machinery to work it. *You* expect the mine to pay while the machinery is going in.'

A week or two later we went through all the arguments again, but this time in new company. Weatherstone had left and Ian Pritchard had been brought down from West Africa to take over. With him had come his assistant, Roy Paulson, who was now to become company secretary and head of the accounts department. I was glad to see them both, but Ian in particular looked white and strained and our greeting was unusually formal.

'I don't think I need tell you,' Jim said, opening the meeting, 'that we're all just as keen to launch the new maga-zine in East Africa as you are. But we've been going into the books. There have been losses which completely upset our balance sheet. I won't go into them now – but I assure you we have no choice in this matter at all.'

'So what have you decided to do about the East African edition?'

'Cocoon it,' Jim replied. 'Cocoon it for a year. In twelve months' time, when we have built up our reserves – which I must ask you to help us do – we can return and push ahead. But now it's right out.'

'Quite out of the question,' Ian agreed.

Roy nodded agreement. 'Not a hope.'

'Well, Jim,' I said, 'it's your money, not mine. If you don't want to spend it on promoting an East African edition, I can't make you. But don't let's deceive ourselves.'

'In what way?'

'Don't imagine you *can* "cocoon" the edition and go back in a year. We are disappointing everyone over the new paper – staff, advertisers, distributors, circulation workers, the public. They've all been told we're doing something big. Now we suddenly find we can't afford to do what we under-took – so we back out. Okay, we're free to do so. But how are they going to receive us if we go back in a year or two and say – "Now we're ready to get started"?'

'We can't do what we can't do. It's far better to go back in twelve months' time with prospects of success than to launch the thing too soon and be a flop. There's no gratitude in business – but there's no resentment either. If we make a go of it in 1961, no one's going to complain we didn't launch it in 1960.'

'I don't think we will launch the thing in 1961,' I said, 'or in 1962. But there's something *more* important.'

103

'Which is?'

'It's these next few years that are going to mean everything in East Africa. That's why we got so much backing from the politicians – they see we can affect crucial issues at a critical time. To tell them we must abdicate for a few years but we'll be back in due course just isn't on. To them it's like saying "We can't send troops for the battle but you can keep us seats for the victory parade." '

'Look, Tom,' said Jim, 'it's no good your being angry or upset over this. I've been concerned with East Africa a lot longer than you have, and I know many more people up there. I feel all this as much as you do, if not more. It's just a matter of simple business necessity – which is something we all have to accept.'

Part of the difficulty of my position at *Drum* was that I was called a 'director' of the firm. But this was a private company, the property of Jim Bailey, and all I knew about the company's affairs was what he chose to tell me. I had no idea how much capital was invested in the business or what dividends, if any, it paid. Indeed I had only learned that our West African edition had for the first time become profitable because the people on the spot, Ian Pritchard and Roy Paulson, told me so when I was up there.

And it was from them that I learned before long what any director of a business would have known at once – the cause of our newest panic. Weatherstone, Jim Bailey's financial manager, had got the firm's figures in a tangle. It had always puzzled me whenever I looked in on him unexpectedly, to find him doing calculations on small pieces of paper which he hastily pushed out of sight under his blotting pad. I had supposed him to be working out why I could not have Peter Magubane's camera lens repaired until next month, or why the broken-down Volkswagen which constituted *Drum*'s means of transport could not be replaced.

But it now appeared that the calculations which kept him so occupied were of a different kind, and that they had brought no benefit to the firm.

8

A Word of Advice

When I got home after being told by Jim Bailey of his intention to 'cocoon' the East African edition, I said to Dorothy, 'I think it's time I finished up with *Drum*.'

'I thought you were beginning to feel that,' she said, 'but why now in particular?'

'We've killed the East African edition. We're saying it's "cocooned" – but I think it's dead.'

'I know you'd set your heart on that – but is it fatal if it has to be given up?'

'Not fatal to the firm, though I think it's a golden opportunity let slip. But it means a lot to me.'

'What does it really mean to you?'

'If we're trying to do something on this continent – then East Africa's the test. The need for a magazine there's obvious and everyone admits it. The door's wide open, and we're being asked in.'

'Then why aren't you going ahead?'

'Because the firm isn't willing to lose quite a modest sum of money there for one year, or possibly two – but only a fraction of what we're cheerfully talking about spending on a printing press.'

'Well, wouldn't a printing press be useful?'

'It might. My own feeling is that it would not. There's far too much printing capacity in South Africa as it is. *Drum*'s much better off buying its printing from someone else rather than putting in expensive machinery and then looking for other work to keep it busy. In any case machinery could still be bought in twelve months' time – but the chance in East Africa won't wait.'

'You're not just thinking this new paper would be profitable because you're so anxious to see it started?'

'Michael Curtis is as sure as I am. I talked to him in Nairobi. Jim's always asking me to find someone to put money into his business – and Michael would do it. He said so. He's started a newspaper publishing business in Kenya backed by the Aga Khan, and they'd come in with us on the new edition.'

'Well – what did Jim say to that?'

'He said "Fine!" at first. Now he's decided to "cocoon" Curtis too.'

Dorothy came over, sat beside me and took my hand. 'I know how much you've put into all this, Hoppy, and I understand your disappointment. But aren't you making exactly the same mistake you made at *Picture Post*?'

'What's that?'

'Not recognizing that the one who pays the piper calls the tune. You think that because you've put your ideas and a terrific amount of work into something, that gives you the right to decide how it should be handled.'

'Well?'

'Ideally, maybe, it should give you the right. But in fact, as you well know, the power belongs to the one who puts up the cash. You may not like it, but that's the way things are.'

'Of course I know that,' I replied irritably.

'But you don't act as if you knew it. If your employer chooses to do something you think is wrong, you can't stop him. It's his property. He can do what he likes with it. He needn't listen to you.' She paused. 'And there's something else as well.'

'What's that?'

'Working too hard for too long hours – as you do – makes the person you're working for suspicious.'

'Suspicious of what?'

106

'Suspicious that a man who gives his time and energy in this way isn't doing it for a salary. He's got plans of his own. And in this case – you must admit – Jim Bailey would be right. You *do* have plans of your own. And you *are* continually trying to put them into effect.'

'I wouldn't be much use to anyone if I didn't.'

'Not if you didn't try at all. But from an employer's point of view you'd be more valuable to *him* if you tried *less* – because he'd be getting more of his own way. Can't you understand?'

'Understand what?'

'You give your loyalty and effort to what you feel a particular project ought to be – in this case a wonderful picture magazine. You think of *Drums* springing up all over Africa – in all the English-speaking territories. You see them raising the cultural standard . . . increasing knowledge . . . helping new countries to unite – and also providing a training ground for writers, photographers and so on. But an employer doesn't *want* you putting all your efforts into realizing your visions. He expects you to support *his* interests in the form in which he sees them.'

'Then he's wanting power as well as profit. He's wanting it both ways.'

'Exactly. What's so surprising about that?'

I could give no answer, but a day or two later I came back to the question. 'What d'you think Jim Bailey really wants? Is he in this to help the African? To make money? Or to build a position for himself?'

'All three. But not in that order.'

'What really comes first for him?'

'Having his own way. He wants to dominate. You refuse to be dominated and challenge him all the time. It isn't sensible, Hoppy. If you were more tactful and in less of a hurry, you'd get much more done with less conflict and anxiety.'

I thought for a minute. 'It's Africa that's in a hurry. Everything's going to happen in the next five years when all these countries get their independence. After that a new pattern

will be set – of cooperation or of fighting one another.
Of tyrants springing up, or decent government. Looking
towards the East, or to the West. It's *all* going to be decided
– and the chance to influence the course of things is now.'

'That may be true, but it isn't the whole story.'

'What's being missed out?'

'You blame the man you're working for because he wants
the lot – profit, the exercise of power, plus credit for high
ideals. You think he ought to be satisfied providing he makes
a lot of cash. If he listened to you he very well might make
big profits – but why should he be satisfied with cash? Why
shouldn't he want more, just as you do?'

'I don't want profits. I only want a reasonable salary to
live on.'

'That's *not* all, Hoppy. If it were, there wouldn't be any
conflict between you two. I know you want to make a
wonderful paper too – that comes much higher on your list
than it does on Jim Bailey's. But even that isn't the *only*
thing you're after, is it?'

'What else am I after?'

'You're after making a position for yourself. You're a
visionary all right, but also you've ambitions. You don't
only want to do something worthwhile in Africa, you want
to be recognized as having done it. You're too concerned
with personal success.'

'What harm does that do?'

'Think! Rich men aren't fools where their own advantage
is at stake. Bailey can see – just as Hulton, or at least his
wife Nika, could see – that you're building a position for
yourself. Not for *him*. Your attitude is that he's welcome to
the profit, but you're going to do the job and get the credit.
D'you wonder he's suspicious of you?'

'It seems,' I said, after a minute or two, 'that I'm a bloody
fool. I ought to have seen all this for myself. I didn't. . . .
Blind as a bat!'

'D'you want to know what I think?' Dorothy asked.

'Of course I do.'

'I think you take *Drum* a great deal too seriously. It may

108

be that you won't be able to do a lot with the magazine – and if you can't that's just too bad. But you've learned a great deal about Africa. You've travelled all over the place. You've been up to West Africa I don't know how many times. You've got to understand and like Africans. If it isn't *Drum*, it'll be something else. Stop taking it all so much to heart.'

We were having a drink on our balcony, seven floors up, looking out towards Zoo Lake and the hills beyond. After a minute or two of silence Dorothy asked, 'What d'you really think about *Drum*? Is it worth going on with it, or isn't it?'

'I doubt it,' I said. '*Drum* needs a big injection of money, courage and faith, and a great drive to expand.'

'Whereas?'

'Whereas our policy is always to cut down and contract. So we live in an endless series of economy campaigns – scraping our own bones for enough sustenance to march another mile, discharging the soldiers because uniforms cost too much, and eating the horses because they need to be given hay.'

'I understand, Hoppy, how frustrated you feel, and if you can't stand it any longer you should leave. But *can* you? What's your position?'

'I signed on for two years. My time's up next month.'

'Think it over for a week then. Remember, you'll miss your friends on the staff and the bustle of the life – just as you missed it when you left *Picture Post*. But if you want to get out – *do*.'

'You haven't asked,' I said, 'how we'll manage if I leave.'

Dorothy patted my arm. 'That's one thing I never worry about with Hoppy. If you make less, we'll live on less. But I've never any doubts as to whether you can earn a living. All ducks know how to swim.'

When the end of the month came, I wrote to Jim Bailey saying I would like to finish at the end of my two years, and that after our recent conversation and the two notes he had recently sent me, I felt sure this would meet his wishes too. He wrote back, seemingly in surprise, to say he did not want me to leave and hoped I would remain with the firm for a long time. Would I reconsider the position and stay on?

This made me hesitate. I had become very attached to the staff, particularly to the half dozen members – in West Africa as well as in South Africa – who I felt were developing and getting some benefit from our working together. Secondly, even though I seemed to be making little headway, I was reluctant to write off an attempt in which I had invested so much energy, which had brought me halfway across the world, and on which I had set out with such high hopes. Moreover – in the course of the last week, and probably because of a remark Dorothy had let fall – I had the idea that it might be possible to give our firm some of the financial weight and consistency of policy it lacked, by forming an alliance or partnership with one of the local newspaper groups. When I put this possibility directly to Jim Bailey, he said he would be only too happy to join forces with such an organization, providing it could be done on reasonable terms. So in the end, after talking it all over with Dorothy once more, I decided to stay on for at least another year. My salary was improved, and in return I agreed that, if I should later decide to leave, I would work out a full six months' notice. That fixed matters for the next eighteen months.

And so began the year 1960, which was to be a momentous one for us, and in which the continent of Africa would dominate the world's headlines month after month almost without a pause.

9
Shooting at Sharpeville

The year which was to be a turning point for many of us, as well as for the continent we lived in, opened happily for *Drum* staff. Ian Berry won the highest award open to any cameraman in the Commonwealth at that time – the *Encyclopaedia Britannica* prize for the best sequence of pictures taken during 1959. The award had been won a number of times in earlier days by our cameramen on *Picture Post*, but this was the first time it had been carried off by anyone outside Fleet Street, let alone a photographer from overseas. Ian won with a set of pictures of a witch doctor at work which we had used over four pages in *Drum*, but which I had difficulty in persuading him to send in at all. 'I suppose the subject's interesting – but they're not really up to much as pictures,' he had said. Since the pictures had had to be taken in a small unlit room he had for once been obliged to use flash, a practice he detested; he would almost have preferred not to win the award rather than to win with a set of flash pictures. At the same time Peter Magubane won a South African competition open to all non-white photographers. For a magazine employing only two cameramen, it was perhaps unique that each in a single month should have won the highest award open to him.

This was in January. In February came a speech by the visiting British prime minister, Harold Macmillan, which added a new phrase to the language and jarred the complacency of Afrikaner politicians in the stability and permanence

111

of the artificial world they had created, a complacency which would be shaken almost to pieces by the events of the following two or three months.

I had heard Macmillan make a short speech at a Johannesburg garden party which contained nothing but rotund platitudes. His speech in Cape Town, however, was a different matter altogether. I listened to it in the offices of *Drum*'s sister paper, a popular tabloid called *Golden City Post*, in the company of Can Themba who had joined *Post* as a reporter, Ronnie Manyosi, the *Post*'s news editor, and three or four other Africans from our two staffs. South Africa at this time was still within the Commonwealth, and the British premier's speech to the two houses of the Union parliament had been eagerly anticipated; there were hopes that he would openly denounce the arch enemy and oppressor, Dr Verwoerd, who, though he did not invent apartheid, had established it as the basis of Nationalist policy and enshrined it in a code of laws covering almost every aspect of daily life. The Africans listened with mounting disappointment. Heard among the teacups, the warning and rebuke, the careful dissociation from Nationalist policy and its inevitable consequences, slid by with only slight effect. But on the 230 listeners from the Union parliament who were getting it full in the face, the impression was very different:

It is our aim, in the countries for which we bear responsibility, not only to raise the material standards of living, but to create a society which respects the rights of individuals – a society in which men are given the right to grow to their full stature.

And that must, in our view, include the opportunity to have an increasing share in political power and responsibility; a society finally in which individual merit – and individual merit alone – is the criterion for a man's advancement, whether political or economic.

The most striking of all the impressions he had formed during his tour of Africa, Macmillan told his audience, was of the strength of African national consciousness:

In different places it takes different forms. But it is happening everywhere. The wind of change is blowing throughout the continent. . . .

The British Foreign Secretary, Mr Selwyn Lloyd, has summed up the British attitude thus:

'In those territories where different races or tribes live side-by-side, the task is to ensure that all the people may enjoy security and freedom and the chance to contribute as individuals to the progress and well-being of these countries. We reject the idea of any inherent superiority of one race over another. Our policy, therefore, is non-racial.

'It offers a future in which Africans, Europeans, Asians, the peoples of the Pacific and others with whom we are concerned, will play their full part as citizens in the countries where they live, and in which feelings of race will be submerged in loyalty to new nations.'

Smoothly the polished phrases rolled out of the office radio. When the prime minister had finished, Can shrugged and Ronnie turned away. Nor did it seem to me sitting beside them that anything had been said that could cause a shock. It was only when Dr Verwoerd began his reply, hesitating and audibly searching for his words, that I realized what was happening nearly a thousand miles away in Cape Town. Next day the *Rand Daily Mail*'s gallery correspondent described the scene.

The face of the South African Prime Minister grew slowly more pale and more tense. It stared stonily ahead as if listening to increasingly bad news. It gave the impression of a loose mask trying forcefully to keep itself in position.

Mr Macmillan gradually developed a faintly scientific manner, more and more like a family doctor offering a friendly solution on excessive indulgence. He understood what the situation was: the difficulties that drove us to do what we did. But then came the grave warning, retaining the friendship of Africa for the West meant more to the West than supporting the racial policies of a handful of white men in South Africa. . . .

There was hardly any surprise among those watching that only half of the listeners applauded the speech. Minister Paul Sauer was so enthusiastic that he applauded more than anybody. But the rest looked fixedly at Dr Verwoerd. The South African Prime Minister

113

was obviously very angry indeed. He began to stumble through his impromptu opening sentences. Listeners stirred with embarrassment. . . .

In the year's unfolding drama the speech we had not thought much of would play a powerful part. The 'wind of change' would blow through many editorial columns and whistle through many political orations. In the townships along the Reef copies of Macmillan's speech, cut from newspapers and pasted on to wood or cardboard so that they would not fall to pieces, had soon become treasured possessions. Read, re-read and passed from hand to hand, they were familiar even in shebeens. And within a couple of months Nationalist MPs would be blaming Macmillan's words for the new spirit of defiance which had burst out, they said, at Sharpeville, and which looked for a week or two as though it might bring down the whole artificial structure of apartheid and open the way for a new order in South Africa.

Early in March Dorothy and I moved home. We wanted more space and to be nearer the country, so we rented a flat in a new block two or three miles out, with a garden on one side and school playing fields on the other. I took two weeks out of the holiday owing me to help Dorothy – who redecorated the whole flat herself – over the move. During the fortnight I was away Humphrey Tyler had already done most of the work of preparing the new issue of *Drum*, and when I got back we were faced with a difficult decision.

For years black politics in South Africa had been domi-nated by the ANC – the African National Congress. 'Congress' was run on conventional party lines or as though it were a white trade union, with an annual subscription, elected officials, lists of members, party cards, branch offices, Roneoed circulars, office rent, telephone accounts – the lot! It claimed a paid-up membership of 120,000, but probably there were not more than two or three thousand who were active, and the organization was only kept from falling open at the seams by the personal nobility and leadership of 'Chief' Luthuli, with the devoted backing of some few dozen leaders

114

who were continually harried by the police and frequently in and out of prison. But though few were willing to exert themselves for Congress, most Africans gave it their sympathy, as did a small number of liberal whites, and it stood to the world outside as the main expression of African political consciousness inside the Union. There was one *E 01 2* paradox about the ANC. For years its leadership had been moderate – 'feeble' was the word its opponents used – but it had also for some time been under the influence of a body called the Congress of Democrats. This was a body with a mainly white leadership, some Asian support, and a strong Communist influence.

On these two points – of a supposed Communist trend and an excessive influence from whites and Indians – there had lately grown up inside Congress a challenge from a loosely knit group known as the Africanists. Though they were not always candid about stating it, the Africanists wanted an almost completely African state, to which only Africans and Coloureds would belong by right, but to which, they sometimes said, whites and Asians who accepted African authority might be admitted as citizens. Though they were little known to the country at large, we had already published two or three articles about them in *Drum*. They had attempted to carry the day at Congress meetings in Durban and elsewhere, but had been defeated, and during 1959 they began to organize a separate political movement under the letters PAC – Pan-African Congress – and to build up connections with other Pan-Africanist movements in different parts of Africa. When, following later successes, the movement became popular, it was generally known not, like the ANC, by its initials, but by the initials spoken as a word – 'Pac': 'Oh, he's a "Pac" man', or 'There are a lot of "Pac" supporters in East London'.

Gradually during the past year a leadership had emerged for the new movement with, at its head, a remarkable young man, Robert Mangaliso ('Wonderful') Sobukwe, a lecturer in Bantu Studies at the University of the Witwatersrand. I had several times met and talked with Sobukwe and with

115

some of his associates, such as Peter Raboroko. I found him an unusual mixture; he had a handsome person and agreeable presence; he gave the impression of thinking more than he was prepared to say; his quiet, polished manner suggesting the educated negro more than the African politician. But when he wrote *Drum* an article outlining his views – which included a united continent ruled by a single central government – I found it curiously naive. I felt we could not even publish it without listing some of the obvious objections – which, by agreement with him, we did; and one or two African political figures in other parts of the continent to whom I later showed the piece dismissed it as utterly impractical.

Sobukwe and his associates had spent the last months of 1959 and the early days of 1960 travelling around the country in a Volkswagen bus given them by sympathizers, building up the new party. Their efforts and eloquence had gained a good deal of support, particularly among the younger people, but this was largely confined to a few cities, among them Cape Town and Port Elizabeth. One of those they had influenced most strongly in the Cape was a young student, Philip Kgosana, who, after the Sharpeville shootings, would lead an extraordinary march of blacks in the Cape on the parliament in Cape Town, which made Kgosana famous for a month and came within an inch of wringing big concessions from a shaken government – concessions they would undoubtedly later have revoked.

PAC did not believe in elaborate organization; their aim was to exploit deep-seated African grievances by a series of dramatic gestures. Of ANC leadership they were strongly critical, arguing that Luthuli ought to have disregarded the government ban confining him to his home town, gone openly about the country speaking, and been arrested and imprisoned. 'When our time comes,' they declared, 'we will send our leaders to jail first. That is where leaders belong – in Front.' Being so loosely organized, the PAC had no chain of command through whom activities could be set in motion. Instead they had made a curious arrangement giving

116

Dorothy Kingsmill as she was when the author met her in the late 1940s. Hugh Kingsmill, her husband, the novelist and biographer, died in 1949. Tom Hopkinson and Dorothy married in 1953 and lived in London till 1958 when they went out to South Africa

Below: Dorothy and the author in Johannesburg in 1961 after opening an exhibition of work by African artists

Above: Drum photographer kicked and hustled by police in a Johannesburg street, March 1961. The occasion was non-political — a pop star's visit!

Right: Peter Magubane taken by cops into a police building. Four young cops then locked themselves into a room with him, but before they could give him the treatment, a major ordered his release

'The Face That Should Shock the World.' Sidney Andrews, *Drum's* office-boy, after being beaten up in a police car while it was driven slowly around Johannesburg streets. The author, called out at night by two of Sidney's colleagues, managed to get him taken to hospital, where photographer Ian Berry took this picture. The police charged Sidney with assault but lost the case, largely because of this evidence. Sidney then sued the police, who settled out of court for £250, enough to buy him a small house of his own. The case was a celebrated one at the time, 1959, and 'The Face that Should Shock the World' was the caption used by the *Daily Mirror*

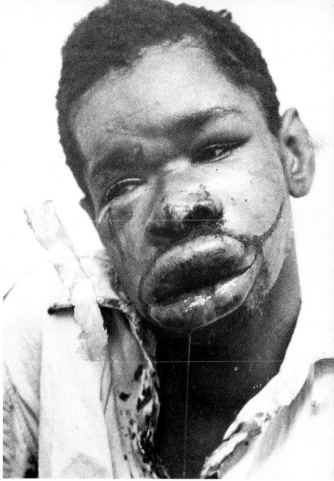

Left: Casey Motsisi, as he appeared in court to give evidence for Sidney. The police attorney demanded to know why he was bandaged. 'I walked into a wall,' said Casey, but did not add that it was a shebeen wall

Sharpeville Shootings.
In March 1960 the whole of South Africa was shaken when police opened fire on a peaceful crowd at Sharpeville, killing 69 Africans and wounding 180. *Drum* photographer Ian Berry took the only pictures of the actual firing, and a *Drum* journalist, Humphrey Tyler, wrote the sole eye-witness account
Below: Africans burning their passes in the belief that the hated system would soon be ended by world pressure

'My God, She's Gone!' When police opened fire, children in the crowd thought it was a game, and ran laughing. But the bullets were real

their president, Sobukwe, the power to call upon his followers for action at any time on three days' notice.

Early in March it had become known that Sobukwe would call a press conference on Friday 18 March, at which he would instruct his followers what they were to do on the following Monday 21 March, and it was this piece of timing which set us our complicated problem. The normal day for *Drum*'s April issue to go on sale would be Wednesday 23 March, and its contents would have to be passed for press almost a week earlier, on the day before Sobukwe's announcement would be made.

During the two weeks I had been away, Humphrey Tyler and Benson Dyantyi had been keeping close to the Africanists, attending their meetings and conferences, and had come to the conclusion that at his press conference on 18 March Sobukwe was going to make a dramatic call for action – a call which would meet with a much greater response than was generally expected. They wanted us to play the story big in our April issue, thus giving *Drum* the chance of an extraordinary scoop, since no other paper was taking the PAC movement seriously. Against this was the likelihood that Sobukwe's call, like so many 'calls for action' in South Africa before and since, would go unanswered. *Drum* would then look foolish. Publicity given to the breakaway movement would also get us in bad odour with the ANC – and with Luthuli whom I knew and liked – and bring us more trouble with the police authorities and the Special Branch.

Humphrey and Benson wanted me to see the Africanist leaders, attend a couple of their meetings and form my own impression. My view was the opposite. 'You've done all that. You've formed an impression of what the leaders are planning and how the followers will react. I'll try and get the feeling of the opposition and the inert mass. Then we'll put our impressions together.'

Golden City Post, I knew, kept in close touch with the ANC and, as it happened, were meeting its leaders on the following Sunday to hear what they thought of PAC's prospects. I therefore arranged to attend the meeting at

117

which the leaders, who included Nelson Mandela, Duma Nokwe and Robert Rhresha, were asked to say what would happen in a week's time when the call for action came. 'Absolutely nothing,' was the unanimous opinion.

I waited till the leaders had spoken and then said, 'You're all dismissing this crowd of breakaways because they don't have the things you've got – typed lists of members, offices with phones, a national organization. But they don't *want* these things. They argue that membership lists are only good for getting your followers arrested, and phones for being tapped. They believe they can cut out all machinery and laborious organization and get through to the people, not by talk but by example. People, they say, are angry and fed up, only waiting for a lead. If they choose the right issue – and the biggest issue, they claim, is the pass laws – and if their leaders are prepared to be arrested and go to prison, they will set off a chain reaction. Their refusal to accept the pass laws will run right across the country like a bush fire.'

There was silence for a moment, then somebody broke out: 'It *can't* work! You can't get action that way. It will fail, and the few who take any notice will be rounded up and penalized, as they always are. Sobukwe is leading the people into trouble with no real chance of success. His plan is completely irresponsible.'

Among those who had asembled was a lawyer–politician, and it was his remarks which – as events later proved – went directly to the point. 'Looked at in the way you've put it, the scheme just *might* come off. But there's one thing these people are overlooking.'

'What's that?'

'Their policy is to go along to the police stations in masses on the appointed day, say they've given up carrying passes, and demand to be arrested. They intend to flood the police stations, cram the law courts, fill all the prisons, making it impossible to go on arresting people and leading finally to a breakdown of the whole pass system. They have a slogan: "No bail. No defence. No fine." The aim won't be to keep out of prison, but to get in. As soon as they're released,

118

they'll all refuse to carry passes and get themselves arrested and imprisoned all over again. . . . It sounds good – but the plan's got one fatal weakness.'

'Which is?'

'They're expecting to be sent to prison for three weeks for not carrying a pass, come out, hold a few meetings, then get re-arrested and go back inside. That may happen to a few harmless followers, but when it comes to the point the leaders won't be sent to jail for three weeks for not carrying passes, they'll be sent to jail for three years for conspiracy or sedition. And what will happen to the movement when anyone who tries to give an active lead is certain to get three years?'

I called a meeting of the staff at which I reported what I had heard, and we argued our policy out among ourselves. Finally we agreed that we would lead the paper with an article called 'Who are the Africanists?' In it we would tell the story of the movement's growth, leading up to the present attempt. We would illustrate it with action pictures of the leaders addressing meetings, with a short biography as caption under each, and we would put a catch line on the cover calling attention to the story inside. But though we would give the facts, we would not take sides or advocate action. The readers would simply be given the fullest information on the personalities and issues. I also arranged with the circulation department to speed things up and put the magazine on sale two days early, not on Wednesday but on Monday, the day the 'call for action' was due to take effect. On the Sunday I phoned the editor of the *Rand Daily Mail* to ask whether his staff expected anything to happen. He answered that all was quiet and they fully expected it to remain so. I also spoke to the editor of *Golden City Post* who, as a final check before publishing his weekend edition, had phoned the police. They told him they were not taking the PAC threat seriously and that no one else should do so either.

So we came to the Monday of Sharpeville. We had laid our plans on Saturday, disposing our tiny staff to what

119

seemed the best advantage. Benson Dyantyi and Peter Magubane, with our only car, were to meet at daybreak in Orlando
and stick close to Sobukwe from then on. He was visited
very early by the Special Branch and Peter took pictures of
him talking to his followers and surrendering himself, with
a handful of companions, at the police station. They were
ordered to wait while discussion went on inside as to what
to do with them. A phone call from Alexandra, a township
on the other side of Johannesburg, told us that a mere dozen
PAC men had turned up there to claim arrest. Down in
Durban thirteen had done the same, and elsewhere in the
country everything seemed normal. We had all been in the
office since the very early morning, and by about ten the
feeling spread that nothing was going to happen, and those
who sympathized with PAC were looking despondent.
Suddenly the phone went. It was one of Ian Berry's contacts
saying that the police had opened fire in Evaton, a location
near Vereeniging, thirty miles or so away, and that the
people were in a state of excitement and had started cutting
the telephone wires. Soon afterwards came another call
saying that trouble was boiling up at Sharpeville. None of
us knew where Sharpeville was, but we soon found it was
another location outside Vereeniging, comparatively new,
with an adult population of about 15,000. Ian was raring to
be off, but our only car was in Orlando.

'What about your own?'

'Laid up.'

'Oh – hell. Take mine. Try and not get it shot up,' and I
threw him the keys.

'Can I go too?' called Humphrey. He looked so eager that
though I would have been glad to have him around in case
one of us had to rush out and bail members of our staff, I
could not refuse, and in a minute they were both out of the
building. On such a day I did not dare leave the office and
was just having a sandwich some time after two o'clock
when Humphrey rang through.

'There's been one hell of a mess-up here. Masses of people
shot – just like a bloody battlefield.'

120

'Where at?'

'Sharpeville.'

'Where are you calling from?'

'A café near Vanderbijl Park. We're wondering whether to go back and look for more, or come on home.'

'Did Ian get pictures?'

'Yes.'

'Are they safe? Has he had his films pinched?'

'Not so far.'

'Then for God's sake don't stick around. Come on in with what you've got.'

By 3.30, dusty and excited, they were back in the building. Ian sat checking his cameras over and counting his rolls of film while Humphrey talked. They had had a close-up of the whole incident which was even now hitting the world's press like a bomb and making the name of Sharpeville both odious and renowned. They were the only two journalists who had been there among the crowd or close to it when the firing started. One other cameraman – Warwick Robinson of the *Rand Daily Mail* with the *Mail*'s crime reporter, Harold Sacks – had been inside with the police. The rest were nowhere.

'Hell!' Humphrey kept saying. 'They were just mowing the people down, kids and all. And Ian was dodging in and out among the bloody bullets taking his little pictures! He just ran out in the middle and knelt down. Hell! *What* a cameraman! He's nuts, of course! Completely nuts! He just ran out into the middle and knelt down. . . . Hell! And then halfway through he just thought he'd try the other camera and switched over.'

When he'd finished his story, I asked: 'What about my car?'

'Hell!' exclaimed Humphrey, fishing in his pocket for the keys. '*Is* yours a lucky car! Not a bloody scratch! And the *Mail* car which went in just behind us has got two bullets in the back and the windscreen shattered by a stone.'

Ian printed up his pictures. He had got the crowd running towards him, many of them children, many of them still laughing, thinking it was all a game, thinking the police were firing blanks to scare them. He had got a woman lying dead and the man beside her staring stupefied at his bloodstained hand. But he had got something more – a picture that was going to be produced dramatically later on at the Sharpeville Inquiry when police officers denied there had been any firing from the Saracen armoured cars. It showed two policemen – one with a revolver and one with a Sten gun – firing into the fleeing crowd, and the policeman with the revolver reloading after emptying his magazine. In the course of a couple of minutes and at the risk of his life, he had taken a handful of pictures that were to be historic. At the Sharpeville Inquiry later on he was to utter, in his diffident, hesitating manner, a sentence that would do more to destroy the official picture of a savage horde baying for the lives of a hundred and fifty policemen than volumes of argument. He was asked if, while walking alone and unarmed among the crowd some minutes before the shooting, he had experienced any difficulty or sense of danger. Ian thought for a moment, then replied: 'I had to say "Excuse me" once or twice in order to get past.'

When the two of them had had a cup of tea, Humphrey went off to write his story while it was still fresh. We were all in a strange state of mind: horrified by the tragedy; excited and disturbed as to what would be its consequences; amazed at the way our gamble on the Africanists had succeeded; elated that *Drum* should be the only paper in the world to have got pictures and an eye-witness account; perplexed as to what to do with this precious material now we had it. Our April issue had been published only that morning – how could we wait till May?

'Don't worry,' I said. 'Get it all written down and the pictures printed. Maybe we can produce a special issue of everything that happens this week. Have it on sale in a fortnight's time.'

We did not guess that it would be six months before – under the Emergency Regulations soon to be brought in – we should be able to publish Ian's pictures, and that by the time it was possible to print Humphrey's article Sharpeville would have become ancient history. Here, however, is what he wrote. It appeared in London in the *Observer*, and in South Africa in Patrick Duncan's courageous and independent magazine, *Contact*, as well as in the United States.

We went into Sharpeville the back way, behind a grey police car, and three Saracens. As we drove through the fringes of the township many people shouted the Pan-Africanist slogan '*Izwe Lethu*', which means 'Our Land', or gave the thumbs up freedom salute and shouted 'Afrika!'

They were grinning, cheerful and nobody seemed to be afraid. Some kids waved to policemen who were sitting on Saracens, and two policemen on one of the Saracens waved back. It was like a Sunday outing, except that we knew that Major Att. Spengler, head of the Rand Security Branch, was in the front car, and that there were bullets in the Saracens' guns.

Spengler led the convoy towards Sharpeville police station, and policemen on Saracens obligingly signalled left and right turns in the road to us, and when they were slowing down. Perhaps they thought we were members of the Security Branch. Then we caught a glimpse of a crowd around the police station at the top of a long rise ahead. Abruptly Spengler turned his car around and the Saracens followed.

We followed the convoy to the main gates of the township where policemen were stopping all cars from town. We stayed on the township side of the barricade. Then Spengler was off again, and his Saracens. We were going back to the police station, but this time there was a difference.

The policemen were all inside their Saracens and the hatches were battened down. The police were looking at Sharpeville through chinks in their armour plating. But the residents did not regard the tanks with concern; they were interested, and some of them grinned. There were crowds in the streets as we approached the police station. There were plenty of police, too, wearing more guns and ammunition than uniforms.

Major Spengler and his Saracens drove through the policemen around the police station and we hesitated. Then we parked our car and Berry went to see what he could photograph. Every time a policeman looked at him he whisked into the crowds. Then an African approached him and said he was the local Pan-Africanist leader. He told Berry his organization was against violence and that the crowd was there for a peaceful demonstration.

The crowd swelled around Berry, listening to what their leader said. But Berry thought the police would come too, so he said: 'For goodness' sake, get these people to move.' The leader spoke to the people around him and they dispersed immediately.

In the meantime I decided to drive through the police cordon and find Berry. I hooted and some policemen moved away but others looked more closely at me. Then a constable shoved the butt of his rifle against my car's windscreen and another pointed his rifle at my chest. A policeman in a tunic leant into the car, red in the face and explosive.

He shouted: 'Have you got a permit to be in this location? Have you got a permit?' I said no. He shouted: 'Get out! Get out! Get out or I'll arrest you on the spot, d'you understand?' He had his police gun in his holster and a black pistol tucked into the top of his pants. He seemed almost hysterical. I backed down about twenty yards and waited for Berry where I had left him.

Then Berry came back and we decided to go around to the other side of the police station. This was about seven minutes before the police opened fire and the crowd seemed perfectly amiable. It certainly never crossed our minds that they would attack us or anybody.

We drove around to the other side of the police station and we parked in a big field. We could see a couple of Saracens sticking above the heads of the crowd ahead of us, just more than one hundred yards away. The crowd seemed loosely gathered around them and on the fringes people were walking in and out and some kids playing. I certainly could not see more than about 3000.

I said to Berry: 'This is going to go on all day.' And he replied, 'Let's hang on for a bit anyway.' Then there was a report, over to the right it seemed, away from the police station.

'That's a shot,' said Berry.

I was still wondering if it was, when there were sudden shrill cries of *'Izwe Lethu'* – women's voices it sounded – from near the police, and I could see a small section of the crowd swirl around the Saracens and hands went up in the Africanist salute.

Then the shooting started. A gun opened up toc-toc-toc-toc and another and another. The shots had a deep sound.

'Here it comes,' said Berry, and he leapt out of the car with two cameras. He crouched in the grass taking pictures. The first rush was on us, and then past. There were hundreds of women. Some of these people were laughing, probably thinking the police were firing blanks. But they were not.

Bodies were falling behind them and among them. One woman

124

was hit about ten yards from our car. Her companion, a young man, went back when she fell. He thought she had stumbled. He turned her over in the grass. Then he saw that her chest was shot away. He looked at his hand. There was blood on it. He said: 'My God, she's gone.'

There were hundreds of kids running too. One had on an old black coat and he held it behind his head as he ran, to save his head from bullets, I suppose. Some of the children were leaping like rabbits, hardly as tall as the grass. Some of them were hit too.

Still there was shooting. One policeman was standing on top of a Saracen and it looked as if he was firing his Sten gun into the fleeing crowd. He was moving slowly from side to side. It looked as if he were panning a movie camera – from the hip. Two other policemen were on the Saracens with him. It looked as if they were firing pistols, but I could not hear pistol shots separate from the toc-toc-toc of the automatic guns.

Most of the bodies were strewn in the road which runs alongside the field we were in. I saw one man who had been lying still get up, dazed, and walk a few paces. Then he fell in a heap. A woman sat with her head cupped in her hands. One by one the guns stopped shooting. There was nobody moving in our field except Berry. The rest were wounded or dead. There was no crowd any more. It was very quiet.

Berry ran back to the car with his cameras and he said, 'Let's go before they get my film.'

We tried to find a way out of the township that did not lead past the police on the main road. Nobody molested us as we drove around the township looking for the back way. We could not find it so we went out on the main road, looking straight ahead. Nobody stopped us.

I heard no warning to the crowd to disperse before the shooting started. Yet the police had had all morning to rig up a public address system which they could have used and I understand that Saracens carry loudspeakers. Nor was there a warning volley. When the shooting started it did not stop until there was no moving thing in the huge open space in front of the police.

I have heard that the police claim that they were in desperate danger because the mob was stoning them. But only three policemen were reported to have been hit by stones and more than 200 Africans were mowed down. So there seems to be some disparity here. I have also heard that the crowd shot at police. But before the police opened fire I heard only one shot, and that seemed to come from a long way away.

I was told that the crowd around the police were armed with ferocious weapons, and that these littered the area around the police station after the crowd fled. But I did not see them, although I have looked very carefully at pictures of the death scene. And when I was there I saw only shoes and hats and a few bicycles left behind among the bodies.

It is also extraordinary that the police did not use the leaders of the crowd to keep order. This had been done earlier that morning at Bophelong township, Vanderbijl Park. A mild-mannered and calm White, Mr Knoetze, township manager, and the local Pan-Africanist leader kept everything there completely under control. Only one person was killed in Bophelong. He was Steven Mathe, nineteen years old. A policeman shot him because he was throwing stones. Tough stuff!

And it seems to me that tough stuff was behind the killing at Sharpeville. The crowd gave me no reason to feel scared, though I moved among them without any distinguishing mark to protect me, quite obvious in my white skin.

I think the police were scared though. And I think the crowd knew it.

That final shrill cry by the women before the shooting started certainly sounded much more like a jeer than a battle-cry. It did not sound like a battle-cry at all. And while the policeman who told me to get out of Sharpeville was red in the face and almost hysterical, the first wave of the crowd that ran past me when the shooting began was still laughing.

A sad postscript to the Sharpeville shooting was written for me at a small café in Vanderbijl Park. Vanderbijl Park was pretty close, I imagine, to Dr Verwoerd's apartheid ideal that day. There were no Africans there. Whites were working the petrol bowsers in the garages and pumping up tyres. Other White workmen were just standing around because the factories were closed for lack of Africans. The place was pure White.

No bread was delivered to the little café that morning; no milk, no other foods either; nor any minerals.

'It looks pretty bad,' I said to the White woman behind the counter.

'Yes,' she said. 'They should shoot all these bloody kaffirs dead, and they'll all come back to work tomorrow,' she said.

When the death roll of Sharpeville was completed, there were 69 dead and 180 wounded. Before the figures had been received, a Nationalist MP, Mr Carel de Wet, said in the House of Assembly: 'It is a matter of concern to me that only one person was killed.' When a United Party member, Major van der Byl, declared that this was 'a terrible remark to make', Dr Verwoerd intervened to say that Mr de Wet's remark had been completely misinterpreted. All he had done was to plead for order. It was shocking that one Christian should attach such a meaning to the words of another Christian.

Over the radio, Col. Pienaar, the officer in command of the police who opened fire, added his own Christian plea for order. The Africans, he said 'had it coming to them. . . . They'll have to learn the hard way.'

There is a footnote to this account of Sharpeville. Peter Magubane provided it in a book of his pictures published nearly twenty years later, the magnificent record* of a heroic life in which he has spent years in prison and no fewer than 586 days in solitary confinement, simply for following his career as a photojournalist and without ever once having been convicted of a crime. Throughout it all he has stead-fastly refused to give up his South African nationality and now at last has broken through to become an international celebrity, free to come and go unhindered. He, too, had been at Sharpeville on 21 March 1960.

I had a hard time getting into the area, which was all fenced off, but I got in there only three minutes after the shooting and was able to take a few pictures. I had never seen so many people dead before; I could not work easily. When I got back to the office Tom Hopkinson was very much angry with me. I did not have the pictures he expected me to have. I had taken pictures from a distance. I did not have the close-ups which would have shown the grimness of the situation. Hopkinson warned me that if I was going to get shocked in circumstances like this I would never make it as a news photographer. From that day I made up my mind whenever I find myself in a situation like Sharpeville I shall think of my pictures first before anything. I no longer get shocked; I am a feelingless beast while taking photographs. It is only after I

*Magubane's South Africa, Secker and Warburg, London, 1978.

complete my assignment that I think of the dangers that surrounded me, the tragedies that befell my people.

When the Sharpeville victims were buried I had a chance to cover the funeral, and this time I made sure to do the job right. The editor was pleased with my pictures. A number of them were syndicated all over the world. I remember, by the way, an incident during that service. Reverend Mahabane was speaking and said, 'God has given and now he has taken.' He was nearly killed. The people went mad, saying, 'God has not taken these people, these people were shot dead by the police. Why don't you say God has given and the South African police has taken?'

10
Echoes of the Storm

Today, so long after the event, it is hard to re-experience the climate of the period just following the Sharpeville shootings. The news had gone round the world in a few hours and the English-speaking newspapers – much more widely read in South Africa than their rivals in Afrikaans – published extensive quotes from overseas opinion. To the blacks the sense that the world was looking on in shock and horror brought new hope, and many even among the Afrikaner Nationalists were horrified at what had happened and distrustful of their own government's explanations. If the official statement were true that '. . . the disturbances resulted from a planned demonstration of about 20,000 Natives in which demonstrators attacked the police with assorted weapons, including firearms', and that 'The demonstrators shot first, and the police were forced to fire in self-defence', how was it that not a single policeman had been injured and none of their vehicles damaged, compared to 250 killed or wounded among the Africans? Throughout the country there was a feeling that changes must now be made, and that in the course of the next few weeks anything might happen. Again and again, in conversations and editorials alike, one heard or read: 'The country has reached a turning point. Things can never be the same again.' Among those who believed in the necessity for change there was a sense of urgency and that it was essential not to let the moment slip.

As we talked the situation over in the *Drum* office next

morning, Nat Nakasa said: 'You know we can't just leave it like this – two hundred and fifty African people dead and wounded, and the rest of us do absolutely nothing – as though it were some kind of a little mistake.'

'What d'you suggest?'

'Chief Luthuli should declare a Day of Mourning, and the whole country stay away from work as a sign of respect.'

Luthuli was contacted and, after consulting his chief followers, agreed, and Monday 28 March, just one week after the shootings, was fixed on as the date. The Day of Mourning was by far the most impressive African demonstration I had ever seen. It did not depend on organization for its success and to that extent justified the arguments of Robert Sobukwe and the PAC. It was an emotional response to a widely publicized appeal, following a disaster which shocked the whole country, white and black alike. Along the Reef and in the Cape the stay-away was practically complete. During the day the townships were quiet, but towards evening violence started up, mainly stone-throwing and burning of buildings. Mobs began to gather around the stations towards nightfall, lying in wait for those who had been to work, chasing and beating them.

During the morning I drove out with Ian Berry and a few visiting journalists and cameramen on a tour of the townships. Orlando was quiet, so we drove on to Moroka. The streets were deserted, except here and there a woman or child hurrying along with food or milk. We stopped at a house known to our driver, and knocked. Like almost all township houses, it was a tiny dwelling – not much more than a garage split into rooms. For a moment there was silence, then someone from inside recognized the driver through the window, and in a moment a dozen or fifteen men came pouring out. They told us they had organized a pass-burning which was just about to start. Soon other doors opened all up the street and in no time there was a crowd of sixty or seventy people.

'Look,' I said to a man who seemed to be in authority – he proved to be an ANC official. 'If the cops turn up suddenly, we'll all be pinched for holding an illegal assembly. Send away all those who have nothing to do with this, and let the others collect on some open ground with a view in all directions.'

The official shouted a few words; the women and children, with most of the men, vanished as rapidly as they had appeared. Then he and about a dozen others led the way to a patch of waste ground. They were carrying a quarter-filled sack and what appeared to be a bottle of gin, which was actually paraffin. When they reached their chosen spot, the leader shook out the sack, poured the paraffin over and began burning about seventy of the precious and detested documents. Though there was no kind of ceremony, he managed to give dignity and an air of ritual to the occasion. As the passes – cloth-bound books with a large number of stiff pages – caught fire, men seized one in each hand and began to dance and shout, waving the blazing passes in the air. I was surprised by their readiness to be photographed in this highly illegal activity. When a Fleet Street cameraman who was with us wanted them to pose grinning over the bonfire into his camera, even those who had been doing no burning rushed to get into the picture.

Ian's quickness and resource astonished me. I was still wondering how he could get anything usable from this artificial arrangement, when I saw he had already darted to one side. From there no one was looking into the lens, and the scene as the men pranced and waved their unfolded passes over the little fire looked like some strange tribal ceremony. Next day when we printed up the pictures, he had got three or four vivid shots in which half-burned passes, with the flames curling up from the opening pages, looked like fiery flowers dangling before the exultant faces; and he had one close-up of a kneeling man, his face intent and brooding as at an incantation, pressing his charred pass into the flames.

As the week went by excitement mounted. Three Africans working for the South African Broadcasting Corporation were sacked; one had put on a record of a song which had strong patriotic associations for his African listeners. Two had stayed away from work on the Day of Mourning; as marked men, they or their families would certainly have been attacked had they not done so. Their sacking led to a campaign in the townships where gangs of youths went round the houses pulling out all the Rediffusion sets. Many were thrown into the streets and burned. They also cut down the poles carrying the wires, and – when these were re-erected during the week – went round and cut them down again.

'I was listening to a lovely jazz programme last night,' Can told us, 'when a lot of young chaps came in. They tore the machine out with the wires, and flung it all into the street. It was no good arguing. Then late at night I was in another house when we heard someone scrambling about on the roof. I wondered what the hell was up, when a voice called out: "Don't worry down there in the house. There's no danger to you people. We're only tearing the radio wires off all the houses." '

The government's reaction to all this was stony-faced. The shootings, Dr Verwoerd told the House of Assembly, were the result of 'attempts to organize a massive revolt'. The way in which the police handled the situation had 'earned the gratitude of everyone'. He congratulated them on the way they had controlled themselves and placed the blame for the violence, not on pass laws or police, but on the newspapers, adding that the ANC was 'no less culpable' than the PAC for what was happening. He thus paved the way, as the ANC leaders had foreseen, for legislation which would ban the ANC – who had opposed the pass demonstrations – equally with the PAC, who were behind them.

Immediately following the Day of Mourning mass arrests began: on Tuesday 29 March more than 200 blacks and whites; early in April, hundreds more. Emergency Regulations brought in on 30 March, and made retrospective for four days, virtually put the country under martial law. The government could arrest and imprison anyone they pleased for thirty days, without giving any reason, bringing any charge, or making the fact of the arrest public. After the thirty days, notice of detention had to be tabled before both Houses of Parliament within fourteen days. This meant that anyone could be imprisoned without charge – or without even the intention of bringing any charge – for over six weeks. Many in fact were imprisoned for the whole period of the Emergency, late March to the end of August, without having any idea why they had been arrested – some of them had not been active in politics for years – the government indemnifying itself by special legislation against any legal actions which might otherwise have been brought.

Moreover, in terms of the Public Safety Act it was forbidden to publish – *or even to pass on to another person* – the names of people arrested under the regulations. Strict new laws controlled all newspapers and magazines, indeed every form of publication including gramophone records and tape recordings. Before these Emergency Regulations were withdrawn it was generally estimated that about 23,000 persons were in prison. The vast majority of these were Africans, described in official pronouncements as '*tsotsis*', 'idlers', 'workless', 'troublemakers' and so on, some thousands of whom were held in a disused mine, and it was forbidden to print any description – much less any photograph – showing the conditions in which prisoners were held.

In addition the Minister of Justice, Mr Erasmus, announced that 'in order to halt the reign of terror', penalties for intimidation and victimization would be increased tenfold. On 8 April, following yet another series of dawn arrests, the minister announced the Unlawful Organizations Act, banning altogether the ANC, PAC, and 'certain other organizations'. They remain banned to this day, and their offices, in London and elsewhere, are from time to time still raided by hirelings of the South African government.

While the excitement was still intense, I was called away to Ghana with our business manager, Ian Pritchard. By a caprice of the Nkrumah government *Drum* had been banned precisely at this moment on the allegation that the magazine was 'under the direct or indirect influence of the South

African government'. But the fact that the charge was laughable only made it more difficult to answer. The real reason, it soon emerged, was resentment at the success of a publication imported from outside the country, compounded by *Drum*'s failure to understand the way political life had developed in Ghana, and the consequent necessity to make itself friends in high places who – whether for love, money or both – would support the magazine in time of crisis. As it was, Pritchard and I spent a frenzied week interviewing ministers and entertaining a short list of *Drum*'s 'influential friends' given us by Jim Bailey. Our talks with the ministers made it plain that the only person who could lift the ban was the one who had imposed it, Nkrumah himself, and he refused to meet us. The 'influential friends', both Ghanaian and white, were happy to be entertained and generous with their advice. Its value was summed up in a letter one of them – a leading adviser to the Ghanaian government on economic and industrial matters from the UK – wrote to Jim Bailey. In it he explained that 'no useful purpose would be served by my taking action *at this point.* Later on, however, when you have seen the President and got the whole matter sorted out, I can step in and add my plea.' It was, I thought, a less eloquent expression of Dr Johnson's letter to Lord Chesterfield a couple of hundred years earlier:★ 'Is not a Patron, my Lord, one who looks with unconcern on a man struggling for life in the water, and, when he has reached ground, encumbers him with help?'

While still engaged in these negotiations we heard on the radio the startling news that Dr Verwoerd had been shot. All our difficulties in South Africa, *Drum*'s headquarters and base, would now be much intensified. It was agreed therefore that Jim Bailey would stay on in Ghana to negotiate, while Pritchard and I returned to Johannesburg at once. Almost our last experience before leaving was a raid on the two-room *Drum* office in Accra by Ghanaian Special Branch

★February 1755.

police, seeking evidence of our being under the influence of the South African government.

'What d'you think about that?' Ian asked.

'If the Special Branch found what they were looking for in the *Drum* office,' I said, 'it's more than anyone else has been able to during all the time we've been out here.'

From the airport at Johannesburg Ian Pritchard and I drove to the printing works where a new edition of *Drum* was being put to press. Under the Emergency Regulations we felt obliged to read every word and caption several times over, and a lawyer was there to read it with us. I had already been handed a confidential message from a friendly MP who had spent a morning with one of the Nationalist ministers.

'They mean to close you down,' was the message carried by hand from Cape Town where parliament was in session, for in these days everyone was extremely careful of the post. 'Give them the slightest excuse, and they'll be on to you at once.'

We had scarcely settled to our task of going through the pages when a call came from the office: 'Come back at once! There's a raid on by the Special Branch.'

Ian and I ran down to my car and drove as quickly as we could. Three members of the Special Branch were in the office, two of them men I knew from previous visits. The lieutenant in charge held up a copy of our April issue which had carried the 'Africanist' story.

'I must tell you we are thinking of bringing a prosecution against you for this issue of *Drum* – and I want to ask you a number of questions in connection with it.'

I felt enormous relief. If all they had come about was the April issue, we must be in the clear. I had been fearing some members of our staff might be more deeply involved in politics than I knew.

'May I ask you a question first?' I said.

'Yes.'

'Is this prosecution to be brought under the Emergency Regulations?'

135

'Well, in fact it will be – yes.'

'And do you know which day the Emergency Regulations came into force?'

They did not, and a discussion followed among themselves. In the end, however, they took our word for it that the regulations had been brought in on 30 March and made retrospective by four days.

'Okay – but what's that got to do with this prosecution?'

'D'you know when this magazine went on sale?'

He held it up. 'You can see. There's the date "April" on it.'

'It's dated "April",' I said, 'because ours is a monthly magazine, and we have to try to sell all through the month. But it was actually on sale on 21 March – nearly a full week before the Emergency Regulations took effect, and ten days before they were introduced.'

Our police visitors looked dubious. Suddenly I remembered that the Afrikaans evening paper, *Die Vaderland*, had printed much of our article about the Africanists on the day after it came out. This copy of *Die Vaderland* must be still in my office, and I went to fetch it. The Special Branch men turned the pages over. There it all was, quoted from the previous day's *Drum*, in a reliable Afrikaans newspaper published on March the twenty-second.

'But this issue of yours is still on sale? It's on sale now – although the Emergency Regulations have been in force for two weeks?'

'Quite right,' I said. 'But nobody said it ought not to be on sale. This is the first time the question has even been discussed.'

Our visitors left. Their stay had been short, and perfectly civil. Next day we learned that the distributing organizations had been ordered to recall and hand over all unsold copies of the April issue. It meant some loss to the firm. However, as the magazine had now been on sale for a clear three weeks we felt we had little cause for complaint.

The Special Branch, naturally enough, had been unable to believe we had simply backed a hunch that the Africanists meant business, and suspected some sinister relationship between us and them. But they clearly could not prosecute us under the Emergency Regulations for an article published long before these came into force, and the scoop had given a big stimulus to sales so that there remained only a few thousand copies scattered about the country for the police to lay their hands on.

On 7 April, while we were still up in Ghana, there had been a second wave of pre-dawn arrests and by now a large number of those, both white and black, who had been in any way associated with liberal or progressive politics, were in prison. Others, feeling the net closing, had fled the country. Numbers more had taken to a hide-and-seek life. They attended to their normal interests by day, but slept away from home. Since arrests took place in the early hours of the morning they relied on being given some warning by their families, and so being able to slip across the borders into Basutoland or Swaziland. Respectable citizens who had avoided taking part in politics but worked in close contact with Africans and mixed with them on terms of friendship, lived in this way with a small hand-case ready packed. One made a nest for himself in a loft in his own outhouse. It commanded a view of the front door and had a back entrance by which he planned to creep quietly off through the bushes to a lane where his car stood all night, ready fuelled.

Since phones were tapped, families worked out codes by which wives could let husbands know if the police had called: 'The postman's been', 'Your uncle was asking for you just now', 'The man from the Prudential wants you', and so on. And as, under the special regulations now in force, it was illegal for a wife even to tell her friends that her husband was in prison, one got used to being given ambiguous messages in reply to phone calls: 'John's away in Pretoria. We don't know when he'll be back.'

One morning as we were going down in the lift, Dorothy said to me: 'When's your turn coming, Hoppy?'

'I don't know. How should I?'

137

'Would they imprison or deport you?'

'Deport me, I should think. But who can say?'

'Well, I've just about got our flat in perfect order – but if we have to pack up everything and leave, I'm quite prepared. It's been well worth while.'

'I don't think we'll have to go.'

'Well – I don't *want* to go because I'm happy here and I love this country. . . . You don't think you ought to take any precautions, do you, like the others?'

'Sleep somewhere else, you mean? No. Why be harassed? Let's have all the normal life we can. We can start being harassed when I'm pinched. And I'll have to sleep away then anyway.'

In the office Cecil Eprile, the *Golden City Post* editor, called a meeting with Jim Bailey and myself. He wanted to know whether, in view of all the arrests, the management would stand by us and look after our families if we were sent to prison.

'Certainly,' said Jim. 'If an editor is sent to prison in the execution of his duty, the firm will give him full support. But we don't want our editors in prison. The real question is not "What does the firm do about editors who go to prison?", but "What can we all do to ensure that none of them goes there?" '

'I shouldn't mind a bit of prison,' said Cecil. 'It would be a rest cure.'

'But we don't pay editors to have rest cures,' said Jim. 'One way would be the system they had in nineteenth-century France.'

'What was that?' I asked.

'Each paper had an editor specially to go to prison. He was imprisoned and well paid for it, and the real editor got on with the work.'

'What do you think about that idea?' Cecil asked me.

'Not much. I'd rather do my own going to prison. Anyway it could only work in a society which paid great respect to legal forms. Here, if editors sheltered behind dummies, the government would just pass a law enabling them to disregard the dummies and pinch the people really responsible – and I must say I should think it justified. So we would only discredit ourselves and get pinched just the same.'

Jim smiled. 'The main thing is for you both to exercise all possible care. Everything you print should be read by the lawyers first. If you see that's done, and if you are both thoroughly familiar with all the regulations, then it'll be your own fault if you get shut up.'

The attempt on Dr Verwoerd's life, coming so closely after Sharpeville, had opened up a split in the ruling Nationalist Party which from the middle of April offered a fresh gleam of hope. On the nineteenth, at the Union Festival Celebrations, Paul Sauer, Minister of Lands, made a dramatic speech. 'The old book of South Africa was closed a month ago at Sharpeville,' he declared. For the immediate future, South Africa 'must re-consider in earnestness and honesty her whole approach to the Native question'. 'An important adjustment' would have to be made to the reference (pass) books system; the Native must be given hope for a happy existence; and he called for higher wages in urban industries.

Since Mr Sauer, besides being a minister of long standing, was also chairman of the cabinet and acted on the prime minister's behalf during his incapacitation, his speech seemed highly significant. Was there going to be a change of heart – and policy – at last?

The answer was not long in coming. Next day Mr Eric Louw, Minister of External Affairs and leader of the extremists in the absence of Verwoerd, bluntly stated in the House of Assembly that no one but the prime minister was entitled to make any statement of basic policy. In other words, Mr Sauer should shut up and toe the party line. Next day another extremist, Mr B. J. Vorster, later himself to become prime minister, rubbed it in: 'Recently doubts have arisen even among Nationalists as to whether we are on the right road, but there is no reason for panic.' There was, he said, no emergency in South Africa, only local disturbances because the Bantu had been excited to riot from the pulpit and by the overseas press. Political rights were demanded for urban

Natives because they worked for the white man. But although he was dependent on the Bantu for his labour, the European was doing him a favour by providing him with work and a livelihood.

The campaign declaring, 'We've done nothing wrong so there's no need for any change of policy,' was accompanied by one of personal adulation for Dr Verwoerd. There had always been reservations in the minds of many Afrikaners on the ground that Dr Verwoerd was a Hollander and not one of themselves. This new publicity aimed at making him a kind of honorary Afrikaner. He had shed his blood for the fatherland and therefore was mystically linked with the soil of South Africa. In addition, a statement from his doctors that the bullets fired into him had missed killing him 'by a hair's breadth' was made the basis of propaganda, sustained by newspaper writers, in pulpits and in public speeches, to the effect that only the direct intervention of God, diverting the bullets at the last fraction of a second from the fatal spot, had saved Verwoerd's life. He was thus more than ever under the personal protection of the Deity, and the people he led could be surer than ever that they were God's Chosen and that anyone who opposed their policies was trying to thwart the purposes of the Almighty.

Meanwhile the leaders of what Mr Erasmus, Minister of Justice, called 'the reign of terror' had still to be punished. On 4 May Robert Sobukwe was sentenced to three years' imprisonment for 'incitement to commit an offence as a protest against the Pass Laws' – just as the ANC leaders had forecast he would be. His lieutenant, Potlako Leballo, fiery orator and the national secretary of the PAC, was sentenced to two years; while other leaders who had either surrendered or stayed to face the music received varying sentences.

Not all the leaders could be found. Peter Raboroko, Peter Molotsi and some others had fled the country and showed up in Ghana before long. Matthew Nkoana, who had lately been working for *Drum* as a freelance, was given eighteen months. He appeared in the dock with 141 other Africans and acted as spokesman for them all, addressing the court almost without a pause for half a day, covering the whole field of South African politics. Once again, as when he appeared to give evidence for Sidney, Matthew – who, as a boy, had wanted to become a lawyer, but whose parents could never find the money – succeeded in dominating a legal scene. When the magistrate, after hearing what Matthew had to say, addressed the men to deliver sentence, there was shuffling and occasional interjections till at last the magistrate appealed to Matthew to secure him a quiet hearing.

'Yes,' said Matthew, 'I spoke for more than three hours, and it's only fair we give you a chance to speak. But I would like to point out that a lot of the things you've said are very provocative.'

'You also,' the magistrate replied, 'said a lot of things which were very provocative.'

A year later the staffs of *Drum* and *Post*, with assistance from Jim Bailey, would raise the money to pay the fine which would absolve Matthew from finishing his prison sentence. He was around Johannesburg and the locations for a few months, still looking like a black undergraduate and arguing politics with anyone who would stop and listen. But it was not long before charges under the Suppression of Communism Act were brought against him, and in December 1961 he was convicted of 'wrongfully and unlawfully performing an act or acts calculated to further the achievements of the objects of Communism'. This time his sentence was one of three years. Matthew appealed, but by the time his case came up he had left the country for the arduous and painful life of a political exile.

So in a series of convictions, the hopes that had been raised petered out, and Afrikaner Nationalism, having reassured itself that it had no sin on its conscience and that God was as ever firmly on its side, decided that it had no lesson at all to learn from the Sharpeville massacre.

11

Cameramen in the Congo

Ian Berry's spectacular success at Sharpeville – when dozens of overseas photographers were in South Africa anticipating trouble, and he alone got pictures of the action – coming on top of his winning the *Encyclopaedia Britannica* award earlier in the year, had made him a very hot property indeed. Bombarded with offers from overseas, he naturally asked whether *Drum* could increase his all too modest salary. I could not answer as I wished because I was at that moment being pressed to fire Berry on the grounds that there was room in the magazine for only two or three picture stories by him each month, and that if he were employed by someone else he could do these few stories for us, but at less cost. So far I had ignored the pressure since, apart from the fact that I could not fire someone who was working excellently, I was not going to kick away one of the two pillars on which our magazine rested. Working in the peculiar conditions of South Africa, it was essential to have both a white and a black cameraman, because there were many situations in which one could operate and not the other. Moreover I was convinced that, in Africa's 'Independence Year' of 1960, the news would come increasingly from other parts of Africa – in which Ian, with a British passport, could travel freely, and Peter, with no passport, could not travel at all. In addition, as regards both Ian and Peter, I felt like a manager with two good fighters or a producer with

142

two stars; I would sooner lose an ear than let either of them go.

The offer which most attracted Ian came from the renowned Magnum cooperative agency in Paris, and together we worked out a scheme whereby, while remaining a *Drum* cameraman, Ian could also freelance for Magnum, the money so earned going partly to himself and partly to the firm. It was the kind of complicated arrangement I dislike, but the advantages far outweighed the drawbacks since it meant, first, that we kept Ian; and, second, that we should secure picture stories from other parts of Africa where *Drum* would never send on account of cost.

Our arrangement was agreed early in June, and the first assignment proposed by Magnum was due near the end of the same month – the independence celebrations of the former Belgian Congo.

I had been to make final arrangements with Ian Pritchard when, as I was going out of his office, he called after me: 'Why don't you go up there with Ian yourself?'

'Can I?'

'Yes – why not? Arrange the work with Humphrey.'

'I'm coming with you,' I told Ian.

'Good,' Ian replied in the curiously vague language he employed. 'You can speak the bloody whatsit and carry my spare thingummies. It's hell trying to shoot both colour and black and white unless there's someone to give you a hand with all the doo-dahs.'

In Leopoldville we were lucky to find a friend already installed. Jim Bell, in charge of the *Time-Life* office in Johannesburg, was a thrusting, tireless baldhead who had been up to the Congo half a dozen times before independence. He lent me his notes on the political situation: extraordinarily detailed and complete, they supplied far more information than could ever find its way into his magazines, and he gave up the next morning to taking us on a quick run round the city. Our immediate need was to secure press passes; and here, in our first task on our first day, we came up against that blank wall upon which so many journalists would exhaust, and a few destroy, themselves in the next few months – the barrier of Congolese military bloody-mindedness.

The office issuing passes was inside the Palais de la Nation, an imposing building with a central dome and pillared portico, where the newborn parliament would meet. But to get to this office it was necessary to go past the sentry on the gate – and he would let no one in who had not already got a pass to show. We argued with the sentry until I could see he was about to lose his temper – and he had a long, thin bayonet and a loaded rifle – then arranged for Jim Bell, who already had a pass, to go through and speak to the Belgian official. The Belgian shouted to the soldier to let us through, but he took not the least notice, and it was only when the official actually came out and escorted us into the Palais, keeping between us and the sentry, that we were able to obtain passes. Similar incidents would happen to myself and other journalists in different parts of the Congo many times in future weeks, and it became commonplace to be summoned to a press conference by Lumumba – or later on by Tshombe – and then driven away by sentries on the door, despite the shouts and cries from Congolese officials to let us in.

Ian was anxious to get pictures of the top Belgian officials concerned with the handover of power and I to hear what they said about the Congo's future. So when I learned there was to be a cocktail party at the residence of the governor of the province, I suggested we drive out there and gatecrash it. The residence, a few miles out of town, was an imposing villa whose main room, on the first floor, was reached by an elegant curved staircase. One side of the room opened on to a wide balcony covered with grass, delightful to the feet. There were window boxes all round, and a superb view over the vast, misty Congo river. Everyone from both sides was at the party, and as soon as I could I went up to Governor-General Cornelis and asked if he felt confident about the country's future after his countrymen had gone home in a few days' time.

'Yes,' he said. 'Quite satisfied. Everything will be all right. We've got a government – that is the great thing!'

He must, I suggested, have had an extremely difficult few weeks.

'M'yes. But I know everyone well. All the time I have understood the people I am dealing with. After all, I've been out here twenty-seven years.'

Did he anticipate trouble when his countrymen actually left? After all, the country was vast and had not been united long.

'No. The worst is over. All should now be well.'

Would he be staying on for a time himself?

'No. I am due to leave in a couple of days.'

I sensed a note of satisfaction in this last reply and asked whether he would come back to the Congo, if invited.

'Possibly – though not in any official capacity.'

I also had a talk with Kasavubu, the new head of state. He was cordial but null, and extremely pleased that in less than a week's time the splendid villa where we were meeting would be his.

Our next few days were spent photographing official celebrations, openings of parliament, ceremonial parades and banquets. But even beneath these official occasions there already ran a mounting current of excitement and distrust.

'Why d'you wear this piece of foliage?' I asked some young men in the crowd, apparently waiting to cheer their new leaders.

The first two would not reply. The third declared: 'This is a sacred herb. It makes us fearless in battle. Nothing can harm us if we are wearing this.' He fingered his green spray proudly – but whom, I wondered, did he and his friends mean to fight after the Belgians had departed?

Gradually the tension mounted, despite a nightly curfew at eight o'clock and the presence everywhere of the Force Publique, the Congo's police force army, officered by Belgians. A day or two before independence, when there was a big reception at the Palais, we arrived early to secure a good position. Crowds had already assembled and more

145

and more people came piling in, lining the streets and scrambling over an ornamental fountain which offered a vantage point. What everyone was waiting for was the procession of cars bringing the new president, Kasavubu, the new prime minister, Lumumba, and all the other twenty-odd ministers, each in his new black Mercedes limousine.

However, an hour before the official party arrived, an old car and a van drove into the open space between the Palais and the fountain. Three or four men scrambled out and rapidly set up a loudspeaker through which a small man – climbing up on to the roof of his stationary car – harangued the crowd. The small man had an unusual appearance, combining the thrust-out chin and arrogant eye of a Mussolini with the toothbrush moustache, strutting walk and flow of angry eloquence made familiar by another dictator. For half an hour he talked on, denouncing the leaders in whose honour the crowd had supposedly assembled. Lumumba, he cried, had promised him a top job in his government. Now Lumumba had gone back on his promise, and he had been squeezed out. His party, he declared, would not accept this. Nor would they accept the results of the recent elections – the first in the Congo's history – since they 'do not truly reflect the importance of our party in the life of the Republic'.

The small man, I learned, was Albert Kalonji, an important chief of the Baluba. A month or two later, following the secession of Katanga under Tshombe, he would seize the opportunity to declare independent his own 'Diamond State' of South Kasai, with an army of a few hundred uniformed soldiers plus a great many armed tribesmen. In place of a capital, he would have some fifty villas lent to him and his entourage by the Belgian company who owned the diamond mines and the town of Bakwanga – really no more than a residential suburb set down on the bare veldt – which was now his, as well as their, headquarters. Here he would be dependent on the company, not merely for revenue and accommodation, but for water, fuel and food – flown in to the single landing strip. Established here, Kalonji conferred on himself a new title – 'The

146

Mulopwe' – which, he explained, meant that he was not only a great tribal chief and head of his own independent state but also entitled to semi-divine prestige. The title, though no doubt comforting to Kalonji, seemed to have little practical effect, since almost the only success achieved by the disintegrated and incompetent army of Lumumba would be to rout Kalonji's Balubas and kill about a thousand of them.

After strutting around for some minutes Kalonji drove off, and almost at once the ministers started to appear. Ian shot his pictures, and we set out to walk back to our hotel. The Palais was a couple of miles out of town, the other journalists had all left, and there was not the least hope of getting a taxi. We had not gone far when we heard shouting and saw, coming up the road behind us, a hundred and fifty or more women, supporters of Kalonji. They had linked arms and were sweeping along, thirty abreast. Big and powerfully built, they made a fine sight as they stormed ahead, turbanned, shouting, their loose robes swirling round them and the dust of the boulevards rising in clouds. Ian was soon running backwards in front of them, dropping on one knee every now and then to snatch a shot. For a few minutes we ran with the women, then they took a side turning and we were left standing at a crossroads. We were still in the residential suburbs, a district of pleasant villas with wide gardens full of flowering shrubs and palms, and I was looking for the road which would lead us back to town, when there came a shout from Ian: 'Hell, what's this?'

Fifty yards away was a square, into which armoured cars and lorries full of troops had begun to pour. We ran to see what was happening. Further up the road leading back into the city was a crowd, shouting and brandishing sticks, some hundreds more of Kalonji's supporters trying to join up with the main body. This crowd was being held back by a thin line of Congolese soldiers under a Belgian officer, and the motorized troops filling the square were evidently reinforcements he had summoned.

Suddenly a jeep in the square began to move. It ran rapidly up the road towards the crowd and a Congolese soldier

147

standing in the back began to fire. He was not firing directly at the crowd, but lobbing canisters which turned over and over in the air and then fell, hissing, among their feet. Clouds of smoke fizzed out of every canister and a pool of emptiness formed round it in the crowd. I did not understand what was going on, but Ian, with more experience of riots, cried out delightedly: 'They're using tear gas!' He thrust his camera bag into my hands, tied his handkerchief round his nose, dodged past the soldiers in the square and disappeared up the road into the trouble.

I tried to follow, but as soon as I got into the tear gas area I was driven back choking and with streaming eyes. Three times I tried, and each time turned away. After about five minutes, looking up the road, I could see that the crowd had been driven out from the confinement of the houses to where the road ran between fields and the gas could get away. I put my handkerchief over my face and ran to overtake Ian, now hard at work.

Within arm's length of us, a strange, slow-motion struggle was going on. The crowd, packed tight, many wheeling bicycles and some women carrying babies, was being herded in reluctant flight along the tarmac. Deep ditches on either side stopped the people breaking out into the fields. Eight Congolese soldiers under a Belgian officer were hounding them along. The soldiers wore steel helmets clamped down over their brows, ears and necks; they had goggles against the gas, and carried rifles with long bayonets fixed. The officer had a revolver, stick and whistle.

They did not fire shots nor stab into vitals with the bayonets, though there were one or two men in the crowd with streaming head wounds. They just herded the people before them up the road, bashing them on arms and shoulders with their rifle butts, nipping in to crack heavily down with rubber truncheons, and kicking. Particularly they kicked the bicycles, their heavy boots crunching in the mudguards and the spokes.

There was one tall young soldier who had inwardly gone mad. Sweat streamed down his harsh features and only the presence of his officer prevented him from killing. His special victim was a small man in a yellow vest. Printed on the vest in black letters were the words MANGEZ LE POISSON DU MARCO. Yellow Vest dived, turned, twisted, but was always finding himself at the tail of the crowd, and the tall soldier would be after him with murderous eyes. In and out of the batons, kicks and curses, Ian was dodging – dropping on one knee as a soldier brought the butt of his rifle down on a woman's back; standing on tiptoe to catch the angry scowl of a protester whose bicycle had been kicked in. Hastily he handed some of his gear to me, then slid back into the fight. Not only the soldiers were shouting at him. Some of the other cameramen – four had magically appeared like vultures – shouted at him too: out of envy.

Soon, as suddenly as it had begun, the action ended. The road ran out into the town and the people scattered. The soldiers pushed back their helmets and mopped their streaming brows. 'Thank God for a bit of action!' Ian shouted. 'I shouldn't be surprised if I haven't got a couple of decent pictures in that brouhaha. Did you see the way the tall thin guy was lamming into the little fellow with his yellow whatsit? And how that officer at the same time urged the soldiers on and held them back? Should have been a scene in a movie. . . .'

Ian, slight, bearded, diffident, was in his element when there was trouble. He came to life like a racing man when he sees the horses in the paddock or an Italian at sight of a pretty woman. Normally he spoke little and was inclined to say still less when bored and fed up. When he *did* talk, it was in language of Kafkaesque vagueness: 'What about going round to the howsit and sending off the other thingummy?' In the hunt for pictures he was inexhaustible. Often, as I settled down to a half hour's reading, I would hear the suggestion, soft but insistent as the voice of conscience: 'Don't you think we ought *just* to slip up to the so-and-so, and try to grab a couple of shots of old who-ha? I'm sure the last ones I got were under-exposed.'

Through Ian I soon got to know other cameramen on this

assignment. Barry von Below worked for an evening paper, the Johannesburg *Star*. Short, sturdy, a jockey in build, I would see him darting in and out of trouble in a well-cut suit with an inch of elegant shirt cuff flapping round his wrist. He was never satisfied with his work, and always sure someone else had done better than he did. Off duty, Barry enjoyed talking about books. He had read and thought a lot.

'Have you read *Dr Zhivago*? What do you think of it?' But before I could reply, he had interrupted himself: 'I say, Ernie's not here! I bet he's on to something. He was on the spot yesterday when that Belgian was arrested. Just half a shake while I see if he's in his room. Hang on to my drink, someone!'

The missing man, another South African, was Ernie Christie. Alert, dapper, grinning, always on the ball, he knew just what was due to happen every day, knew the times of planes and the situations of post offices – whom to approach for permits, passes, facilities, free cars. He would slip in everywhere with a Cockney smile and no French. 'Just stand out of the light, mate, while I get my picture,' and the bewildered Belgian official or sweating Congolese sergeant, instead of thrusting him away, would hold his spare camera or push the crowd aside. Unlike Barry – who always thought his pictures ought to have been better – Ernie was constantly delighted with his own success. 'Wonderful stuff this morning!' he would say as he joined us for a beer. 'Cops pitching into the Congolese like mad. Only waited till I arrived to get started. Then as soon as the *Life* boys showed up, they packed it in. Couldn't have been better!' He rubbed his hands with satisfaction.

He seemed the hundred per cent happy extrovert. But Ernie really *did* have ulcers, so his drive and bustle took their toll. And when things failed to go well – as when a young Congolese civil servant snatched King Baudouin's sword on the far side of town – his face wore an aggrieved expression as if the least you'd expect was a telegram warning him to be on the spot.

Tall, lean, bespectacled Larry Burrows had worked for

Life for seventeen years. English by birth, he was by now indistinguishable from an American except for a gentleness not usual with American newsmen. Working for *Life* meant all the newest equipment; cars at his service all day instead of struggling for taxis; a hired interpreter; now and then a charter plane or helicopter. Yet, with all the lavishness of *Life* and *Time*, it came down in the end to the man himself.

I was in the city the day before independence, and the king was due to give the whole place away tomorrow. I had walked to the boulevard to watch his arrival and now sat at a table drinking, waiting.

There was a stir in the crowd and a few motorcyclists hammered by. 'This must be it,' I thought and jumped up on a café chair. More motorcyclists – and then, running like hares, but stopping every few moments to swing round and shoot, there tore past me Ernie and Barry, Ian and Larry Burrows. They had dropped their coats somewhere and their damp shirts flapped against their backs. Sweat streamed into their eyes. The crowd and police kept getting in their way. But they ran while I watched, for a quarter of a mile, constantly turning to shoot at the slow-moving royal car. Ernie, once a well-known footballer, was the least in trouble – dodging and darting up the wing. Barry, more worried than ever, scudded up the middle of the road. Ian, scarf flying, ran with a high, loping trot. Larry, white and exhausted, ready to drop, held grimly on. He explained it afterwards in the hotel with his own particular mannerism of speech.

'We were in a lorry – an' that. The four of us. We were following the king – an' that – into the city. The Belgians, of course, had the first lorry. It was all fixed up with stands – an' that – so they could shoot down into his car. The French had the next best, just like they always do. . . . We were given the last lorry – right at the back. Well, we're just coming into the town – with all the people cheering an' that – when our lorry breaks down.'

'Belgians fixed it,' grunted Barry, nodding grimly.

'We think we've had it now, so we all hop down – cursin'

an' that. Ernie spots that the king's going round two sides of a square, and if we cut across the middle we can get in front of him. But there's a line of troops in the way and the crowd an' that behind.'

'Yes,' said Ian, cutting in, 'and Ernie just takes one look, shouts "Follow me" – and busts his way through the line of soldiers. One chap I saw would have stuck him with his bayonet, only by then Ernie was halfway across the square.'

'Well, then,' Larry continued, 'we have to dive through this crowd and the line of troops again over the other side – and we find we're in front of the king's car, an' that. We run like hell, an' that, and we shoot our pictures. Backwards.'

He laid his hand on his silk shirt with its embroidered monogram. 'You know when that sod of a driver pulled the lorry up suddenly?'

'Yes,' they agreed.

'I was flung up against the corner post. I think I've bust a rib, an' that.'

He had.

It was a long time since I'd been out on a job with cameramen. Dismissing from my mind a couple I would come across later in Katanga, the cameramen I was with in the Congo were a bunch of true professionals; quick-witted as weasels, hard-boiled as jockeys; wary, astute, hard-working. Always alert to steal a march, they were equally ready to share a chance, give a lift or cover up for a man who had missed the boat.

Their company did me good. I kept wishing I had a paper that could hire the lot.*

* * *

*Of these four brave men, Larry Burrows died in February 1971 when the helicopter from which he was covering the Vietnam war was shot down. Ernie Christie killed himself in March 1979, flying his light aircraft into a block of Johannesburg flats during an emotional crisis. Ian Berry is still with Magnum as a freelance cameraman of international renown; and Barry von Below is picture editor of the Johannesburg *Star*, to which he gave so many years of service as a troubleshooting photographer.

After a week of intense activity Ian was as near to being satisfied as I had ever known him. But I still hankered after one thing. I wanted to interview Lumumba.

'Oh hell,' said Ian. 'Everyone's trying that one on. You'll never get him, and if you do he won't say anything. Cut it out, and let's go round the townships again. Yesterday the Force Publique were simply carving one chap up – only I couldn't get close enough to photograph the pieces.'

I persisted, but Lumumba proved no easy prey. I began with his secretary, Mandolo, going up to him in the lounge of the Memling Hotel, nerve centre of Leopoldville where all the strands of public and journalistic life crossed and entangled.

'But certainly! An interview for your paper with the prime minister? Delighted! Where are you staying? The Stanley. I shall ring you there as soon as I have fixed the appointment.'

More cautiously I approached the mysterious Mme X, part Italian, part Creole, loaned as 'adviser' to Lumumba, it was rumoured, by Sekou Touré of Guinea. Circuitously, with many compliments and tentative propitiatory phrases, I led up to the question of the interview – towards which I invited her to use some fragment of her enormous influence. For a moment I believed we were there; a decision in my favour was struggling across that pallid countenance which seemed to have been built up – like composite pictures of twentieth-century man – by laying pictures of all nations over each other and printing out the highest common factor. But just then a shadow fell. It was Jason Sendwe, Lumumba's choice to take charge of the province of Katanga as soon as ever the troublesome Moishe Tshombe should have been eliminated.

'Jason!' she exclaimed delightedly. 'You will take me out to lunch! And as for your interview, monsieur – you can depend on me. You can depend on me!' she assured me over her shoulder as she vanished.

I went next to the office of Lumumba's newspaper. On the first four visits the place was closed – a new experience for me in newspaper offices. On the fifth I found the door

153

open and walked in. A young Congolese sat with his feet
up on a desk, eating a potato. We conversed in a sort of
pidgin French.

'Monsieur Lumumba, he no come here. Why he want
come here? Monsieur Lumumba print paper so he become
prime minister of Congo. Now he prime minister – why he
want come office more?'

'But doesn't his paper still appear?'

'Sometimes yes. Sometimes no.'

'What do you do here then?'

'Me circulation manager and chief of staff. . . . Also head
political executive,' he added as an afterthought. I took him
for a caretaker or the man who passed copies out to the
street sellers.

'Look,' I said, 'I have an urgent message for the prime
minister. Can you give me his telephone number?'

He shook his head – then, catching sight of the hundred-
franc note. 'Telephone number? To ring prime minister?'

I nodded.

The political executive fished in a drawer, pulled out a
scrap of paper and carefully printed out the number 81.82.
Two days and about fourteen telephone calls later, I learned
that the number he had sold me was that of the nightwatch-
man in the National Museum. It was time now for a frontal
attack. On the evening of Independence Day, at the state
banquet for a thousand guests, seeing that Lumumba had
not spoken a word for ten minutes to the Belgian dignitaries
on either side, and having noted that his bodyguard was
securely drinking in the press bar, I went directly up to him.

'Mr Prime Minister,' I began, 'I am in your country on
behalf of one of the leading European picture magazines. In
the past few days my cameraman and I have made a truly
impressive record, both of the ceremonies surrounding independence and also of popular reactions. One thing is still
missing – a short interview with yourself on the future of
the Congo.'

Lumumba said nothing.

'As prime minister – and as leader of one of the parties

which has stood consistently for the unity of the Congo – your views are of intense interest to readers overseas.'

Still no answer.

If politeness fails, I thought, try something different. 'There has also,' I added, 'been much criticism about your speech when you attacked the Belgians at the ceremony of transferring power. The speech is said to have been out of place. Have you anything to reply?'

Lumumba looked up. He was a tall, thin man, of considerable presence, wearing his evening clothes and his sash – some order, I imagined, recently conferred – with an air. He had a small goatee, not thick but wispy. As with many Africans, the hair on his face seemed to grow hesitantly, giving the impression that once this soft beard were shaved away it would be the work of months to grow another. About his mouth there was something sardonic and contemptuous, but his eyes – behind powerful lenses – had a formidable glow. His hands were large with twiggy fingers, which he clasped and unclasped as he spoke.

'*Criticism of my speech*? Surely it was plain enough? What could anyone find to criticize in *that*?'

'Your critics, Monsieur Prime Minister, say this was a formal occasion calling for a formal response – and you made it the occasion for an attack.'

'Every occasion is a proper one for saying what is true. The Belgians have done next to nothing for my country. Am I expected to *praise* them for this remarkable achievement? What would my followers think of me if I did?'

Lumumba's Belgian neighbours were beginning to show interest. A waiter hovered near with a fresh course.

'It is exactly these points on which my paper is anxious to secure your views. If I may stay and discuss them now, I shall be happy to do so – but if you prefer me to call at some more convenient time. . . .'

'Be at my house before eight o'clock tomorrow morning. You know my house? Well then – tomorrow morning. But be sure you are there by eight o'clock.'

I found Ian. He had been photographing some painted

belly dancers in a tent, described as 'Grande Demonstration Folklorique'.

'It's in the bag,' I said.

The Belgian diplomat was bowing courteously. 'Which of you two gentlemen is Lord Dundee?' he asked.

It was tempting, but it clearly wouldn't work out. 'Neither of us is Lord Dundee,' I answered. 'We are two English journalists whom Monsieur Lumumba instructed to come here at eight o'clock for an interview.'

His face fell but clearly once in, you were elected. 'I'm afraid you may have to wait some time,' he said. 'This is our morning for receiving state representatives.' He looked round the room. 'Those who will shortly become ambassadors.'

I answered that we were prepared to wait and turned to consider my fellow diplomats. 'Which country do you represent?' I asked a grey-haired figure sitting next to me. He hesitated, then replied not in French but in English: 'I am from Saudi Arabia. That gentleman opposite is from Iraq. Next to him is the representative of Iran. The group in the corner is of Liberia.'

'And the tall gentleman?' I asked, indicating a handsome Nordic figure whom he had not yet identified.

'He is the future ambassador from Nebbidge.'

I racked my brains. Though my education was old-fashioned, I doubted if there could be a whole country I had never heard of, especially a European country.

'From *what* country did you say?' I asked again.

'From Nebbidge,' the future ambassador repeated crossly.

At that moment a tall, handsome presence with a square jaw, clipped moustache and greying hair was shown into the room, accompanied by a man I knew to be the British consul.

'Bulldog Drummond,' Ian whispered.

'Lord Dundee,' I whispered back. At that moment it suddenly struck me where to find 'Nebbidge' on the map.

My informant had lapsed into French – the language of diplomacy. It was Norvège from which the handsome Nordic figure came. After a short wait a door into the passage by which we had come in was opened, and a secretary came out from what was clearly the prime minister's study. He shook hands cordially with Lord Dundee and led him and the consul inside.

During the next hour only one person among those waiting gained admission. A dapper little man seated unobtrusively behind the curtain, he was clearly nobody's ambassador but might have been a small Levantine trader. However, when the secretary next came out he caught his eye and smiled. The secretary nodded. The little man – now seen to be carrying a large silver tray wrapped in tissue paper – got up and vanished, bowing, into the interior. In ten minutes or so we saw him emerge into the passage and make his smiling way to the front door without his tray.

After a couple of hours everyone was restive. One or two of the diplomats got up and walked about, shrugging their shoulders at each other.

'Let's pack it in,' Ian whispered. 'God knows what we may be missing in the streets.'

'Give it half an hour,' I hedged. It was now 10.30. Punctually at quarter to eleven the door of Lumumba's study opened and he came through, followed by his secretary. We all stood up as he made the circuit, shaking every hand. I nudged Ian: 'Get cracking. This is all we'll get.' He followed the prime minister round the room, snapping away in the half light.

When he reached the door by which he had come in, the prime minister turned and faced us: 'Gentlemen, I am happy indeed to see you here. I welcome you personally, and I welcome you as the representatives of your various countries. I give a particular welcome to the representative of a fellow African nation' – he looked at the Liberian delegate – 'whom we know we can number among our true friends. I should have liked,' he went on, 'to talk to all you gentlemen individually. Unfortunately I have just received an urgent

157

summons from the head of state which renders that impossible. Here, however, is my secretary' – pushing him forward. 'Monsieur Mandolo is an excellent secretary, in whom I have complete confidence. I hope you will stay and talk with him. He will write in his notebook whatever you wish to convey to me. He and I will go through the notebook this evening, and it will be exactly as if you had conversed with me in person. . . . But now, gentlemen, to my great regret, I must say goodbye.'

As the prime minister left the room, the future ambassadors glanced meaningfully at one another and strode out to their cars. All passed the waiting secretary without a word.

'It is no kindness to a country,' I wrote that evening in my notebook, 'when its independence comes too suddenly, since its leaders lack any chance of learning how to cope with the enormous difficulties of their task.'

12

Man Hunt

The Congo's Independence Day was Thursday 30 June 1960, and by the evening of the following day Ian and I had almost completed our assignment. At intervals throughout our stay he had posted off packets of photographs to the Magnum agency in Paris, and we should be taking back with us to Johannesburg on the Monday enough to fill half an issue of *Drum*. As we sat drinking in the bar of the Memling Hotel with our fellow journalists – Americans, British and South Africans drank together, and the French and Belgians on their own – we felt satisfied and relaxed. Then, during that night, there was trouble at a village near the airport, several houses burned down and about twenty people injured. On the Saturday morning, when we drove out there, the ruins were still smouldering and there were slogans daubed over the scorched walls, but little to photograph. However the city was full of rumours, and in the evening someone handed me a slip of paper with the name DENDALA printed on it in capitals – I have the slip of paper by me as I write.

Dendala, or Dendale, is a suburb of Leopoldville, part of the African quarter and a stronghold of the Bakongo people; Kasavubu, the Congo's president and leader of the numerous Bakongo tribe, had obtained his first electoral mandate as burgomaster of Dendala. The slip bore only the name, but having nothing else to go by Ian and I decided to get up early and go out there next morning, and Barry von Below said he'd come with us. The first taxi we took wanted not

only the usual hundred francs an hour, but to be filled up
with petrol too, so we ditched him and took another out to
Dendala.

Wide tarmac roads met our gaze. Broad dusty fringes, the
equivalent of other roads, ran beyond them on both sides of
the central one, and beyond them straggled walls of mud or
stucco, occasionally dwindling to a fence or merging into
shops, a bar, some houses. At right angles, dusty tracks
too rough for anything but bicycles wandered off among
dwellings of baked mud or wattle, roofed with corrugated
iron or matting. Being Sunday, the streets were crowded,
partly with women out shopping or on their way to church,
but mainly with a throng of men and boys in white shirts
with khaki shorts or trousers. Many were carrying sticks
and the air smelt of danger. I caught sight of a spiral of smoke
ahead and directed the driver towards it. It was coming
from a brand-new bicycle, lying under a tree with its tyres
burning. There was something oddly sinister about this sight
– a bicycle burning quietly and the passers by taking no
notice – and I was certain now we should see trouble.

From time to time as we drove along we caught sight of
a swirl of movement among the white-clad youth. Tension
seemed about to spark off action, but by the time the car
reached the spot there was nothing to be seen, and through
it all the people went on with their shopping and flocked
steadily into the churches where mass was being celebrated.
A lovely girl, not more than fifteen years old, was passing
close beside us on the pavement. She wore a white dress and
a round white hat, held her little head high and clasped a
prayer book to her tiny waist. I must have been gazing at
her with visible delight, because the driver called over his
shoulder: 'You want that girl? I get her for you tonight. You
tell me where you stay – I go now and. . . .'

'My God!' came a shout from Ian. 'What's that over there?
Quick! Tell him to drive across there – *now*!'

'Go on up the street and turn,' I told the driver. 'Then
come slowly back down the far side. Keep right into the
gutter.'

160

'Quick! Quick! For Christ's sake, hurry!' Barry shouted.
It was a man hunt.

A big, powerfully built fellow in a white sleeveless vest
was running through the crowd, pounding along slowly but
determinedly like a rugby player through a crowd of would-
be tacklers. His pursuers dodged after him, slashing and
beating, some with sticks or strips of rubber cut from car
tyres; one or two had iron bars, and everyone, as they saw
him coming, joined in with whatever was handy – some
even slipping off their shoes to crack at him. We were right
into the gutter now, keeping slow pace with the runner, Ian
and Barry shooting through open windows. The man was
tiring fast, but most of the blows fell glancingly and he kept
going. Now he stumbled, coming heavily down on to one
knee, but he forced himself up and held on, waving his arms
before him like a swimmer. They were throwing stones at
him too, not the pebbles boys chuck at one another's heads,
but quite big stones, small boulders such as go into an
English garden wall. Suddenly somebody ran up and threw
a bicycle full in his path. The runner trod on it, slipped, and
came crashing down immediately in front of us.

The taxi stopped, and the two cameramen worked fever-
ishly focusing and snapping, then all at once the crowd
closed round him. I saw one pursuer run up and kick the
fallen man full in the face, while another began systematically
cutting into his back with a long rubber strip. I realized that
they meant to go on hacking away at him till he no longer
twitched. Beside myself with rage, I slipped out of the taxi,
took two steps to the spot, and stood over the man. '*Assez!
Assez!*' I shouted furiously. '*Laissez-le!*' I had no feeling at
all that the crowd might attack me; on the contrary, I knew
quite certainly they wouldn't. But I was afraid they might
seize hold of the man, drag him away from me, and finish
him off out of my reach. When two or three boys rushed in
with their sticks and slashed again, I shouted at them so
fiercely that they shrank away. Directly facing me, a yard
away, was a Congolese in a blue shirt. I looked at him, he

looked at me. I saw he was on my side and he put his arms up to hold back those nearest to him.

What was to be done next? I could hear Ian and Barry shouting to me from the taxi: 'Come back, you bloody fool. You *can't* do that! Come back!'

I thought, we can shove this chap into the back between us and get him to hospital. I called out, suggesting we do this. 'No! No!' they said. 'Come back, for God's sake!

I daren't take my eye off the crowd, but managed to glance at the driver. He was laughing heartily. I made signs that we should take the injured man into the car, but the driver flatly refused, since the man's back was a mass of blood and dust. Suddenly, as I hesitated, the hunted man got up, staggered into the road, crossed it unharmed, and began to trot, slowly and brokenly, down one of the side turnings. A few boys followed, hitting at him in a desultory way as if their heart were no longer in it. I followed too for a moment till I saw he would get away. It was amazing to me that he could still get up and run; his face was a pulpy mass, with smashed lips hanging loose like Sidney's when the cops had hammered him, and his back was striped as if he had been flogged, great dull red scores whose open edges were grey with dust. His blood was splashed over my trousers.

'God, Tom!' said Barry as I slipped back into the car. 'You mustn't do that – you're a journalist.'

'Well, thank God we're all safe,' said Ian as the car slid off. The driver was still laughing.

We spent the rest of the morning in the African part of the city. As tension heightened we didn't care to be on our own, so we attached ourselves to a patrol of military police, four jeeps with about sixteen Congolese under a Belgian officer. His patrol ran up and down the streets continuously. Whenever he saw a man being beaten up he would stop to rescue him, order him to point out his attackers, or, if he were too badly hurt, push him into a jeep to be carried to hospital.

'How long have you been at this job?' I asked.

'I was called back from my holiday in January 1959, when

the first trouble started. I've hardly had a day off since,' he said, wearily mopping his strained face.

Suddenly he let out a shout. Dave Snell, a *Time-Life* writer who had joined on to our convoy during the morning, was coming towards us, walking awkwardly, peering constantly back over his shoulder. Dave was a heavily built man wearing shorts and a coloured baseball cap. In one of his shirt pockets was a row of ballpoint pens, in the other a row of cigars. As he came nearer we could see why he looked so anxiously around, for close behind him trod an evil troll, his steel helmet jammed over his eyes, his wickedly thin bayonet in the small of Dave Snell's back.

The officer roared a second time. Sullenly, reluctantly, as though robbed of his booty, the troll slunk off. Dave passed the officer a cigar. 'For God's sake,' he said to us all as he bit off the end, 'keep close to me. With me and my men here, you're safe. Don't wander off! That little chap was from the Force Publique – their own officers can hardly handle them, and if you get into their hands there's damn all I can do for you.'

'What's the cause of the trouble?' I asked, as we rested for a moment by the jeeps. 'Why are these chaps being hunted by the others?'

'Tribal hostility. . . . The fact is that we Belgians have played up tribal differences and encouraged tribal organization. It makes things easier for the politicians – or they think it does – because they can keep people divided. But it makes life a bloody sight harder for us.'

'Why?'

'Because the people never really settle down together. Take this whole Cité Indigène, with its various suburbs such as this one – it's all part of the territory of the Bakongo tribe. It looks like an African suburb anywhere to you and me, but to them it's their particular tribal land. Into this territory in the last years have been brought thousands of men from other tribes. Fellows with some bit of skill – lorry drivers, machine operators, builders, or whatever it may be; they find themselves a lodging and settle down. . . . During the week, when everyone's at work, it's okay. But when there's a Sunday or a holiday, trouble starts.'

'What starts it?'

'Well, you see these chaps we keep picking up – chaps who've been knocked about, like this one crying now inside the jeep?'

I nodded.

'You notice they're a different type from the others? The Bakongo on the whole are small and slight. As individuals they're docile. When I go like this to a Bakongo' – and he thrust his helmeted face into mine with a grimace – 'he's frightened and gives back. If I'm questioning him he spills the beans. The Bakongo are only dangerous in a mass – these others are mainly Bayakas.' $E \, o t \, 3$.

'What are they like?'

'As you see – physically different. Squat, heavily built, often with a rather brutal expression. They're also individualists – much more courageous and more arrogant than the Bakongo. Trouble starts because one of them behaves arrogantly or says something tactless. Or else a number of Bakongo get into a pack and just turn on any Bayaka they come across. That's where the Bayaka's physical difference lands him in trouble – he's so easily spotted.'

'What d'you do with all the chaps you're pulling in?'

'Take the injured to hospital.'

'And the others?'

'Give the troublemakers a taste of their own medicine.' He waved his arm and shouted to his men; we all piled into our vehicles and drove off. Later that morning when we stopped at a police station, we got a glimpse of the troublemakers' 'medicine'. At the back of the station was a bare space surrounded by high walls, and in the dust, each a yard or two apart from the next, squatted perhaps fifty men, each holding a paving stone above his head. Walking among the ranks were half a dozen uniformed Congolese who delivered a sharp kick to any man who lowered his paving stone, while in each corner three or four more police kept guard with automatic weapons. It was a rough way of dispensing justice, but it was clearly impossible to bring all these men to trial or to obtain evidence if they were tried, and after seeing what I had that morning I felt that at times justice needs to be rough. Most of the men, we were told, would be kept there for a few hours and then sent home. In all, according to the midday radio, some eighty to ninety people had been taken to hospital that morning and some 150–200 arrested. Astonishingly no one, it seemed, had yet been killed.

As we paid our taxi driver off and took down his name for future journeys, he shook his head sagely at us: 'When things like this are going on continually, where will it all end?'

Later that day, everyone else having gone off on business of their own, I sat by myself in the bar. Even the barman had gone, leaving a tape running; a guitar strummed softly through familiar tunes but kept coming back to. . . .

> As I was out walking one day in Laredo
> As I wandered out in Laredo one day. . . .

What, I asked myself, was the meaning of the morning's incident? While we were driving up and down, even when we first saw the lone man running, I had no intention of intervening. Indeed I never *had* had any intention of intervening because conscious intention had not come into the matter. One moment I was sitting in the car observing, and the next, seeing the group of men and boys – and some of them were no more than boys – moving in to kill a fellow human being, I was filled with such blind rage that I wouldn't have cared if they'd all been armed with guns and pickaxes. . . .

But what *was* this rage? Where did it come from? What was it about?

By degrees three threads, three strands of feeling, began to disentangle. The first was our common humanity. It was unbearable for human beings to have so little regard for the value and frailty of life, for all that has been built up and inherited by us from the past, for our shared hopes for

165

the future, as to cut a fellow man to bits for sport – for entertainment even, for some were actually laughing as they hacked and slashed.

The second strand of rage came from my experience of the last two or three years – and was due to the fact that these were black men killing a fellow black. Africans in South Africa assume as a matter of course that cruelty and brutality come from the white man. Leave us Africans to ourselves, get the detested white man off our backs, and we are all brothers. But here the white man had got off their backs, had already handed over power, within a few days would be gone – and his going, it appeared, was to be the signal for a mass slaughter of Africans by one another. That also made me mad.

The third strand had no idealism in it and no logic. It derived from vanity. I was insulted – not as a man or human being but as myself – that a rabble should suppose I would look quietly on without protest at their deadly sport.

These three thoughts – when in fact there had been no time to think consciously at all – had touched off a blinding rage which exploded me out of the car into the crowd. It was perhaps the first purely free action – without consideration and regardless of all consequences – I had ever taken in my fifty-five years of life, and I felt as though some huge burden I did not even know I was carrying had been lifted off my back.

The little incident, like similar incidents which must have happened to others in those months, would have passed unnoticed if my companions had not happened to be pressmen. But on our return Ian Berry was asked by the columnist of the *Rand Daily Mail*, Dennis Craig, for a paragraph or two on his experiences. He passed the story on and next day it had reached London, as also had photographs from the Magnum agency, which were published in the *Daily Express*, as well as all over South Africa and in *Paris-Match*.

Dramatic as our glimpses of trouble had seemed, they were little compared to what happened two days later when the

Force Publique revolted. On this army of 25,000 men, drawn from different tribes all over the country, law and order in the Congo had depended under the Belgians, and it was planned that it would similarly so depend under the new government. The soldiers, however, had other ideas. They had watched political and other powers being handed over to their own people by the whites, yet they were expected to remain orderly and obedient under a few hundred Belgian officers. They had not even been given a big pay rise. Nor was there in the force that community of feeling which unites men of different races in a common pride and sense of service; on the contrary, men and officers lived completely separate lives, so that the revolt took the officers as well as the whole country by surprise. On the very eve of the mutiny, at an American Fourth of July party, the commander of the Force, General Janssens, made the ludicrous pronouncement: 'The Force Publique? It is my creation. It is absolutely loyal. I have made my dispositions.' Three days after making it he had been dismissed and left the country, a bewildered man.

At the Njili airport outside Leopoldville, from which crowds of whites, now thoroughly alarmed, were trying to leave the country, a pitched battle took place between men of the Force Publique and Belgian paratroops brought in to restore order. When Ian saw in the Johannesburg *Star* just after our return the picture Barry von Below had taken of half a dozen nuns crouched under the airport counter as the bullets ricocheted over them, he remarked: 'That settles it. No one'll look at the stuff we took three days ago. It's been knocked right out. I *knew* we ought really to stay on.'

'I couldn't stay anyway,' I said. 'We'll only just get the next issue through as it is. But what d'you want to do now?'

'Go back, of course. Soonest possible.'

'Well, cable Magnum and see if they'll back us. If they'll do that, we might get away next week.'

Ian's series of pictures taken on the troubled Sunday morning had been a best-selling series, and I was pretty sure Magnum would want him to return. I hesitated to suggest the idea to Dorothy, but when I did, she said at once: 'Do what you think best. I don't like your going, but it's for you to decide.'

By the time we were due to leave, Tshombe had declared Katanga independent, there had been riots in his capital, Elisabethville, and the Belgians were now pouring out of there as confusedly as they had poured out of Leopoldville the week before. Magnum cabled from Paris urging Ian to go this time to Katanga, offering substantial guarantees and asking that if possible I should go with him again. *Drum*'s South African edition for August had just been completed. By a lucky arrangement of timetables there was a ten-day gap before the printers would need copy for the two West African editions, and so, just before mid-July, we were off again.

At Ndola, in Northern Rhodesia, the airport was flooded with refugees, mainly women and children on their way to Salisbury from where they would be flown direct to Brussels. The Rhodesians had set up a system of emergency aid, and there were feeding arrangements for grown-ups and children, and rest rooms with doctors and nurses in attendance.

At Elisabethville airport, which we reached in the late afternoon, there were again crowds of refugees. All customs and immigration services had broken down; arriving passengers collected their own luggage and looked around for some means of getting into town. Would-be departing passengers – some of whom had driven hundreds of miles with whatever possesssions they could load into their cars – sat disconsolately about on suitcases waiting for planes or information. This breakdown of formalities seemed a blessing at the time, but later it would prove one among many factors that would land us in trouble.

A bus took us to town where we got a room at a hotel. It was still functioning, but the town was almost empty. Shops were closed. There were guards on the post office and radio station. Armed patrols moved continuously through the streets. There were no women to be seen, or so few that everyone turned and gazed at each one as she passed, to see whether she was worth gazing at or not. An early curfew was in force, but hearing there was to be a meeting that night of the Provincial House of Assembly – a rumour which was untrue – Ian and I set out to walk there through the darkness. The streets were deserted and without lighting, so that it was not long before we were rounded up and taken to the police station. As we were escorted inside, I glimpsed a scene that would have made a telling photograph – but it was far too dark to shoot and we were in enough difficulty for the moment without adding to it. In the open courtyard, a few yards from us and shadowy as ghosts in the faint light reflected off the walls, four Africans were kneeling with hands above their heads. As many black police kept watch over them with Sten guns, fingers on triggers. All around were stacked piles of recovered loot – furniture, kitchen utensils, radios, a heap of bicycles.

We were soon on easy terms with the sweaty-faced and exhausted Belgian officers, and I arranged with one that he would take us on his midnight rounds of the Cité Indigène. From Ian's point of view it was a wasted night. Rioting had been checked and in the whole city of darkness we saw not a gleam from any door or window; the sole sign of movement picked up in our headlights came from two gloomily copulating dogs. Outside many of the houses stood piles of goods carefully stacked as if to be collected by removal men. 'Loot!' the officer told us. 'We shot a few looters and got things under control, and now people are frightened we shall come round and search their homes. So they bring out their loot and stack it at street corners, and we drive round with lorries and recover it.'

I got an excellent impression of the Belgian officer in all but one respect – and in that, I thought, must lie the explanation as to how it was possible for the Force Publique to be in a state of imminent revolt while the officers remained quite unaware of their feelings. Our officer was tough, fearless, systematic, an admirable officer in all respects except that he lacked contact with his men, and clearly did not think it necessary, or perhaps even proper, for him to have any. Part of his work that night as he drove us round was to call in on various sub-police stations and outposts to hear how things were going. In most there would be a dozen Congolese soldier-police under a sergeant. We would drive straight into the courtyard. A sentry would turn the guard out and call the sergeant, routine questions would be asked, and we would be on our way.

But at no point was there anything like human friendliness. These men, after all, were alone in their small outpost, in a city torn with riots a few days before and where at any time fresh trouble might break out. Yet never was there one question which showed interest or concern for the men themselves – as to whether they'd had their food, were glad of a quiet night, or any of the questions a natural sympathy suggests. Nor was there any friendly recognition between man and man – they might have been enemy outposts the officer was inspecting. I was to be struck by the same thing a year later when travelling round big agricultural estates and factories in remote parts of the Congo where two or three Belgians, unarmed, would have charge of an area containing tens of thousands of Congolese. A dozen times then I noticed a Congolese – perhaps in charge of a machine being demonstrated or of some particular operation on an estate – waiting after doing what he was asked, visibly hoping for a friendly word, a nod or smile from the Belgian showing me round; waiting, but very rarely getting it. Yet the same Belgian manager would assure me: 'Our relations with our Congolese employees are excellent. They are all delighted to have us back.'

On the whole, I believe, the record has been unjust to the Belgians in the Congo, who had done a lot more in the way of education, health services, agricultural development and so on than they were given credit for. But much of this practical work was undermined by a monumental tactlessness in the area of human contact, which appeared to extend from the poorest *colon* scratching a living on his plot to the highest state officials.

In Elisabethville we stayed only a few days. Having found out that numbers of the rebels were being held prisoner at two points, we managed to wangle our way in. Some hundreds, perhaps as many as two thousand, were in the open on a sports ground. They made a strange impression, in a uniform that looked like denim overalls, and confined by a loose roll of barbed wire such as might be used to keep cows off a cricket pitch. But outside the wire walked soldiers with automatic weapons, and machine guns were sighted on them from press boxes and stands.

Ian, having taken his close-ups, slipped up into the grandstand and secured two or three of the finest pictures he took on this trip, showing the whole body of prisoners huddled together with bowed heads, and the guards standing over them. Meanwhile, chatting around, I learned that there was another mass of prisoners confined out on an airfield in an empty hangar, so we drove out there quickly. At first everyone denied that there were any prisoners there and ordered us to clear off, but we chose a route for leaving which led us past the hangars, and drove slowly.

'Stop a minute!' I told the driver, and when the engine was switched off we could hear it – the whole hangar vibrating as if full of angry bees. We got out of the car and after a minute or two found an officer, showed him our permit to photograph the men on the sports ground, and managed to convince him that it applied to the hangar too. It was packed to bursting; from time to time the sliding doors would be rolled back a couple of feet and two or three men allowed out to the latrine or to get a drink of water, always under guard. These were more of the 'rebels' who had turned on their officers a few days before, been disarmed, and were now waiting to be shipped off in trains to the districts from which they had originally been recruited. Later, when Tshombe issued a national call to arms to resist the United Nations attempting to end his separate regime, most of them would come flocking back – 'rebels' no longer – to be issued with the same weapons which had been taken from them and to resume their military careers where they left off.

Every afternoon at about three we assembled at Tshombe's villa for his press conference. Tshombe, smartly dressed and easy-mannered, would welcome us and read – with manifest interest as to what was coming next – what was supposed to be his own communiqué for the day. This would be followed by questions, which he dealt with or diverted easily. He was loquacious, natural, charming – but there was often a contradiction between his features. He would smile with eyes or lips while his forehead wrinkled into a frown. With him at the conference would be one or two of his ministers and also Colonel Weber, the Belgian parachute commander whose forces had put down the revolt.

One day after the conference ended, Ian and I decided to go and see Colonel Weber. If we could get him to talk, he might give us an idea where trouble could still be found. The parachute colonel made an impressive figure with his grey hair, grey eyes, tanned skin and a smooth face sloping forwards to a powerful chin. He had the air of genial brutality common to many successful soldiers, making you feel that if he had to shoot you he would do it with a handshake and a smile. We started by asking him about his position in an independent Katanga. He had it all quite clear.

'I am not under the control of President Tshombe. I am under the control of my home government in Belgium. For the present my government has told me to obey whatever orders President Tshombe gives me, so I do so. If my government gives me different orders tomorrow, I shall obey those too. At this moment I wish to go to Brussels. I should like to see the king in order to explain my work here, and ask his permission to continue. . . .'

We asked him about the military situation. 'In Katanga all is quiet. My troops are going out from all centres. . . . The revolt is under control. . . . The rebels are being disbanded. . . .'

'What do you believe was the cause of the revolt?' I inquired.

'It was Lumumba who inspired and fomented it,' the colonel answered. 'We have definite evidence in our hands.

172

The revolt of the Force Publique was organized by Lumumba.'

As the revolt had done more than any one thing to destroy Lumumba's position, and as in its first days he had rushed desperately around with Kasavubu, trying at the risk of his life to calm it down and insisting – until it became hopeless to do so any longer – on the appointment of Belgians to key defence posts, this seemed a most unlikely action for Lumumba to have taken. I did not, however, raise that question; instead I asked: 'Since all is now quiet in Katanga, that implies there is trouble somewhere else. Where would you say is the most troubled spot at this moment?'

'At Luluabourg in the Kasai things are not too good,' the colonel told us. Ian kicked my ankle. The kick meant – 'Don't waste any more time. We've got what we came for. The problem will be to find a plane going to Luluabourg. Pack all this in and let's get started.'

We shook hands and left. It had been a pleasant interview. There are people who like the company of journalists, just as there are others who detest us. Both Tshombe and Weber, I felt, in their different ways liked having journalists around: it gave them a pleasing sense of being at the centre of interest, even, at that moment, of world interest. In return they treated pressmen with good temper and consideration, and Weber at least had told us the truth wherever it did not conflict with official policy. Such factors, I believe, influenced journalists more than they should in helping to clothe the artificial state of Katanga with an appearance of reality – an appearance which would not last long.

13

'You Are Belgian Spies!'

'People aren't going to Luluabourg any more – they're getting out,' the man in the Sabena office told us.

'Will there be a plane?'

'I don't know if there'll be a plane. But if there is, you'll have no trouble getting on.'

There was a plane. It flew the 700-odd miles to Luluabourg in a series of short hops. Two newsreel men had had the same idea and travelled with us. Nominally rivals, working for different continental programmes, they had reached a friendly understanding. Neither was to take any unnecessary risk, and they would work out their expenses together in case their bosses happened to know each other and check up. . . . 'I say, have you had a man in the Congo, Frans?' 'Yes, Hans.' 'Well, what has he charged you for the flight to Luluabourg?'

Of all the confused situations in the Congo, that at Lulua-bourg in mid-July was the most complex and explosive. Luluabourg, a tiny, modern city with a huge hut town of Africans a mile away, was the capital of the Kasai, most central of the six provinces making up the ex-Belgian Congo. Political control, following the May general election, was in the hands of Lumumba's supporters, but the whole state was split by a great tribal feud – strong in several other provinces but dominating everything in the Kasai – between the Luluas and the Balubas, who had been their subjects. The Luluas, a proud but rather primitive people, had clung to their early way of life. When the Belgians came the Luluas wanted nothing to do with them, their organization, or the religion they brought with them. The Balubas – alert, intelligent, adaptable – made friends with the invaders, learned all they could from them, and had soon become the holders of the best-paid jobs as clerks, foremen, telephone operators and machine minders, and the manipulators, under the Belgians, of much administrative power in a host of minor ways. This powerful position, gained partly through hard work and partly through the Balubas' cohesion and mutual support, had long been resented by the Luluas, who now – with the departure of the Belgians – feared they were going to be dominated by a people who had formerly been their slaves, so they determined to take action first.

The revolt of the Force Publique, running like wildfire across the Congo, broke out in Luluabourg as well. The rebels attacked the Europeans, who shut themselves into a big office building in the heart of the town and suffered for a day or two a kind of desultory siege. Then, a few days before Ian and I flew in, the Belgian paras arrived. They dropped into the bush a few miles away and converged on the airport, which they seized. They entered the town, raised the 'siege' of the Europeans and escorted all who wished to leave to the airport – from which they were flown off by degrees – and then dug themselves in. The fact that the 'siege' had not been exactly bloodthirsty was shown by the fact that some fifty men and two women refused to be evacuated. They had made a hotel in the town their headquarters, from which they seldom ventured out except in cars, several at a time, and armed.

There was extreme resentment in the town over the action of the paras, who – said the Congolese – had created a military operation where none was necessary, with a loss of Congolese life that could easily have been avoided. The paras in their pits and trenches had the opposite opinion. They felt themselves to be the defenders of white civilization against hordes of mutinous barbarians and were only disappointed that the hordes seemed reluctant to fling themselves against their automatic weapons. That was the picture held by the men. The officers, who had contact with Belgian officers of the Force Publique – a number of whom courageously continued to live in camp with their men, though not allowed to exercise command – had received from them a view of the situation which was more confused and therefore closer to reality. Between the Belgians on the airfield and the Congolese five miles away in the city there was no contact except for the visits of these Force Publique officers.

On our arrival we reported to the commandant. He warned us strongly against going into the town, except in a jeep with an escort of his men for a quick in-and-out glimpse, and hospitably said he would find us a blanket and probably something to eat later on. We thanked him for his offer, which I had already made up my mind not to accept, for we should get no pictures and little idea of what was going on by sitting on the airfield. We therefore started to look around.

On the airport's control tower a couple of machine-gun posts had been established, and from the top we saw an unexpected sight. Though there were only fifty Europeans left in the town, there were hundreds of cars lined up below us. We went down to examine them, and the cars told their own story. They were mainly new, for the owners had been prosperous: a number had only a few thousand miles on the clock. Some were unlocked and a few had the ignition keys still in position. A number, dusty or spattered with mud, must have come hundreds of miles on their last journey; others looked as though they had been washed down that morning – and almost every one was full of luggage. Clearly the refugees had loaded all they could into their cars, only to find on reaching the airport that they could take no more than a suitcase or two on the plane. Luggage lay open on the back seats, the contents scattered about in the search, perhaps, for some special possession: women's clothes and shoes; baskets of food; children's books and toys, a huge teddy bear. Some had hopefully brought large trunks and packing cases half across the province, only to abandon them

176

here at the last minute. From the condition of the cars one could see something of the owners' state of mind. The majority had simply been parked and left there – 'We shall never come back; someone might as well have our belongings.' Others were locked and the windows wound up, as if the owner half expected to come back before long and drive away. A few had been deliberately driven into each other and remained with shattered windscreens, clinging to each other's bumpers like boxers in a clinch. And just one or two drivers had evidently gone round with hammers or tyre levers, wrecking all they could before leaving.

'What'll become of them all?' we asked a paratrooper.

'God knows!' he said. 'You can take one if you like, as far as I'm concerned. The only thing is you won't have any papers for it. You may get shot as a looter somewhere along the line – and if you get it to the border, you've *still* no papers. They may haul you up there for having pinched it. Take a chance if you like, but I doubt if it's worth the risk.'

Just on the edge of the airfield at the farthest point reached by the paratroops' patrols, stood a small hotel in a clump of trees and bushes called the Oasis. Before the flight, it had evidently been the favourite place for Luluabourgers looking for a night out. There was a restaurant with a dance floor, a cinema and night club, and chalets in the grounds for those who had reasons for not going home. I suggested to the others that we all stay at the Oasis instead of dossing down in the airport building. We would get a bed and a bath, possibly a decent meal, and if we took two adjacent rooms between the four of us we could probably look after ourselves. We had been warned that Congolese – as well as paratroop patrols – visited the Oasis, and that a night or two previously three Belgian civilians staying there had been dragged out of their rooms and beaten up.

The Greek proprietor welcomed us. We noticed that the half dozen cars parked outside his door had all had their tyres stabbed through with bayonets, and the proprietor told us that two evenings previously when the 'rebels' came round he had hidden in the loft and only been saved by the action

177

of his Congolese steward, who called to the soldiers to come and have a drink on the house at the very moment when they were starting to go up into the loft with their bayonets. After a couple of drinks, happily, they had forgotten their intention of visiting the loft.

We enjoyed a bath, a meal and sleep with no interference from outside, and when Ian and I appeared for breakfast next morning the two newsreel men were already hard at work.

'What are you charging for lunch on the way up?'

'It was free. They gave it us on the plane.'

'I know – but you've got to put down *something*.'

'Say a hundred and fifty francs.'

'Okay – plus fifty for drinks, eh? What are we paying at this place?'

'Two-fifty a night.'

'Better make that five hundred, don't you think? Otherwise the balance of everything gets upset. . . . Plus another fifty for phone calls, and fifty for odds-and-sods?'

'Now – hire of car for going into Luluabourg. . . . What are you putting down for that?'

'But we agreed last night not to go into town. You haven't changed your mind, have you?'

'Of course not – and there aren't any cars to hire anyway. But it would look natural to hire a car – and we didn't *ask* our ruddy companies to send us here.'

I made a sign to Ian, who was finishing his coffee, to slip away and join me outside.

'I can't take this any longer. We had two hours of it yesterday.'

'What d'you think we should do?'

'Go into town.'

'But we've no transport.'

'I can fix that. We'll stand by the roadside a couple of hundred yards up where our friends here won't see us, and thumb a lift into Luluabourg. There are certain to be cars going in with people who have jobs, lorries with vegetables

– or something. The important thing is they must be Congolese, not whites, for getting us past the searchpoints.'

'Okay. Just let me grab my cameras and I'm with you.'

We hadn't long to wait. The first car we thumbed slowed down for us. It was full already, but the Congolese moved up to make room. I at once told them who we were and what we were doing, knowing that if we were questioned at the searchpoints it would all have to come out, and it would help if they could declare that we'd told them the same story. Twice we were stopped by patrols, but each time the driver vouched for us and we got through. He put us down at the 'white' hotel in the middle of Luluabourg, and, not for the first or last time from a Congolese, we were shown real kindness.

'I don't know how you're going to get back,' he said. 'How d'you think you can manage it?'

'We don't. We're hoping for the best.'

'Well – I'll be going out around midday. You and your friend be here at half past twelve, and I'll take you out with me in the car.'

I thanked him and shook hands. It was just nine o'clock. Half past twelve seemed a very long way off.

Talking it over, Ian and I had made up our minds that the first thing we must do was to secure some kind of permit which we would pin on to our shirts. By looking preoccupied and walking quickly as if late for an appointment, a journalist can often get by unnoticed, or at least unstopped. But taking pictures is a different matter; first, it's obvious, and, second, it's suspect. Walking up the street, Ian with his camera under his jacket, every face stopped and turned; I could see them in the shop windows without looking round. But there were very few faces and not many shop windows. No shop was open and many had their windows boarded up or broken. In a quarter of a mile of the main boulevard we passed fewer than twenty people – all Congolese, all men, all in white shirts and shorts. Everyone stared, and no one smiled.

At the first military post we stopped to tell our story.

179

Here there were a dozen soldiers with two jeeps and some automatic rifles. We asked for *Monsieur le Capitaine*, who proved to be a sergeant major, bespectacled, with a small Hitler moustache, but friendly and glad to smoke a cigarette. All we want, we say, is a permit to walk quietly about the streets of this handsome city for an hour or two and take one or two photographs of the principal sights, in order to show the outside world that all is calm.

'Photographs? But this is certainly a matter for the colonel. It cannot be decided by a non-commissioned officer.'

Taken to the colonel in a jeep, I show him the one copy of *Drum* I have brought with me and explain what it is we want. The colonel asks if he may keep the magazine, to which I agree – an agreement we regret later in the day. He then tells us that permission to take photographs is not a military but a political decision, and can only be obtained at the main government office. There, after much argument, it is decided that we have to see Monsieur le Ministre des Affaires Intérieures himself. After half an hour's wait, Monsieur Luhata sees us. We are now in a much colder climate. Luhata is a highly intelligent and capable young man, but he is also suspicious. He takes down particulars, asks us to hand over our passports, and says he will consult the president. May we take a picture of the minister? No. If any pictures are to be taken, it will be proper to begin by taking the president.

We wait an hour, an hour and a half. The sky has become overcast, and suddenly there is a crack of thunder overhead, followed by another, and a heavy downpour. Now from the gardens outside the government buildings comes the echo of a shot. Then half a dozen more. We make an excuse and move to the windows. A few dozen white-shirted Congolese are rushing up the street, away towards the country, out of town. Two jeeps race by with automatic weapons ready.

'Hell!' says Ian. 'They're starting a bloody war out there. Let's go down and see what's happening.'

180

Congo 1960: Before the Storm.
The author waiting to obtain passes for
Independence ceremonies in the capital,
Leopoldville, soon renamed Kinshasa.
Delays were interminable, confusion
endless. But order was still being main-
tained by the *Force Publique* and the Belgians
were confident that all would be well

The new President, Kasavubu,
welcomes the South African chargé
d'affaires. The author and Ian Berry,
who have gatecrashed the party, learn all
they can

Left: Lumumba, the ill-fated Prime
Minister, with his Belgian staff — all
shortly to leave the country

A Street Incident.
On the Sunday morning following the Congo's Independence, the author and three cameramen have gone out to a suburb of Leopoldville. All seems peaceful, pavements are thronged mainly with churchgoers. Suddenly there is a swirl in the crowd and a man appea running for his life fron a crowd armed with clubs, torn-down iron palings and strips cut from old tyres. A bicycle, thrown in his path, crashes him to the ground

The runner has fallen and the pack close in for the kill

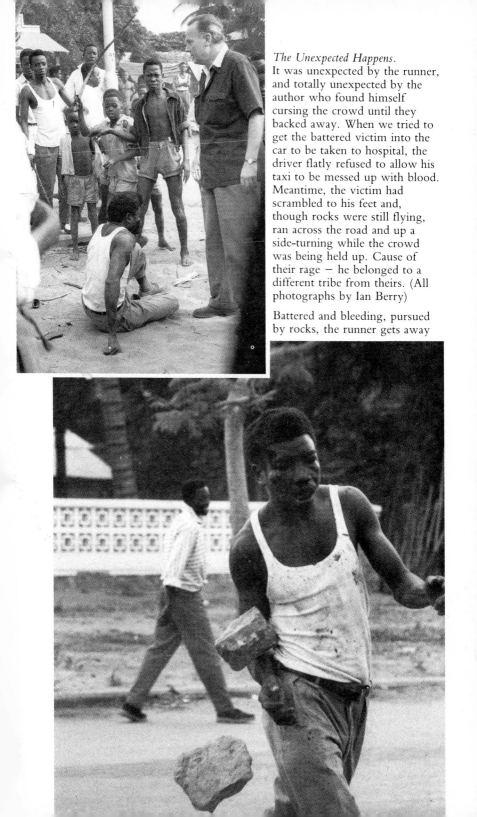

The Unexpected Happens.
It was unexpected by the runner, and totally unexpected by the author who found himself cursing the crowd until they backed away. When we tried to get the battered victim into the car to be taken to hospital, the driver flatly refused to allow his taxi to be messed up with blood. Meantime, the victim had scrambled to his feet and, though rocks were still flying, ran across the road and up a side-turning while the crowd was being held up. Cause of their rage — he belonged to a different tribe from theirs. (All photographs by Ian Berry)

Battered and bleeding, pursued by rocks, the runner gets away

The Governor Opens the New Centre.
March 1963, and the Rt Hon. Malcolm
Macdonald, Governor of Kenya, opens
the first-ever training centre for African
journalists, in Nairobi. Students come
from all over East and Central Africa.
Later, a similar centre would be set in
Lagos for West African journalists.
During the six years the courses lasted,
more than 300 African newspaper and
radio men learned to take over the posts
white men had filled before the great
tide of African independence

Below: Tom and Dorothy Hopkinson
today

Meher Baba (1894-1969).
Avatar Meher Baba as he looked when
the author and Dorothy first met him in
the early 1950s. From that point he
exercised a growing influence over their
lives. Baba founded no new religion. His
message to mankind is: 'I come not to
teach but to awaken'

'Better not move just yet. We're being looked at with suspicion.'

Another quarter of an hour's wait, and we are sent for. Monsieur Mukenge, president of the Kasai, a slightly built young man with a sardonic face, sits at a big desk at the end of a long room. The Minister of the Interior sits at a corner of the desk facing him. Between the two is a young man whom I take to be a clerk, but who is – it soon appears – a security officer. We are waved to seats, and told to tell our story. Everything I say the president notes down. It is not an encouraging beginning.

'You tell me,' the president asks, 'that you were in Leopoldville two weeks ago?' I nod. 'Yet you have no stamp in your passports for Leopoldville. How is that?'

I am certain there must be a stamp, but this is a passport on which I have travelled over Africa for the last two and a half years. It is full of stamps, and, not expecting to do much reading, I have left my glasses at the hotel and can only gaze blankly at the pages. At last Ian finds the stamp, almost invisible against a whole-page visa for the Congo obtained a month ago in Johannesburg.

'Ah!' says the president. '*Now* I begin to understand! You are really South Africans calling yourselves "English". What contacts have you been having with the Belgians?'

I explained that we arrived in Elisabethville five days ago and came up to the Kasai only last night.

'Then where are your stamps for entry at Elisabethville?'

Now we are getting really entangled. I explain that, when we landed at E'ville, there was such confusion over the departure of refugees that no passports were being stamped. It sounds so thin I almost wonder myself whether it is true.

Now the president turns his attention to Ian Berry's passport. Ian – a handsome young man of twenty-six with a beard and wavy hair – is represented in his passport by a fat-cheeked, pop-eyed boy in his teens. The president tosses it down with a sarcastic laugh. 'Why! it does not even begin to look like the same person! It's an insult to our intelligence to pretend this is a genuine passport belonging to that man.'

181

Once again, in the most fluent French I can manage, I make excuses. My friend is a young man. Until a year ago he was a student and found it convenient to travel as a student; this is a picture of him from those days. It's true, I concede, that it doesn't look much like him now and we ought perhaps to have had it renewed – however, we were forced to leave in a hurry and so on . . . and so on.

'And what paper do you say you represent?'

'The magazine *Drum*. It is published mainly in South Africa, with editions also in Ghana and Nigeria.'

'There – I said you were South Africans! What kind of a magazine is this which is published in Johannesburg?'

Patiently I explain. *Drum* is a magazine mainly for Africans. Though published in South Africa, it supports their interests and deals with their activities. I had a copy with me, but it was taken by a colonel at one of his military posts. If the president cares to send for it, he can prove what I am saying. Travelling for this magazine, I have met on friendly terms many of the present-day African leaders – Monsieur Nyerere, Monsieur Mboya, Chief Luthuli – only the other day my friend and I had the pleasure of meeting and photographing Monsieur Lumumba.

'Again what you tell me is absurd. There can be no magazine which supports the Africans published in Johannesburg. The South African government would not allow it – that is obvious to anyone. *I believe you are Belgian spies*. Where did you and your companion spend last night? With the Belgian soldiers on the airfield?'

'No. We stayed just outside the town, at the Oasis Hotel.'

'Good. We shall check up.'

I feel nothing but relief as the president himself dials the Oasis. Now at last some part of our story is going to be confirmed. Exactly the opposite happens. The manager of the Oasis, scenting trouble, takes the safe course and denies that we ever slept there.

'There were two English journalists here for dinner, but they went away afterwards and did not spend the night.'

The president turns to us with scorn. Clearly, he thinks we are not only spies but clumsy ones.

All I can do now is start talking. Let him send one of his men back to the hotel with us immediately. We will show him our room with our luggage still in it, and our names must be in the hotel register. Then, feeling we are getting deeper and deeper into difficulties, I sense that our only hope is to stop defending ourselves, and angrily let fly.

Why are we being treated like this, I demand? Why, when we have taken the trouble to come and see the Congolese side of things, are we being persecuted? Nothing would be easier for us than to sit in the airport and write about murder and violence in Luluabourg. There are other journalists who never leave the airport, but instead we have decided to come and find out for ourselves. Does the president really wish that all accounts of events in the Kasai should be written from the Belgian airport – if so, he need not be surprised if they take a Belgian point of view. We are two English journalists of good standing, living and working in South Africa. We have come to the Congo not out of hostility but because we wish to know and tell the truth. If this is the reception to be expected, then I think other journalists will be wise to stay away and make up their stories at a safe distance. We acted in good faith in presenting ourselves to his military outpost. Now we ask for some good faith in return.

For the first time we feel a small response. The president says he will give us one more chance. We have spoken of photographing Monsieur Lumumba two weeks ago in Leopoldville. He will phone through to Monsieur Lumumba and inquire. . . . We've had it now, I think. How can the prime minister of the Congo – who must have talked to 150 journalists at least during independence week – possibly remember Ian Berry and myself, present at his house by accident among a number of diplomats?

But our luck is turning. Somewhere along the line there is a strike of telephone operators, and the president cannot be put through. He himself is still suspicious, but the other two, the security man and the minister of the interior, have come round invisibly, mysteriously, to our side. Neither of them says a word, but we all feel the division. Four people round the desk now think we are *not* spies. Four to one, instead of two against three. The president says nothing. He rings a bell, and his *chef de cabinet* brings in a folder of official papers which, ignoring the rest of us, he starts to sign. The telephone rings: 'No!' he shouts. 'All that *bagarre* this morning was nothing but a scare. No bombs were dropped – it was thunder. The Belgians remain quietly at the airport. There are some of our army who are soldiers – but there are *others.* . . .' He leaves the rest unsaid and goes back to signing papers.

He signs the last one, then turns to his *chef de cabinet.* 'These two English journalists may go round the town and take pictures in the streets. They will be accompanied by two soldiers to see that there are no incidents. But they are not to come back into the town once they have left. Tomorrow they must leave the Kasai. You will be personally responsible.' A pause, and then he adds: 'But first you will give them something to eat.' He holds out a hand. We see for the first time something like a smile, and we are dismissed.

For two or three hours we are driven around in a jeep. Apart from a few families of Balubas making their getaway with furniture piled high on to shaky lorries or the roofs of aged cars with boiling radiators, there is little to see and less to photograph. Long before six o'clock curfew we are set down by our guide at the Oasis, and here the grimmest joke of the day is still in store for us. We go to our room to wash, only to find that all our belongings have been removed and there is no sign that we ever stayed there. I go to the office and look in the register. If our names were ever entered last night when we filled in various forms for the proprietor, the page has now been cut out.

We ask for our two newsreel acquaintances. They left for the airport, we are told, when they learned we had been arrested. At the proprietor's insistence they took all our

things with them 'for safety'. So, if we had come back to
the hotel under escort in order to point out our luggage as
proof of our stay, we should have found a completely empty
room and a proprietor with his lies ready prepared.

We slept that night at the airport, Ian on the counter
where they issue the tickets, I in two deckchairs. Late in the
afternoon we cadged a lift in a paratroop plane to Kamina,
the great military base, where the Belgians put us up for the
night and gave us food. During the meal – which was in a
huge mess seating hundreds – a Belgian Air Force officer ran
wild and began hitting and kicking the Congolese stewards.
His friends soon sat him down again and one of them told
us what had happened. A plane bringing in troops, piloted
by one of his friends, had been shot down by chance rifle
fire up in the north of the province. This officer had been
sent up with others to bring in the bodies – which he found
stripped and mutilated. Now, in a delayed reaction, he
attacked the first black men he saw. . . .

And so by troop and cargo planes we got back to Elisabethville, and then on more normally to Salisbury, Johannesburg and *Drum*.

In leaving the Congo, a page or two may be allowed in
explanation of the catastrophe which followed independence.
At the time the Belgians were widely blamed for this on the
grounds that they had done little or nothing for the country.
This was untrue. In fact the Belgians were working on an
original and enlightened plan for the development of their
enormous territory. But their plan had a basic fault in that
they never expected to leave the country altogether;
Belgians, they thought, would continue indefinitely to hold
key positions in the political and social fields, in commerce
and industry, and above all in the armed forces. Moreover
their plan was only half complete when, faced with the tide
of independence sweeping Africa in the late 1950s, they
decided to get out rather than risk becoming involved in a
costly and hopeless colonial war as the French had done in

Indo-China. How had the Belgians landed themselves in this disastrous position?

Though the mouth of the Congo river had been known since the fifteenth century, it was only Stanley's historic journey from east to west in the late 1870s which opened up the heart of the continent, the hinterlands of the enormous river. The Congo was then seen to be a territory of vast agricultural resources and great mineral wealth. Stanley offered his discovery to the British and, when they showed no interest, handed his claim over to King Leopold II of Belgium, under whose agents the country was exploited, virtually as the king's personal possession, with a cruelty and ruthlessness which shocked the world. It was not until 1908, when the Congo was taken over by the Belgian government, that any concern began to be shown for the welfare of its people. These were made up of a large number of tribes with different customs, different languages and in some cases a long tradition of mutual hostility.

In forming their plan for control and development of the Congo, the Belgians had studied the British colonial system and noted its chief features: its use of indirect rule through chiefs and notables; the education and training of an élite, either in Britain or in local institutions modelled on British lines; the introduction by degrees of British constitutional forms and a legal system based on the British pattern, while allowing smaller issues to be decided through tribal chiefs or village councils. The system was relaxed and economical. Voluntary agencies were encouraged to take part in missionary and educational activity; and the development of councils at various levels up to parliamentary bodies, with, more recently, the appearance of 'home-grown' newspapers, allowed a considerable degree of argument over future policy. As against these advantages, British rule had done little to break down tribal and racial barriers, which indeed it often encouraged in order to make government easier. Moreover it had introduced a new form of division between the class of administrators, educationalists and others who had 'white' connections and ambitions, and the mass of people living much as they had always lived, and on whom the new class tended to look down as primitive 'bush' people.

The situation had been summed up for me on one of my earliest visits to West Africa in the use of the expression, a 'been-to'. A 'been-to' meant someone who had been to Britain, where residence for a year or two – perhaps as a trainee with some commercial firm or as a nurse in hospital – conferred on return a status amounting almost to a university degree. 'It's difficult for me to find a wife in this country,' a young Nigerian journalist had complained. 'You see, I'm a "been-to", so I can only marry another "been-to". I don't want a wife who is a "bush" person – she'd only be a handicap in my career.'

The Belgians had also looked critically at the French colonial system, in which élitism was taken much further than under the British. Proud of their culture and their language, the French taught those who learned French at all to speak it perfectly, whereas the British were content for their language to be used, misused and transformed into any kind of pidgin, providing it served the purpose of communication. The phenomenon of *négritude* in former French colonial possessions – that is, the resistance of black intellectuals to domination by an imported European culture – had no parallel in the British-controlled territories, either because the British colonialists brought little or no culture with them, or because they did not take seriously such culture as they did bring.

Black officials in French colonial territories spoke and wrote excellent French; often had polished manners; were concerned about literature and the arts. But even more than in British possessions, their focus of interest lay overseas rather than in their own countries. They were encouraged to go to France for their education and professional qualifications, and, instead of reading newspapers produced by local journalists and full of oddities of expression, they read the French newspapers flown in daily so that they could enjoy 'the best'. Many officials went to France for their holidays, and they and their families looked to Paris, rather than to the capital of their own country, as not only the source of future progress and promotion but also as their intellectual home.

The plan of development worked out by the Belgians was designed to avoid this division between the enlightened few and the backward many. In the Congo there was to be no élite. The whole country was intended to move forward together at an even pace. The period 1908–60 saw the development of an extensive system of primary education, and by 1958 the Congo had the highest literacy rate of any country in Africa. It also had the best colonial medical service, some of the best African housing and one of the highest African living standards.*

Given another ten years, all might have turned out well. But time was not on the Belgian side. In March 1957 the Gold Coast became independent under the name of Ghana, an event which had shattering consequences throughout Africa. By 1958 the tide was already at the door. In Brazzaville, capital of the French Congo only just across the river, General de Gaulle announced that that country was to have self-government. Soon there were violent riots in Leopoldville and the Belgians found it necessary to declare self-government as official policy for the Congo too, and from that moment the race was on. Hasty preparations were made for a general election, but only a tiny minority of Congolese had any experience of government at all, and that only at the level of a few small town councils. The overwhelming mass of people had never had the opportunity to vote for so much as the control of village revenues or the election of officials for a football club.

The Congo was to be self-governing, but where were its leaders to be found? Though primary education was general, there was almost no secondary education and the first half dozen Congolese graduates were only just emerging from the recently opened university. On the very eve of independ-

---

*c.f. 'Congo', by Catherine Hoskyns, from *Africa: a Handbook*, edited by Colin Legum, Anthony Blond, London, 1965.

ence, in June 1960, there was not a single Congolese lawyer, doctor or accountant, and no Congolese soldier above the rank of sergeant. General Mobutu, who would later govern the country, was at this time a sergeant like so many others, and would attain general's rank by self-promotion.

The general election of May 1960, which immediately preceded independence, was the first in the history of the Congo. It was contested by about a hundred political parties and from the general confusion the leading figure to emerge was Patrice Lumumba. He had managed to build up something approaching a national organization by promising posts in his government to the leaders of various groups in return for their support. But even though he appointed no fewer than thirty-five ministers he could not fulfil his promises. Powerful men were left discontented and hostile, and those such as Tshombe and Kalonji who felt strong enough to break away soon did so.

When at his cocktail party Governor-General Cornelis, then about to leave the country, had said to me: 'We have got a government. That is the great thing!' what he was really saying was: 'Somehow or other – thank God! – a government of *some* sort has been pieced together. The correct processes have been gone through and the necessary formalities observed. We have handed over to the Congolese a neatly packaged constitution, worked out in Brussels by lawyers and political experts. Now it's up to Lumumba and the rest of them to make it work! If possible.'

14

Last Days with *Drum*

As we approached the end of 1960, I had to decide whether to stay on with *Drum* or leave. I had undertaken to work a further year from January 1960 and then to give six months' notice if I were not staying on. The real problem, over which Dorothy and I had many discussions, was whether Jim Bailey and I could ever manage to work harmoniously together.

His difficulties with me were considerable, and there was justice in his complaints, constantly repeated in long memoranda which he would leave for me before setting off on a visit to England, West Africa or his stud farm down in the Cape. The chief ones were that:

1. I wanted my own way too much.
2. I was touchy and resentful of criticism.
3. I had no proper regard for financial difficulties, and tried to push ahead too fast for the means at his disposal. Out of this had grown his conviction that I saw everything through my experience of the lavish world of Fleet Street, and so failed to adapt myself to the totally different circumstances of South Africa.

My difficulties with Bailey could be briefly stated too:

1. He reached decisions crucial to the magazine without any discussion until after his mind had been made up; only then did he call me in 'to talk over future plans'. I was thus in the position of having to argue against a decision already

190

reached, and what ought to have been the joint examination of a problem became first an argument, and then a row.

2. We had not, and never had had, any concerted plan for *Drum*'s development beyond selling as many copies as possible and getting in all the advertising we could. This lack of an overall plan was particularly damaging since we had so many territories to cover, and it was this living from hand to mouth – hoping for the best without ever providing against the worst – which had landed us in such messes as the ban in Ghana.

3. About finance I agreed that we had different attitudes, and that in general I assumed that if one followed the right course, the money would come in. But I objected that it was difficult to be governed by financial considerations when, though nominally a director, I never saw the firm's financial picture, depending on such indications as he from time to time threw out.

But behind these practical sources of disagreement – which we ought to have been able to get over with goodwill on both sides – lay another, more fundamental and also more nebulous, a difference in our attitude to life as basic as that which makes one man gloomy and another optimistic, something we could no more change than we could the colour of our skins. This affected in particular our way of relating to each other and the staff. Born into a wealthy family, Jim had inherited something like a fortune from his father, Sir Abe Bailey, the Johannesburg mining millionaire, racehorse owner and associate of Cecil Rhodes. The fortune had been tied down in various ways and shared with others in the family, but from the outset Jim had never been anything but rich. His mother, Lady Bailey, an adventurous aviator, had made notable, even historic, solo flights in a light aircraft. There was ample courage, enterprise and drive in such parentage, but it did not appear that the children when young had enjoyed much warmth and sympathy, except for what they could give to one another.

In the manner of his everyday life Jim appeared to be reacting against, rather than following, Sir Abe's lavish style.

He dressed anyhow; preferred cars to be second- or third-hand; ate whatever was going; stayed, when travelling, either with friends or in cheap hotels. Few men with the power to please themselves can have spent less on self-indulgence. During the war he had been a courageous fighter pilot. He had a streak of poetic feeling and had published a book of poems. He was also without any form of racial prejudice.

But either through his parentage or from his background he had derived the rich man's distrust of those around him; the sense that everyone needs to be watched, which I had noticed in other rich men I had known and worked for and which might be called the rich man's occupational disease. All his associates, the sufferer is convinced, are on the make and, if not constantly supervised, will waste and dissipate his money – that money which has given him his position, his protection, his security. And just as all associates are on the make, so all employees and workers tend naturally to slack, to do less than a full day's work for the pay they get. A steady flow of complaint and criticism, however, will hold associates up to the mark, and through them the employees also will be kept on their toes.

If this philosophy of distrust worked out in practice, it would be difficult to fault. But it had not prevented *Drum* from putting unreliable men into key positions, nor from sending to Rhodesia a junior white employee with a considerable sum in cash. He had stayed in the country only long enough to borrow all he could and to cash one or two bouncing cheques before taking the next plane to London with the proceeds. Most firms, no doubt, employ an occasional bad egg, and there are rotten apples, we are told, in every barrel. But to suspect all apples of being rotten affords no guide as to which ones actually are. On the contrary, too widespread distrust tends to defeat itself, and the ruler or employer who suspects all advisers is left in the end surrounded only by those deserving of suspicion. The honest prefer not to work where they are not trusted, and only those remain who intend to exploit whatever opportunities

192

they get, and whose servility in the meantime offers an apparent assurance of devotion.

At the deepest level we are all the creatures of our background and our past, and my own background and experience of life had been very different from Jim Bailey's. Despite superficial resemblances – an 'Englishness' of manner and appearance, an enjoyment of games and sport – we looked on the world from different angles. All my life I had been an employee, and even in the one or two important positions I had held my natural sympathy was with my colleagues rather than with those who paid my salary. To an employer my attitude has always been to make as much profit for him as I could and do my best to increase the value of his properties. I saw my debt to him as a financial one, like his to me. But in the way I did the job I followed my own beliefs and so, he could justifiably argue, served my own ambitions rather than his. And though I was glad when there was friendship, I had never experienced that personal devotion and ardour of loyalty which I have heard three or four of my fellow editors, both in Africa and Britain, publicly express for their proprietors.

On the staff I looked much as I did on myself. I expected them to work hard, which in general they did, and it was an article of faith with me that the way to get the best out of them was to encourage and reward, only complaining when there was obvious need to do so. Decisions were reached in discussion among ourselves, and I never passed on to them demands such as 'the boss wants this', or 'we've got to do it this way to please him'. This protected them from pressurization, but it also meant that I was relating their activities and interest to myself as editor, and not to their paymaster and employer. In acting as I did, I also sometimes made mistakes, sent people on assignments they could not cope with or put them into positions they could not adequately fill.

The point I am making, however, is not that one of these two attitudes, trust or distrust, is right and the other wrong. Both doubtless are right and wrong in differing circumstances. My point is the simpler one that two people whose innate convictions are in this way basically opposed must find it hard to work harmoniously together. If you believe in the stick, you consider the man a fool who offers, or wants to offer, carrots. If you feel in your bones that the creature responds best to carrots and a rewarding pat, it goes against nature to apply the stick.

'Well,' said Dorothy, 'I see you mean to leave, so there's really no more to be said.'

'But d'you think I'm *right* to leave?'

'You're right to leave if you want to leave. If you can't go on any longer, then you must stop and find something else. All the same. . . .'

'What are you *not* saying?'

Dorothy hesitated: 'I don't want to say something that will hurt you.'

'Say it all the same!'

'Well then, you lack resiliency. You take everything connected with your work too seriously. What does it really *matter* whether you get eight extra pages into next month's *Drum*? What does it matter if Jim Bailey decides to start a printing works? Let him go ahead and do it.'

'But he'll lose a lot of money, and then the magazine is bound to suffer.'

'*Let* him lose money – and if, after you've said all you can, he still goes ahead and the magazine suffers, why take it so much to heart? I know less than nothing about business, as you know. In most of the arguments you've had with Jim Bailey, I think your idea has been the right one. But. . . .'

'But what?'

'But you don't need to *have* so many rows. Win one, lose one! And maybe when you're working for someone else you have to lose two – or three – or four – for every one you win. Then *lose* them! One thing Jim Bailey says about you is quite true, you always want your own way.'

I was about to speak, but Dorothy continued: 'Come on, you've made up your mind that you want to go – and I support you a hundred per cent in your decision. But that doesn't alter the facts. . . .'

'What facts?'

'That if you'd been a bit more easy-going – and your outlook wasn't so narrow – you could have gone on working for *Drum* and used the situation to benefit yourself. . . . As a matter of fact, you *have* benefited yourself. Just look at the travel you've had all over the continent, all you've learned and all the African leaders you've met. . . . And you owe this to *Drum*.'

I sat silent. It had occurred to me that I had done exactly what I accused Jim Bailey of doing, discussing a situation which crucially concerned us both only after I had made up my own mind. I began, hesitantly, to try to say something of the sort but Dorothy, sensing my difficulty, used the technique which would always cut me short. 'Well, darling, that's settled. Now what about a drink?'

Big changes were taking place at *Drum* besides my leaving. Humphrey Tyler left for Durban before the year's end. Alan Rake, now that the East Africa office had been disbanded, went to take charge in West Africa. At the end of the year, when Ian Berry won his second *Encyclopaedia Britannica* award in successive years – a unique achievement – for his pictures taken in the Congo, he too moved on to wider fields. During my last few months I saw little of Jim Bailey and, as if by mutual agreement, we avoided argument.

It was now my last evening in the office. I had asked the staff to come round for drinks at their favourite shebeen, outwardly the Classic dry cleaner's. Casey was to organize things so that we got a room to ourselves, and ask Can and anyone else from *Golden City Post* who cared to come along as well.

'There's rather a lot of us,' Casey said, 'so don't all rush in at once. Drift up in twos and threes, and if there's a cop around I'll warn you off.'

When I 'drifted' past the door with Nat, Casey beckoned us in. It was a bare room just behind the shop, which would have been a store room if the shop had been run seriously and not just as a blind. It had a cement floor with a strip of carpet – a relief since the cement was cold – and the only windows, high up in one wall, were pasted over with brown paper so that no one could look in. There was a door that locked and on which someone posted himself as guard, a big chair into which I was put, and various stools, chairs (I recognized a couple which had vanished some while ago from the office), oil drums and boxes with newspaper spread over them. One corner was full of domestic objects belonging to the owner's family, such as a folding pram and a bicycle. The handlebars of the bicycle stuck into my back between the shoulder blades; this irritated me for five minutes, but after that I never looked round or thought of moving, and it was only when I got up to go that I realized I had had one handlebar pressing into me for the last two hours.

People kept drifting in until finally we had all assembled. From *Drum* there were Peter, Nat, Casey, John Taukobong the driver, Victor who had lately joined us as office messenger, and a comparative newcomer, Mike Phahlane, who wrote a column of jazz criticism called Swingcerely Yours, and who, whenever he phoned me up while on a job always began with the words 'Sir, this is your favourite son speaking.' From the *Post* there were Can and the sports editor, Theo, also a freelance writer Duke Ngcobo, a musician known as 'General' Duse, and two or three others I knew less well – about fifteen in all.

Casey called me to the door and, in his urgent whisper which still, after three and a half years, I found difficult to catch, asked what drink to order. We settled for two big case bottles of brandy and a dozen quarts of beer to start with, since I knew my guests liked to drink spirits and beer alternately, and that their favourite spirit was 'mahog', the sweetish brandy which you could feel easing its claws into your liver and stomach the moment it got inside. The General took charge of the bar and poured everyone out a slug of brandy, holding the glasses up to the light to make sure they were all equal; the beer we took as we pleased. After a while came another carefully measured slug, and another free-for-all session with the beer. At first there was an opener, but this soon vanished and from that time on the General opened the beer bottles with his teeth, hooking the metal caps deftly off against a single tusk in his lower jaw, which must have been designed and inserted by nature for that purpose.

Once while he was doing this there was an ugly crack and I thought he had broken it. This gave me the shivers because I knew if he had he would do nothing about it, but simply wait until the stump fell out or wore smooth in course of time – but luckily he had only bitten a piece of glass off the top of the bottle together with the metal cap. We poured that bottle out more carefully than the rest and went on drinking.

Meantime Mike Phahlane had got to work to entertain us. Mike was short-legged and thickset, with an orange complexion and a fringe of black whiskers round his face, ending in a tuft beneath his chin. He had laughing black eyes and a jovial expression, which he could smooth in a flash into contrition and anxiety when I asked him what had happened to a missing photograph. With his swaggering walk and air of cheerful effrontery, with his black suit and black hat, stuck flat on top of his head and turned up all round, he looked like a dissolute chaplain in some African navy of the future. Mike had an ear for dialects, forms of expression and tones of voice, and was always enacting scenes of himself being interviewed by cops who had stopped him on the way home.

He began by giving us the meeting – which had then recently taken place – between Kennedy and Khruschev, doing both men speaking and their interpreters. His 'Russian' got great applause. He went on to do imitations of us all – Casey, summoned back from the shebeen by the news that I was looking for him. Casey, frail, with hunched shoulders, swaying slightly, puffing furiously at a cigarette to try to drown the smell of drink. Benson, with his trick of clapping

197

his hand to his forehead as he came out with some thumping lie as to why he wasn't at work yesterday, and the important political inquiries which had detained him. He also imitated what I supposed were my own soft voice and quiet manner, my way of holding up a finger to claim somebody's attention and saying: '*Nat* – just a second, please'; '*Casey* – if you're not too busy'; '*Edna* – just one or two letters', and 'Oh, by the way, where's Benson?'

By now it had become dark and the room, lit only by a single hanging bulb, cast strange shadows on the lower part of our faces. We looked like creatures in a Daumier lithograph, prisoners perhaps, with our heads rising up out of the darkness of a cell, black shiny heads and a single white one. We were all at least partly drunk. I saw Can surreptitiously push away a further case bottle of brandy, as though fearful of its effect once it began to circulate. The General had spotted it, however, and it was soon measured out as carefully as water to a shipwrecked crew. From time to time someone rattled on the door, and was either allowed in or told bluntly to clear off. Mike, in one of his impersonations, kicked over the big plate in the middle which served as ashtray. The butts still alight started to burn holes in the carpet, and we all stamped on them or splashed beer on the smouldering edges.

And now the tensest part of the evening was beginning. Mike – who would never willingly yield the floor to anyone – was pulled down, and Duke took his place. Duke was a plumpish Zulu from Natal, with a round face and missing tooth. 'Mr Hopkinson,' he started in, 'you have been with us more than three years. We are all glad you are going because of this party. But we are all sorry for the occasion of this party. I am going to say to you now what the Zulu wife says to her husband who is going away. . . .' and he recited a long piece, half-poem, half-prayer, in which the husband is urged by the wife to go since he has to go, but to come back one day and to 'come back clean'.

Mike, who had endured Duke's speech with difficulty, now sprang up again: 'No, no, *I* want to speak. I have

198

something I *must* say' – and he brushed off all restraining hands. He spoke for some time, ending up: 'Sir, you are our father.' Anxious to calm down the general emotion, I pushed him down on to the floor beside me, and said that now I wanted to say something. I told them the past few years had been mixed ones. There were things to think of with pleasure, and others with disappointment. . . . 'The work of an editor isn't to do things himself, it's to extract them from other people. When Casey wrote a funny story, Peter took a good set of pictures or Nat made some complicated subject clear – that was my success, and I was happy. . . . The opposite was true as well.'

I found I was talking almost to myself, looking fixedly down at the carpet. When I paused and the silence became acute, I looked up and saw eyes gazing at me through the smoke as though our lives depended on attention. I told them what I had hoped we should achieve: *Drum*s springing up all over Africa; the office a training ground for journalists and cameramen from which papers not yet in existence would one day draw their staffs. 'You speak of my coming back one day to work with you again. I would be happy to come back under conditions which made it possible for us to achieve the things we failed to do in these last years. But I warn you, if ever I come back it will be to demand far more from you all. Far, far more from everyone.'

Casey, pressing his glass between his hands and with eyes both angry and appealing, was trying to speak.

'Mr Hopkinson,' he began, with a slow and careful articulation, as though he found it physically difficult to enunciate, as perhaps by now he did, 'I don't agree with everything that's been said. Not at all. But I say two things. *Two* things. One, when any of us has a trouble, we come to you. You don't care if a man is black or yellow, bald or covered with fur. You listen to him. If you are able to help him, then you do. That's why Mike, who talked a lot of bullshit, called you the father of the paper.

'The second thing is – you talk of disappointments. Yes,

I'm sure you have had disappointments. Big disappointments. Sometimes from us. Sometimes not from us. But I tell you this. When we go on a job and there are troubles and we want to pack up and go off on the booze, then we would think, "Better not disappoint the old man!" '

Casey looked across at me. I was experiencing intense strain. It was not concerned with what he said, but that he should be able to get it out, as though, if he failed to say what he wanted, he would be left carrying some painful load around inside him.

The words 'old man' evidently struck him as needing explanation: 'We call you that, you understand, not exactly because you are an old man yet – more perhaps oldish, at least compared to us – but because of your position. We feel – "Get done what the old man says we have to do". . . . Well,' he said, looking down into his glass and automatically passing it over to the General to be refilled, 'I guess that's all I have to say. We're glad you've been here. Sorry you're going. And that's all.'

We passed the bottle round. Since some had taken in all they could hold, the rest were free to help themselves. One or two had slipped out and gone home. Henry, the shebeen owner, his other customers having long since vanished, had now settled down with us.

Peter got up. He spoke in an abrupt and jerky manner, not so much addressing us as flinging out sentences for anyone who cared to pick them up. 'What I want to say to you fellows is just one thing. You think you're the same fellows you were when you were sitting in this room three years go. You're not. You may feel the same, but you are *not* the same. None of us is the same. Nat here is not the same. Casey is not the same. I am not the same. We're different people from what we were. We think differently. We work in a different way. We are *not the same*. . . .'

'No,' I said, 'and I am not the same either. Nothing like the same.'

It was growing late, and there would be problems, as always for Africans, about getting home. We straightened ourselves, shook hands all round, and I went through into the back to settle up with Henry.

'So much for the brandy,' he said, 'and so much for the beers.'

'It ought to be more. You've left out the last lot of beers you brought.'

'Oh,' he said, 'that was my contribution.'

I thanked him and went out through the dark store. The rooms were now all empty, and a reek of smoke and drink flowed into them from the room where we had been sitting. In the dark street hovered a group of shadowy forms.

'Has everyone got transport? Can everyone get home?'

'Yes – we're okay,' the voices shouted. 'Goodnight.'

'Goodnight.'

My car was over on a deserted parking lot. John and Victor came with me to carry my two cases full of books and papers from the office. I fumbled with the keys and dropped them.

'I'm all right, John,' I said. 'You think I can't get home, but I shall.'

I climbed in and called goodbye. Once at the wheel I knew the car would take me home. Inside myself I felt completely empty as though the whole contents of my body had been extracted. For the last hour or so, I realized, I had been shivering all over. The room had been stuffy and crowded and I was swimming in drink, but it seemed as though all vital warmth had been drained out of me.

15

South Africa, Farewell

Looking back on this time it seems rash of me to have given up a reasonably well-paid job for no better prospect than to become a freelance in South Africa. I was fifty-six, had responsibilities to my children and to two previous wives. Dorothy and I lived up to our income, had an expensive flat and a car, and our only capital was a few thousand pounds – just enough at that time to have bought us a small flat if we had gone back to England. For the moment though there was enough work to keep me busy. Gollancz had commissioned a book – an 'African Diary'* covering the past few years; I had an article or two to write for London papers and magazines; and I had been asked by the Anglo-American Corporation, who published an impressive quarterly review with the modest title *Optima*, to return to the Congo for a month, travel widely, and produce an objective assessment of the country's economic, social and political life, and its prospects now that the fighting appeared to have died down.

This is not the place for an assessment of the Congo's chances of survival in the early 1960s, nor do I mean to describe my month of travel, but one point impressed me before starting. A requirement for visiting the Congo was the production of a certificate from the South African police

*This would appear as *In the Fiery Continent* during 1962 in Britain, and in the US a year or two later.

saying in effect that there was nothing against me in the record. This had presumably been a requirement of the Belgian authorities – as part of their general cooperation with the South African regime – and had never been cancelled although a Congolese government was now in power. The requirement might well have lapsed, but there was no way of finding this out in Johannesburg and from my earlier experiences I did not want to risk arriving without necessary papers and so perhaps being turned back, or at best wasting a week to get round the situation. I therefore applied to the police authorities, who followed the familiar technique for those of whom the authorities are suspicious, giving no direct refusal but telling me to come back in four days' time. When I did so and the precious slip of paper had not arrived from Pretoria, I was told to return after the weekend – and so on. At last, when there was only one week left before my departure, I went to the Anglo-American office and said it looked as though I should not be able to make the trip and produce the article they wanted.

My contact, a high-up executive, at once rang the Pretoria police and demanded to know why I had not been given clearance. Some sort of objection was evidently raised because he replied sharply: 'But don't you *understand*? Mr Hopkinson is going for *us*. We've asked him to go and we want him to go.' He ended by telling the officer in Pretoria that he would need to make the certificate available for me on Monday without fail – which it was.

The article I wrote on my return was the longest and most thorough piece of reporting I have ever undertaken and took up the first twenty pages of the review.* The Congo had been almost continuously in the news since the upheavals of 1960, and my visit now chanced to coincide with the outbreak of a wholly new war – that between Tshombe's forces in Katanga, led by renegade Belgian and French officers (known among themselves as *les affreux*), and the forces of the United Nations, whose political representative

*Optima, December 1961, pp. 167–186.

in Katanga was Dr Conor Cruise O'Brien. Under these circumstances the *Optima* article proved highly topical and attracted a lot of notice, including one or two editorials in Johannesburg papers. A number of people rang me or spoke to me about it in the street. I was asked to give a few talks and lectures, but more valuable than these was the contact which grew up for me with the principal morning paper in the Transvaal, the *Rand Daily Mail*, and its redoubtable editor, Laurie Gandar.

Dorothy and I had known Gandar and his wife Isobel for the previous couple of years, having been to their home a number of times and they to ours. When I got back from Katanga just as the new 'war' broke out, Laurie asked me to write two articles for his paper explaining how the situation had arisen. These were reproduced by other papers in the group. Their good reception led first to further pieces, and before long to the suggestion that I should come into the office three afternoons a week to write leading articles and features for the leader page, and generally give whatever help I could. This provided the mainstay every freelance must have in order to keep going while payment for casual work is coming in, and my contact with Gandar also served to keep me in closer touch with all that was happening politically in South Africa.

One evening in the middle of 1962, after I had been free-lancing for a year, Dorothy and I went out to dinner with some friends. Among the guests was an elderly man – a Colonel Barnard – who impressed us both. He had apparently been much involved in political life soon after the war, but had despaired of the United Party* and dropped out of the political scene. What he said, in a sentence or two, was that the English-speaking people in South Africa came from

---

*The nominal opposition to the ruling Nationalist Party which had governed the country since the fall of General Smuts in 1948. It was regarded as the party of the English-speaking people and engaged in shadow-boxing with the 'Nats', whose basic policies, however, it did not seriously oppose.

204

a race with great ideals which had made a notable contribution to the world, and that they had no right to abandon these ideals and their faith for the sake of a comfortable life and in order to avoid hostility. They owed it to the non-white peoples as well as to themselves to hold fast to their principles which – being in line with the general progress of mankind – must inevitably triumph in the end.

About a week later at around 2.30 in the morning I woke up with my head full of thoughts and phrases. For a while I tried to go to sleep again but found it impossible, so I went into the study and began to write. Before morning I had written one complete article and part of another, and by the end of three days I had written a series of four, which I called 'A Word to English-speaking South Africans'. I took them to Laurie Gandar, who at once said he wanted to run them on four consecutive days. Much to my surprise the editors of the other leading papers in the group – the *Cape Times*, *Natal Mercury* and the *Port Elizabeth Evening Herald* – decided to run them too, and they appeared in the middle of August 1962, on the heels of a succession of repressive laws, passed or in process of being passed, which the Nationalist government had produced in the aftermath of Sharpeville, once it had started to recover from the shock. These included the notorious 'Death for Sabotage' Bill, aimed primarily not at the planters of bombs and blowers-up of pylons, but at dissenting whites. In the words of the Minister of Justice, Mr Vorster, it was aimed at 'curbing white agitators' – and he went on to accuse the English-language press, the newly formed but still tiny Progressive Party, the Black Sash women's organization and certain clerics, of 'dangerous and irresponsible agitation'. The Sabotage Bill was to be followed by one to standardize education on what were called 'Christian National' lines, plus a Censorship Bill to deal with any aspects of free expression which the Sabotage Bill had failed to cover.

All this legislation was to be supported by a drive to try and secure forty to fifty thousand new settlers every year, with a view to achieving a white population of ten million by the year 2100. One of the aims of the legislation, in addition to the immediate one of 'curbing white agitators', was to get the existing white population regimented and in line before the expected inflow began, and I had written about this in the *Rand Daily Mail* a month or two previously.

All immigrants tend to fall in with the ideas and attitudes of their new country; but if the country is divided and there is a choice of attitudes, they will take their choice. They may be Nationalist, apartheid-conscious; or they may be democratic, disposed to believe that all human beings have a basis of equality.

It is crucial, for Nationalist policy, that they be given no choice. Hence the attacks on the English-language Press – newcomers are far more likely to read English than Afrikaans. Hence the Sabotage Bill – aimed primarily at silencing dissenting whites.

Hence measures to secure a totalitarian grip on the country's system of education.*

The nub of the four new articles lay in the second, entitled 'Values that Must Be Preserved'. To the English reader these values will seem commonplace, but in the climate of South Africa at that time their impact was very different.

In the situation in which we English-speaking people find ourselves, it is essential to be realistic, and to judge our own values with dispassion.

The question forced upon us at this moment is: What are the essential values in our tradition and way of life – and what the symbols and relics of the past, with which, however deeply we revere them, we must be prepared to part? What, we must ask ourselves, do we live by and for? What are we willing to give up in the interests of harmony and peaceful living? And what will we never give up – for any blandishments or in face of any threats? . . .

Those who wanted a republic had the right to test public feeling in a referendum; having gained the day, they had the right to make our form of government republican. Once this is done, there is little point in battles about flags and photographs. Deeply as many of us feel, it is misdirection of energy to fight over symbols when the association they symbolized has been broken off.

*T.H. 'Apartheid: a new mental attitude', *Rand Daily Mail*, 19 June 1962.

If our heritage does not consist of outer forms, such as the monarchy, wherein does it lie? What are the values we must at every cost preserve?

First: Love of justice between man and man, people and people, class and class. This must be expressed in courts of law, independent of the government, to which everyone must have access on equal terms. It is a corollary of this that no Minister, and no government, shall have power to control the courts, to be judge in his own case and to order his own penalties.

It is a further corollary that the law itself must not discriminate. Courts can only interpret the laws laid down. If the law itself discriminates against certain men because of their colour, their origin, their religion or for any similar reason, then the justice the courts dispense cannot be equal.

Courts of law should be concerned with one thing only – guilt or innocence.

Second: Tolerance, and the allowing to every man a right to his own point of view. Men, as men, are entitled to think their thoughts and express them to their fellows. There is no thought a man can have so dangerous as the suppression of thought. Progress comes from the clash of opinions and beliefs, not from marking out a road and ordering everyone to march along it.

Third: Freedom of the Press and of expression. To the democratic way of life, free speech and a free Press are as necessary as independent courts of law. Note that a free Press is not simply the right of journalists to air their views – it is the right of citizens *to hear both sides*.

Fourth: Freedom of conscience and the liberty of education. The right of us all to follow our convictions, and to educate our children in our own faith and ideals.

Fifth: Political power is not a weapon, but a trust. Honestly used, it is a means of raising the less developed to their full stature, and of reaching a just accommodation with minorities. . . .

I put this list forward, not as a maximum but a minimum – the minimum contribution we should insist on making to the life of the Republic.

A great deal is talked and written in this country about South Africa being 'an outpost of Western civilization'. But you can only call yourself an outpost if you are actively upholding and vigorously extending the basic tenets of the civilization you claim to represent.

In respect of all the tenets listed above, our country today is going backwards and not forwards. The government in power has no intention of changing course. Inch by inch and stride by stride it is moving away from democracy towards a totalitarian regime.

What, under these circumstances, can those people – English-speaking, Afrikaans-speaking or of whatever language, who love the tradition of freedom – do to uphold the values we believe to be essential?*

To say that, for the English-speaking readers at whom they were aimed, this series of articles fell flat would be an understatement. To readers concerned with adding a second swimming pool to their garden or putting a fourth car into the garage, talk of this kind was a meaningless, even impertinent, distraction from serious issues. The half dozen letters received by the *Rand Daily Mail*, signed 'Happy English South Africans' and similar *noms de plume*, were either sneers or angry denunciations. But if they had little or no effect on the English-speaking population for whom they were intended, their effect on the Nationalists was dynamic. This was partly a matter of content – an open appeal to the English-speaking people to reject Nationalist policies – but much more to their timing, since their publication coincided with an organized drive in all the provinces to lure the English-speaking people into joining the Nationalist Party. The drive was particularly strong in Natal, where a high proportion of English had settled since early in the nineteenth century, and was already meeting with some success, so that the last thing the Nationalists wanted was an appeal of this kind coming at this moment.

René de Villiers, then the assistant editor of the *Star*, Johannesburg's evening paper, was an Afrikaner, but one of progressive and liberal views as well as an outstanding journalist. He told me that the series had . . . 'really got under the Afrikaner's skin. It has made me think afresh of the importance of "personal" journalism. In our editorial columns we've been banging away for months on just these issues. But when a man or woman comes out publicly and

*T.H., *Rand Daily Mail*, 14 August 1962.

says it all in terms of "me" and "you" – then the effect is altogether different.'

So determined were the Nationalists to counter the series that two leading ministers in the government were assigned, or took on, the task of publicly refuting them. One was the Minister of Information, Frank Waring, a former hero of the rugby field, and the other was the Minister of Transport, Ben Schoeman.

A Mrs Clark, wife of the US Counsellor, told me: 'I was at a lunch of the Constantia Women's Club in Pretoria, an organization of Afrikaner women. There were about two hundred present to hear Frankie Waring speak. He spent his whole time tearing your articles to bits. He had them all there in front of him pinned together, and went through them one by one. At one point he kept saying . . . "Now I *must* control myself. I *must* not lose my temper. . . ." '

René de Villiers, with whom I discussed this, remarked: 'Yes – and I can tell you just what got him. It was your saying that if the English-speaking people choose "to exchange their democratic birthright for a Nationalist one, they will find a welcome – though never a final acceptance of equality – inside the National Party". They could expect in time to form their own separate branches of the National Party, with their own ministers permitted to take part in the shaping of still further restrictive legislation. . . . But let them not imagine they will be able to influence its aims or policies by a hair's breadth.'

However it was when the two ministers, Waring and Schoeman, joined forces to address the rally of the Natal National Party held in Pietermaritzburg, that events took a surprising, and for us in the long run beneficial, turn. The political correspondent of Dr Verwoerd's newspaper *Die Transvaler* was present at the meeting, at which the main subject of discussion was my four articles. After the Minister of Information, Waring, had described me as one who 'stands not with one foot but with both feet in Britain', and Minister B. J. Schoeman had carried on with the attack, English-speaking members of the National Party demanded from the floor, '*Wie is Hopkinson?*' ('Who is this Hopkinson?'). To this a certain Mr E. A. Stirton jumped up and replied, 'He is a bastard.' He did not actually use the word 'bastard' since the way of expressing this accusation or insult in Afrikaans is slightly different: '*Hopkinson se pa was 'n oujongkerel*', ('Hopkinson's father was a bachelor'). This *Die Transvaler* published in its report on 23 August, and a reporter from the *Sunday Times* of Johannesburg who happened to be present rang me up to call my attention to it. I at once rang my lawyer who said he had no doubt this was actionable, and we agreed that he should write at once to the *Transvaler's* editor, Dr G.O. Schultz. I suggested he should include in the letter that I was not taking the matter up primarily on my account but out of respect for my father, the late Archdeacon of Westmorland.

Next day *Die Transvaler* must have come to its journalistic senses, because the paper carried a curious kind of apology on its front page saying that their report of the Natal meeting was 'not intended to cause [me] embarrassment'. In view of their rapid, if half-hearted, apology the matter was eventually settled out of court for the sum of £300 and the payment by *Die Transvaler* of all legal costs.

At this moment Laurie Gandar, one or two of whose principal colleagues in the *Rand Daily Mail* happened to be retiring, made the suggestion that I join the paper full-time. He would concentrate on the political side of the work and the writing of editorials, and I would apply myself to working with the staff on the day-to-day running of the newspaper. The idea appealed to me greatly, since I had met no one I would sooner have worked for and with than Laurie Gandar*, but now out of the blue came a different proposition.

Towards the middle of 1962 newspaper proprietors and

*For his courageous editorship of the *Rand Daily Mail* under most difficult conditions, Gandar was awarded the Gold Medal of the Institute of Journalists in 1964, also the World Press Achievement Award by the American Newspaper Publishing Association in 1966.

editors in East Africa and the then Federation of Rhodesia had made an appeal to the International Press Institute, based at that time in Zurich, to set up some system for the training of African journalists. With the coming of independence all over Africa the white journalists – who had hitherto run the newspapers, magazines and radio stations – were leaving, since there would be no future for them, and such few Africans as already were in journalism had had no chance to gain the necessary training and experience. Jim Rose, the Director of IPI, took a swing round Africa to see the situation for himself, and in the course of it called in at Johannesburg where he was guest of honour at a dinner given by Joel Mervis, editor of the South African *Sunday Times*. I had known Jim Rose when he was literary editor of the London *Observer*, and he now told me of his hope to set up one or two training centres for young African journalists if the money for the project could be found.

During the next two or three months Rose took up fresh work in London and was succeeded at IPI by Rohan Rivett, an Australian editor of high standing. He took a lively interest in the new plan, as also did Michael Curtis, whose newspaper, the *Daily Nation*, was just starting up in Nairobi, and a colleague of his, Charles Hayes. Both of them were members of IPI and among the four of us, in letters and visits between Nairobi and Johannesburg, the details were worked out. The scheme was to be an emergency one for a limited period, aimed at producing a flow of trained African journalists who could fill the gap between the departure of the whites and the setting up by newly independent countries of their own systems of training. Since distances were so vast and cultural differences so great, it was thought necessary to establish two centres, one in East Africa at Nairobi and a second in West Africa, probably in Lagos. If the project got off the ground I was to be the director and find, or try to find, the necessary staff. The scheme might extend over five or six years, after which the work could be taken over by colleges or universities.

In October, while Dorothy and I were in London for the

211

publication of my book *In the Fiery Continent*, we learned
that the Ford Foundation had agreed to fund the scheme for
two years, and the project was announced to the press. There
were still final arrangements to be made and we returned to
Johannesburg to await instructions. On Christmas Eve came
a phone call from Rivett in Zurich saying that everything
was now on line, and asking how soon we could be in
Nairobi. I put my hand over the mouthpiece while I spoke
to Dorothy, and then told him we could pack everything
and be up there in ten days.

My farewell to South Africa had already been made. On 31
October in reviewing my book for the *Cape Times*, Anthony
Delius, a staff journalist and writer, had begun his review
with the sentence: 'Tom Hopkinson may not be the sort of
newly-arrived "true South African" with whom Mr Frank
Waring would crack a bottle of free wine – but his observing
and vivid book, *In the Fiery Continent*, shows that he is the
sort of immigrant South Africa most desperately needs. . . .'

This had stung the Minister of Information to reply in a
letter to the paper★ which appeared under the heading 'True
S.A. Immigrant now Emigrant' and ended with the words:

He [Anthony Delius] is most inspired by this man who is going
to show us a 'true South African immigrant'.

Only on Monday Mr Hopkinson, from London, advised the
Press he had accepted the new chair of journalism at the University
College of East Africa.

What about this clear-eyed immigrant making this country his
home, come what may? Apparently he is looking for his 'greater
opportunities' elsewhere.

Somehow, Mr Delius, I feel your slip is showing.

Anthony Delius, of course, was perfectly capable of
defending himself against Frank Waring, but I too wanted
to answer the minister, particularly as this would be our last
word before leaving South Africa. I accordingly wrote to
the *Cape Times*.

Three months ago, at the Nationalist Party conference in Maritz-

★*Cape Times*, 9 November 1962.

burg, Mr Waring was attacking me on the ground that I had 'not one foot but both feet in Britain'. Now his criticism appears to be that I am going to work in Kenya.

This is no 'professorship' or 'chair'. What has happened is that the newspaper groups of Central and East Africa, acting in enlightened self-interest, have decided that it is folly to draw their journalistic talent from only a small section of the community. In future they intend to seek it among Black as well as White.

With this aim, I have been asked to start a training scheme for African journalists. The Royal College in Nairobi, forming part of the University of East Africa, has generously offered it a home. I am sorry if, by accepting this opportunity, I have exposed your admired contributor, Anthony Delius, to one of Mr Waring's easy sneers.

In leaving South Africa, where my wife and I have lived happily for five years, in spite of those difficulties which any active supporter of Western democratic ideals inevitably meets, I would like to say that I am grateful for my time here, and I wish this country every good gift: in particular the blessings of a truly representative government, a Minister of Justice concerned to uphold the rights of the individual citizen, and a Minister of Information not lacking in dignity or commonsense.★

★*Cape Times*, 27 November 1962.

16
In a New World

Arriving in Nairobi on the night of 10–11 January 1963, we were met at the airport by our friends Michael and Joan Curtis, with whom we were to stay for a short time while we found somewhere to live. Michael, former editor of the *News Chronicle* at the time I was on its staff, was engaged in launching a new tabloid, the *Daily Nation*, backed by the Aga Khan, many of whose Ismaili followers lived in Kenya. The *Nation*'s offices were conveniently near the centre of the town, and I arranged to rent a room from which to get the training scheme organized. The task was not easy. Premises had already been found – a rather rundown villa in the grounds of Royal College, soon to be renamed University College – but I had no staff, no students and no programme of work. To plan everything properly would take months and the need was immediate. So I decided to fix an arbitrary date, 18 March, for the course to open, and wrote at once to all government information offices and radio stations in East and Central Africa, as well as to all independent news-papers – of which there were few indeed – asking if they wished to send any of their staff for training. The area covered was a vast one, from Ethiopia and the Sudan in the north down to the British High Commission Territories in Southern Africa which would become before long the independent states of Lesotho and Botswana. Zambia, Malawi and Southern Rhodesia came into our field, as well as the islands of Mauritius and Zanzibar. For most of this

214

area I had nothing but addresses and a name or two, but in the East African territories of Kenya, Uganda and Tanzania I had friends I could write to or call upon.

Even the writing of these 'announcement' letters involved a number of final decisions. How long was the course to last? What would we provide for those who came on it? What would be the qualifications for acceptance? Normally one might expect to spend weeks arguing such far-reaching decisions, which had now to be settled out of hand. Most students, I knew, would be married, so the length of the course was fixed at six months – the maximum time they could be expected to stay away from their families, and the minimum into which we could cram the necessary training. Our budget would allow us to provide accommodation and food and to pay fares by air or rail, but it would not allow us to provide pocket money. It was therefore a condition that every student while on the course must be given his full salary by his employer which, I reckoned, would serve both to keep their homes going and leave a few pounds a month for personal expenses.

As for qualifications, it would be useless to expect much, and quite impossible to bring candidates for interview over such vast distances. In the end all we asked was that, since English was the only common language in such a mixed group as ours, every student should be able to speak and write English and should have worked for at least two years in some capacity on a newspaper or magazine, in radio or for his government information service.

For several weeks after sending out the announcements I heard nothing. Then the replies started to come in, and it was soon apparent we should get at least a necessary minimum of students. But who was to do the teaching? From the staff of Royal College I could find lecturers on particular subjects, but I needed one helper with newspaper experience – wider and more varied than my own which had been mainly in magazines – and who was also familiar with Africa and African conditions. While working on *Drum* I had been impressed by our correspondent in Rhodesia who offered

215

stories we could use and always sent them in on time, well written and with the pictures captioned. His name was Frank Barton; his wife Maureen was Rhodesian and they had both lived for a number of years in Central Africa.

Frank had twice had papers which he had launched or was working on in Southern Rhodesia closed down by the Welensky regime for being too pro-African. He was a tall man, powerfully built, and though totally committed to African development could be hard when the situation called for it. Coming home one night to find that a burglar had broken into his kitchen, he fought the man for an hour – with only a few brief pauses for breath – until both were too exhausted to continue and the African slipped out by the way he had come in.

When *Drum*'s Cape Town editor, Peter Younghusband, had left to join the London *Daily Mail*, I persuaded Frank and Maureen to come down with their young family to Cape Town, and now wrote urging him to move back north again and help me get the new course started. His acceptance took a big weight off my mind, but my troubles were not yet over. The Royal College had undertaken to put the villa into good order well before the opening date, and there was plenty to be done. The two main rooms must be knocked together to form a lecture room; lavatories and telephones had to be installed; there were many minor repairs and the whole place needed decorating. Every time I went round to the official in charge he assured me the work 'will start tomorrow', but only two weeks before the students were due to assemble nothing had been done, and when I appealed to higher authority in the college I was told I must 'settle the matter myself'.

Since requests had proved useless I looked round for a bludgeon and happily there was one to hand. It had been arranged that our course should be opened by the governor of Kenya, Malcolm MacDonald. I had had some contact with him back in *Picture Post* days, and when I called on him soon after arriving to confirm the arrangement I found him most sympathetic to our venture. He was also, it appeared, the Visitor to Royal College, but had never yet been there in his official capacity, and the principal had been delighted when I told him the governor would be coming to the college to open our course on 18 March.

When I looked in now on the building manager he called out cheerfully: 'Don't worry! We'll be over there tomorrow! Just a few jobs to clear out of the way first.'

'Don't bother to go tomorrow,' I told him. 'You've left everything so late you can't possibly put the place straight by the eighteenth. I'm not having the Governor of Kenya open a course for the International Press Institute in what looks like a broken-down pigsty. I'm calling his visit off.'

He looked at me with horror: 'What on earth do you mean?'

'Just that. I'm on my way to tell your principal he needn't bother to show up on the eighteenth. Then I'm going up to Government House to see Malcolm MacDonald. He's not going to feel very good about being invited here – then put off at the last minute. But that's not my affair. You and the principal can explain it to him together.'

'Oh, for God's sake!' said the man. 'Have a heart! We'll be over there in two hours' time.'

With the building work now going ahead fast, all seemed to be in order – but I had forgotten the power of red tape. Full independence for Kenya was due at the year's end, but in the meantime the Colonial Service ran everything in accordance with the rules. A phone call came from a high official in the Education Department who, having explained who he was, inquired: 'Is it true that you're planning to launch a training course for journalists inside Royal College?'

'It is indeed. It opens later this month.'

'What qualifications have you for starting such a course in a university college?'

Hastily I started to go over a career which showed, I thought, some knowledge of journalism and, by now, some experience of Africa.

'No! No!' my caller interrupted. 'Not *all that*! I mean what *teaching* qualifications have you got?'

217

I was beginning to confess that I had none, when an idea came to me and I replied: 'Well, I don't know if it's to the point, but I'm an MA of Oxford University.' In my day, the MA followed automatically after one had acquired a BA, merely by paying £12 or so to the University. Today no doubt it costs more.

'My dear fellow!' said the voice. '*Of course* that's okay, then! Why on earth didn't you say so in the first place?'

On the day and at the hour appointed, Malcolm MacDonald opened our course with charm and good humour, shaking hands and chatting with each of the newly arrived students in turn. The building was in good condition, newly decorated all through; an Asian firm in the town had made the curtains in two days. In the lecture room there were fifteen desks and typewriters. Each student had a room of his own in the college only a stone's throw away. . . . All that was necessary now was that, over the next six months, they should learn to become journalists.

Next morning we assembled and I outlined the programme of work to be got through together over the next half year. They put a number of questions and then, as I was about to leave, one of them asked: 'Sir, you have told us of the work we are to do, but you have told us nothing about the one who will teach us how to do it. We ask you to speak about yourself.'

We were sitting, not at desks but in a circle, and I looked round the ring of faces – hopeful, intent, bewildered, and one or two suspicious.

'I see you intend to put me on the spot.'

There was an outcry: 'What do you mean? Who has put you on the spot?'

'If I talk to you about myself,' I said, 'when you go out of here you will say to one another: "Our new instructor is a very vain man. This is only our first day at work – and already he has spent half an hour talking about himself!" But if I answer "No, I shall *not* talk about myself", then you will say: "Our new instructor is a very cagey man. He must be hiding something. All we did was ask him to say a little about himself – and he refused to speak!" '

I took off my watch and handed it to the student on my right. 'Aidan here has got my watch. I shall talk for just two minutes about myself – then he will stop me. And each one of you in turn will talk for just two minutes about yourselves. No more. No less. After that we shall have all begun to know each other.'

What we all said of ourselves I no longer remember – except for one student who came from a weekly paper. He gave his name, then added: 'I am an assistant editor. I have been an assistant editor for four weeks because the white man who had my job has gone home. Before that I was a copy boy carrying copy to the printer and proofs back to the journalists. I am an assistant editor who cannot write a story, does not know how to conduct an interview, cannot write a heading to fill a space, cannot mark up a picture to go into the page. . . . I am an assistant editor who knows *nothing*.' He fell silent, and I did not speak but I thought – 'and before you walk out of this place in six months' time, you will do each one of those things as though you'd been doing them all your life'.

It took Frank Barton some weeks to get up from Cape Town, but once he arrived the work really took off. He did the journalistic training, for which he had a natural gift, being clear, forceful and good humoured. I did the administrative work and went through the day's news every morning with the students. In addition I read books with them – a surprising activity for journalists. We had hired from the college an excellent English teacher to give instruction in the language, but what I was trying to do was different – to arouse their interest in books and reading. The system was that they would all read a chapter in the evening and we would talk it over together the next morning. What did it mean? What was the author getting at? How far had he succeeded?

On our various courses we would read a variety of books, but the two authors whose work aroused everyone's interest were George Orwell for his *Animal Farm* and *1984*, and the Nigerian author Chinua Achebe. Achebe's novel *Things Fall Apart* tells how white civilization disrupted the established order of African village life; and his *No Longer at Ease* is the story of a young man from the bush who succumbs, after a hopeful start, to the temptations and corruption of city life. On all these our discussions would be lively: people would contribute their own experiences and tell what had happened to their friends. Though still young – most of them in their late twenties or early thirties – they had themselves in many cases made that prodigious journey across the centuries from a barefoot village life to the world of towering cities and space exploration. The book which aroused most argument, however, was always *Animal Farm*. The fable as a literary form and the fiction of animals and birds that talk are both basic to African culture, and everyone could apply the moral of Orwell's tale to the country they knew best. Later on, when we had brought students from West Africa to join our Nairobi course, one of them put into plain words what others had expressed in roundabout terms: 'I don't know who is this George Orwell. I have never met him. But I tell you one thing about him for certain – he must have lived for a long time in Ghana!'

While all this activity was going on, Dorothy had been looking for a place for us to live. After inspecting two or three houses, agreeable but suburban, on the Nairobi out-skirts, she took me to a large, rather sombre house of reddish stone. Almost the last in a long road, it stood on the very edge of the coffee plantations, beyond which there was nothing for miles but rolling hills, Kikuyu villages and farms. A circular drive ran down to a large porch, above which rose a kind of tower which contained the staircase. There were almost no windows in the front, but a fine outlook at the back where the ground fell steeply away to a small tropical river fringed with banana trees.

'What d'you think of it?' Dorothy asked.

I hesitated. 'Forbidding, but not unfriendly. A bit like "The Fall of the House of Usher." But what do *you* think?'

'It's got big rooms. Parquet floors. There's a lovely kitchen. . . . We can have a study and bathroom each. . . . It's a bit dark inside.'

The garden was messy, full of scraps of flowerbeds, and the darkness came from a row of towering blue gums along one side. Planted much too close together, they could do nothing but shoot up higher and higher into the sky.

'If we cut down all the blue gums,' I suggested, 'and clear the ground at the back. . . .'

The rent was reasonable, but the owners, said Dorothy, didn't really want to let it but to sell. 'Like most other people they're leaving the country and they'd like to get it off their hands.'

'What are they asking for it?'

'Seven thousand pounds.'

'That's reasonable enough for a large house and three acres of ground – but our contract here's only for two years. And if we have to sell up in two years' time there may be no buyers at any price.'

'Have we *got* seven thousand pounds?'

'No – but we could raise most, and fix a mortgage for the rest. It really depends what's going to happen in this country.'

'What do *you* think is going to happen in Kenya?'

'I think peace is going to happen. They've had a revolution. They've got independence. Now they want to get on with being a country. . . . But do *you* think we should buy the house?'

'Yes.'

Dorothy and I had now been married for ten years, during which time I had come to respect her intuitions. Often hesitant and indecisive over trifles, when faced with any serious decision she knew what she thought was right and what would work out best. When she said 'Yes' or 'No', that was what she meant. We bought the house. It was the first we had ever owned and it would be the last. It was a wonderful place to live and when we came to leave would prove a good investment. Meantime it had to be decorated throughout, a task in which Dorothy was in her element since she had a natural gift for colour.

The blue gum trees were quickly felled, and the hillside behind the house cleared of mimosa roots and scrub which served only to harbour snakes and rats. An African contractor chopped the trees down to be sold for timber, and the scrub for charcoal. I let him have the wood for nothing in return for a promise to dig up all the roots.

'Yes,' he swore, 'when you come back here they will all be gone. Every tree root will be gone!'

We were busy at the time and it was three days before I got back to our new property. The roots were all still there; it was the contractor and his men who had vanished – a useful lesson to me not to be so simple-minded. Over the next year or so two stout Kikuyu garden workers would spend much of their time digging up and burning nearly three hundred roots. They also levelled the hillside off into an evenly sloping bank; covered it with coarse, quick growing grass which strangled weeds; created terraces one above the other for an evening stroll; and made a little avenue of datura shrubs whose long tubular flowers in orange, lemon and white gave off an intoxicating scent. The 'avenue' ran down from our garden to the tropical stream and its banana trees, where each of the house and garden workers had a *shamba* or garden of his own to grow whatever he pleased, and hope to harvest the produce before the porcupines got at it.

17

Getting Started

The students, with only one or two exceptions, flung themselves into work with passion. They saw these six months as the means for making a stride forward in their careers, which was understandable; but they also saw them as the opportunity to gain what so much of Africa cries out for – education and a knowledge of the modern world. Some, when they arrived, had little idea of how to study, but they learned quickly from the others. All supposed they could take in far more than was humanly possible in a six months' stay, and, so far from trying to avoid doing what we asked of them, would insist – sometimes with a kind of rage – that we give them more.

Having learned that British journalists use shorthand, they demanded to have this added to the course, and when we pointed out the difficulty of writing shorthand notes in English for those who still thought in their own language, they brushed it aside impatiently: 'We are all thinking in English! You have taught us to think in English. If the English journalists use shorthand, we can use it too. We are not inferior to journalists overseas.'

A similar struggle broke out over learning French. Few before this had ever travelled outside their own countries and I had remarked that, though in Africa as a whole more than eight hundred languages are spoken, one can get around all the cities and towns using only French and English. 'Then *why* are you not teaching us also to speak French? We must learn the French language on this course. You must make it possible for us to talk with our brothers from other African countries.' And when I answered that their time was fully occupied, and that if we took on something new their work in journalism would suffer, there was an outcry. 'This is our only chance to learn! You should not hold us back! You *have* to arrange that we learn French.'

Some of their demands we met, and others bypassed. Merely to correct the work they were doing and plan what to do next week kept Frank and myself hard at it. In addition problems we had not expected would crop up from their lack of educational background. Few had looked at newspapers before this, except casually. Less than half had ever seen a film. Not one, until we took them, had been inside a theatre. Indeed to have got as far as the lecture room and to be tapping out brief news stories on a typewriter was already an immense advance.

In *African Assignment*, the short history of the course he later wrote for the International Press Institute, Frank Barton quotes from a letter written by a student on applying to join one of our courses. His name was Ajwando Abour, and he was a Kenyan, born on the shores of Lake Victoria in the very heart of Africa where his tribe had herded their cattle since time immemorial.

I used to spend a lot of time writing with a twig on my arms and thighs as I herded our cattle. Full of enthusiasm and urged to write, I decided to open a News Agency. The first of its kind. I came across a book in which a line suggested that all one needed to become a writer was a writing table, pens, a notebook and ink. Using a small amount of working capital I decided to open a News Agency in Mombasa. That is how I got into the print.

Only a few years later Abour was a government information officer in Kenya, covering an area twice the size of Greece.

Another student, Aidan Cheche, who would become news editor of Radio Tanzania soon after he left us, noted in a piece of writing done during an exercise that he had seen his

224

first white man only twenty years earlier – a missionary
cycling through his village in a remote part of the country.*

Whenever some gap in general knowledge revealed itself
we would lay on a special lecture at short notice. During
one course there occurred the first budget day of Kenya's
independent government, and we had spent our 'news hour'
discussing the sort of measures the government should introduce. Rather thoughtlessly I asked: 'D'you think it would
be a good thing for the government to make a law doubling
everybody's pay?'

Certainly it would – there was general agreement that all
pay should be doubled! Fearing to embark on the dangerous
waters of gross national product, profit margins, and relations between the public and private sectors, I asked one of
the finance ministers, Mwai Kibaki, to come along and
explain just how a budget is drawn up – which he did with
admirable clarity. Another such special lecture, however,
landed us in an emotional crisis. Important finds had been
made near the coast of bones and skull fragments from man's
early ancestors. Inevitably the subject of evolution came up,
and several demanded to be told: 'Evolution? What is that?'
I did my best, but the theory of evolution is too important,
I considered, for an amateur and there happened to be a well-
known biologist at Royal College who at once agreed to
come over and explain the subject. At the end of an interesting talk a student from Uganda asked how this description
of the universe could be reconciled with the Bible story.
'What about the story of Creation? What about the book of
Genesis? What about Jesus Christ?'

The lecturer was visibly taken aback. 'What *can* you
mean?' He spread his hands out in dismay. '*Jesus Christ*? You
believe in all that? In Father Christmas too? And in gnomes
and fairies?'

After he had gone we had a difficult time. 'Fifty years
ago,' cried the Ugandan who had been to missionary school,

African Assignment, by Frank Barton. International Press Institute,
Zurich, 1969, pp. 23–4.

'you came here with your religion. You took away our own religion and gave us your Christianity. You taught it to us and you told us it was true. . . . Now you come and tell us it is all a lot of nonsense, like Father Christmas. What *are* we to believe?' He was on the verge of tears. Only slowly, over the next hour or so, was some degree of harmony reached between theories of evolution and the Christian faith.

Since families and homes were far away, we tried to find interests for them at weekends. Dorothy would ask ten at a time to lunch on Sunday, and they would spend the afternoon playing records and dancing; Maureen and Frank would invite another group. At other times we would take them to the game parks where one of the wardens would explain about conservation. Once on every course Frank Barton took the whole group to Mombasa to see the workings of a modern port; it was an arduous trip involving two nights in railway carriages, and a great deal of counting to make sure no one had disappeared, or at least that they rejoined the rest in time for the return journey.

There was also a good theatre in Nairobi and when we had enough in the till we would take everyone to see a play. One of the first we saw was Shaw's *Arms and the Man*, and when they learned we were going they insisted I should tell them beforehand what the play was about, and how plays get produced and put on in the theatre. Next evening we were all at the theatre in time except for Fred, the trouble-maker, who arrived half drunk, still arguing about how he had been 'surcharged' by the taxi. But he vanished after the first act and the rest of us were soon deeply involved. One whom we called Bali, a radio man, sitting just behind me, was so carried away that he started to join in and answer the actors. I thought at first he was chatting to a friend, but then, glancing round, saw his anxious gaze locked on the stage and his mouth working. At the play's end, where Sergius utters the final line: 'What a man! *Is* he a man?' Bali could contain himself no longer and shouted his reassurance: 'Yes! Yes! He *is* a man.'

Of the means we used to alleviate their long period of

absence from home the one most looked forward to was the visit to Government House. On the day the course opened Malcolm MacDonald had said, 'I want you to bring everyone up to have dinner with me one evening. Afterwards we can all sit around, have a few drinks and chat.' He was at that time heavily occupied in negotiations for the transfer of power, and I hardly expected his offer to be made good. Towards the end of the course, however, an invitation came – and continued to come for succeeding courses for as long as MacDonald remained in Kenya, first as Governor, then as Governor-General following independence, and finally, at the special request of the Kenyan Government, as High Commissioner.

By this time he had been to our house and we to his; we had also met him at various functions so that Dorothy and I had come to know him fairly well. Unlike most high officials, he was equally lacking in self-importance and in cynicism, an ideal choice at this time when the need above all in Kenya was to spread confidence and good feeling to black and white alike. Short, squarely built, with bright blue eyes, rosy skin and a shock of white hair, he was affable and relaxed in manner but persistent in anything he undertook.

A recent predecessor in office had denounced Jomo Kenyatta as 'a leader to darkness and death', not a helpful description of the man who was certain to become the first head of an independent multi-racial Kenya. MacDonald, from the first day he arrived in the country, set himself to build up an exactly opposite impression, not only throughout the white and Asian communities but within Kenyatta himself, and through him on his supporters. Calling the political leaders together, he assured them that he had come to Kenya for one purpose only, to organize the handing over of power to the future government as rapidly and safely as possible. The many different aspects to be covered – details of the new constitution, legal and political rights, transfer of assets, phasing out of control over the military and police – meant that they had together a huge programme of work to get through before Independence Day. He intended, he said, to

227

hold daily meetings with them and was prepared to work as far into the night as they were prepared to stay. ~~£oS -~~

He put this programme into force at once, and we soon began to hear confirmation from ministers who visited the course or came to dinner in our home. 'We spend all day in cabinet meetings,' one complained, 'and when we finally get back to our offices, there's the whole of our day's work waiting for us.' On top of which they were continually hounded by constituents demanding that their sons be found places in school or their aunts got into hospital. 'I'm giving up my house,' Tom Mboya told us, 'and moving into a flat. With a house everyone can get at me. My own relatives come up from the country, camp out in the garden and demand to be fed and looked after. The constituents don't camp out, but they come to the house at all hours of the day and night. A flat may be small, but at least it will be our own.'

As he drove ahead with the programme of work, MacDonald was also continually affirming and supporting the authority of Kenyatta. When arguments arose he would listen to all points of view and then refer the matter to him for decision. 'We know,' he would say, 'that Jomo Kenyatta is not only the leader of his own people, but the Father of our country as a whole. He has the interests of all races at heart, and we can be sure his decision will be fair and wise.'

What part this deference to 'Mzee' (the Old Man) as a truly national leader played in building up the new Jomo Kenyatta no one now can say with certainty. But before Independence Day came at the end of 1963 the same settlers who had talked of leaving should Kenyatta ever come to power, on account of his reputed links with Mau Mau, were assuring one another that, 'Of course everything will be all right as long as the Old Man's in power. But the trouble is he's old, and if anything happens to him, then the country will really be in trouble.'

Some impression of MacDonald's unusual character and of his influence had naturally reached our students, and they looked forward eagerly to visiting Government House. The entry was imposing, with guards on the gates and servants

in uniforms, but after we had dined and were installed in
the library with drinks, MacDonald chatted for a couple of
minutes to put everyone at ease, and then invited questions.
They were not long in coming, some of them loaded.

'You have lived in many parts of the world, Sir, so you
know many different peoples. Do you think there is any
difference between the abilities of one race and another?'

'There are surface differences, of course. People who live
by the sea are better at handling boats, for instance. But if
you mean basic differences – of being superior or inferior –
then to me all men are equal. Everyone is a person, whatever
his race, or creed, or colour. Only someone who stays at
home and never travels can believe that one is "better" than
another because of his race or tribe – because he is English
and not Russian, or because he is Kikuyu and not Luo. When
I was in China I found that the Chinese look down on the
rest of the world because of their own ancient culture. It's a
wonderful thing to possess an ancient culture, but it doesn't
make one people "better" than another.'

From the safely general, questions moved nearer to the
personal. 'What was your biggest success – the thing you
are proudest of?'

'Getting the Malayans, who were half the population, to
sit down at the table and talk with the minorities – the
Chinese, the Indians and the one per cent of Europeans. I'd
been told they could never be got together in one room. But
they came. We talked the political difficulties out as man to
man – and Malaysia today is the result. A peaceful,
successful, multi-racial state.'

'And what was your biggest blunder?'

'Trying to do the same with the Jews and Arabs in 1938–9
when I was responsible for Palestine. It was a disastrous
mistake. I think it is not possible for Jews and Arabs to work
together. To do so requires compromise, and if you are
convinced of being a hundred per cent right, you cannot
compromise.'

Though his answers were direct, they were also skilful.
One of the Kenyans, familiar with the way British policy

under MacDonald had been reversed, asked a probing question about how far a new governor consults his predecessor when he takes office, 'since his predecessor is already familiar with the situation'. MacDonald answered urbanely that he had the greatest personal respect for all his predecessors, but that when a man takes an important position in government service, he receives instructions from his government – from the foreign minister and the prime minister – and it is *their* orders he has to try and carry out, not those of his predecessor who may have received quite different orders at some earlier time.

Fred, who had been helping himself freely to the whisky, demanded, truculent as ever: 'Why are you not a lord?'

'A lord? So you think I ought to be a lord? Do I *have* to be a lord?'

'Aren't most governors called "Lord" or "sir?" '

'Yes. Most of them are,' MacDonald agreed. 'And I have been asked if I would become a knight, and also if I would become a lord. They said it would make things easier for me because people, particularly in developing countries, would be impressed, and so would listen to me more . . . .'

He paused and Fred broke in: 'But is that not true? Do not people pay respect to lords?'

'Some do, of course,' MacDonald replied. 'But I prefer to be judged as a person. And I think most people would rather talk and listen to somebody just like themselves . . . .'

He came out on to the gravel to see us off and again shook hands all round. Fred only just made it to the bus before the whisky overcame him, but Frank looked after him and the sound of his being overcome was lost in the chorus of goodbyes.

A few days later our first course was due to end, a date to which by now we were looking forward as eagerly as were the students. But first there were the examinations, after which the successful would receive a handsome diploma from the International Press Institute. We had agreed among ourselves and with the Institute in Zurich that these examinations would be real. Our diploma was the first award ever offered to African journalists, and it was essential it should be valued by students and accepted by governments and editors as proof of capacity to do a proper job. It was not to be a soft option, a qualification anyone could pick up simply by attending the course and sitting through so many lectures. If 50 per cent of marks was the figure for a pass and 66 per cent for a distinction, no one was going to be given a diploma or a distinction for anything less.

A day before the examinations started, I was told that Reynaud, the student who had the best record of work to date, was in bed and would not be able to take part. When I went to see him he was leaning against his pillows, restless and dishevelled, but when I took his hand it seemed quite cool and his eyes did not look as though he had a fever.

'What's the matter, Reynaud?'

'Sir, I have a terrible headache. I cannot take part in the examinations.'

'If you cannot take part it will certainly be a pity. You have nothing whatever to fear. Your record of work makes it certain that if you go in and write the papers – even with a headache – you will get your diploma easily. Mr Barton and I will be sorry if you cannot take the examinations, since we naturally want as many of our students as possible to get diplomas. However, one of your fellow students is going to be very happy that you stayed in bed.'

'Why is that?'

'Because, as you know, there is a prize of a new portable typewriter for the student who does best in the examinations. I had imagined that typewriter might very well go back with you to Mauritius for everyone to see who was the best student in Nairobi from all the different countries who have taken part. But, of course, if you don't take the examinations someone else is going to win the typewriter – and it will go back with him to his own country.'

Reynaud was in the examination room next morning, and when the final results were announced, the typewriter duly went back with him to Mauritius.

231

18
Uhuru

Our second course, which began in October 1963 and ran through till late April 1964, took place against a background of dramatic events throughout East Africa. Kenya had gained full internal self-government on 1 June 1963. The Independence Day ceremonies had been fixed for 12 December, and there was rising excitement throughout the country as the day approached. We were used to forecasts of disaster from our white acquaintances, but were surprised when a black friend, a nursery school teacher named Elizabeth, told us her fears.

She was a plump, friendly woman with the perfectly smooth skin many African women keep throughout middle age, probably because their skins were regularly rubbed with oil during infancy. Dorothy was making her a dress, but when Elizabeth called at the house I had to tell her that Dorothy was in bed with dysentery.

'God will care for her,' Elizabeth told me.

'And you? How are you and the children?'

She had two with her, boy and girl twins, whose father was away in Australia learning to be a medical superintendent. 'My little girl,' she said, 'misses her father very much. She writes to him, "Send me some pictures so I can see how you are looking now. Are there other little girls in Australia for you to play with?" But the boy does not write and ask when his father will be coming home. When we went to the airport to see him off, the girl cried all the way.

But the boy did not cry. He said, "Let my father go away and be well educated." '

'How long will your husband be in Australia?'

'He is away still for a year. Meantime I am too much afraid for all of us.'

I thought she must be speaking of money troubles, and asked, 'Can you not manage, with your husband away from the country?'

'It is not that. All of us where I live are afraid. Mzee has come back from London. He is a sensible man, so we hope he will calm the people down. But they are very excited because of Uhuru.* We are afraid we shall all be killed.'

'Killed?' I asked. 'Why should anyone wish to kill you? Surely you, whose home is here, will be all right?'

'We are Christians. Many of the people where I live do not like Christians. They say Christians are not wanting Uhuru, and so they must be killed.'

I was surprised that any of the African population should be fearing independence, but found it to be true of those, like Elizabeth and her husband, who associated much with whites and had adopted a similar pattern of life, as well as of those belonging to smaller, less advanced tribes, who feared domination and hostility by the Kikuyus and Luos. The whites themselves had now lost their earlier anxiety that independence might bring rioting and killings, but there was considerable fear among the farmers of expropriation and among town dwellers of petty violence and robbery. During the period of Mau Mau and the struggles leading up to independence, a number of politicians had promised that when Uhuru came all whites would be compelled to leave, and not only the land itself but everything in the country would belong to Africans. Though the leaders now spoke very differently, echoes of their earlier words remained. Like other white people, we never went out at night without chaining up our windows so that they could not be forced without difficulty, and locking all the doors of ground-

*Independence.

233

floor rooms so that each one would need to be broken into separately. Almost every house in Spring Valley Road where we lived had been burgled in the short time we had lived there. Once, seeing us going through our usual routine before setting out in the evening, our cook Ngani had remarked: 'You need not do that. This house will not be broken into.' Ngani himself, as we knew when we engaged him, was a former Mau Mau; both of us felt that his words were kindly meant, but nevertheless we continued to lock our doors.

Our friends Michael and Joan Curtis, living in a big house in Muthaiga, the fashionable part of Nairobi on the very edge of the forest, were short of garage space and so kept one of their cars out on the drive all night. It was a Volkswagen, a make very popular in East Africa. One night Joan was wakened by slight noises; unidentifiable sounds were suspicious at all times but especially at night, and she went to the window. A group of shadows was flitting around the Volkswagen, executing precise and practised movements like a ballet, and she realized it was a band of Africans taking away the wheels – which, with whatever else they could remove, they would sell in the Asian quarter down by the river. She woke Michael, who got up quietly and dialled 999. Meantime the men worked rapidly on, finally carrying baulks of timber from behind the house to rest the car on now that it had no wheels. The whole task was carried out with no word spoken and the minimum of noise. Only about five minutes after being summoned, the police arrived just as the men dashed off into the forest. A tracker dog was sent for, and late in the morning the police returned. They had followed the thieves ten miles into the forest, and though they had not been able to catch up with them, had chased them so hard as to recover all the wheels.

Lawlessness was in the air. We had often been warned never to stop and give help if we should see a black cyclist lying in the road as though he had met with an accident. Driving home late one evening Frank Barton came on just such a scene. It was so real that he had already almost stopped his car when he remembered the warnings, and decided to drive on up the road on his sidelights, turn around and switch his headlights on. If the man were still lying there, he could go back and help him. But the man was not lying in the road – he had jumped up and was chatting with three others who had come out from hiding behind the trees.

The actual week of *Uhuru* was a round of parties and entertainments, the climax of which was a long drawn out ceremony with bands and much marching of troops in a specially built stadium. As midnight approached two figures marched out side by side, picked out by searchlights – the heavy figure of Jomo Kenyatta and the slim one of Prince Philip – for the crowning moment of the transfer of power, the hauling down of the Union Jack and the raising of Kenya's black, red and green flag with its crossed spears and shields. Next day the story would be all over the town that, as the two men approached the dais, Prince Philip had asked Jomo, 'Sure you don't want to change your mind?'

Independence Day came at the very height of the rainy season. Since early November there had been regular downpours – a good omen – and though only showers fell during the ceremony, the rain poured down as soon as it was over. Thousands of cars had arrived, and most had parked wherever they could about the countryside. Frank and I had come on our own, leaving our wives at home, since we had no idea what time all this would end. We had taken too little note of where we left the car and stumbled around in the long grass until two in the morning looking for it. Just as I concluded it had been stolen and we must walk the several miles back into town, we came upon it and, by following Mboya's official car with its police escort, slipped through the throng and home.

Early that morning Dorothy and I had given our two house men and the two gardeners or *shamba* men the day off, with some money, beer and a packet of cigarettes each to celebrate *Uhuru*. They would not be back until next day and so Dorothy was on her own, and we had agreed that on no account would she open a door or window if anyone should knock or try to enter. It was nearly three when I reached home and she told me what had happened. Long after midnight when she was already sound asleep, she had been wakened by a crash at the back of the house and went to a window to look out. Our back door was reached up a flight of steps on which stood a couple of dustbins. A would-be housebreaker, trying to reach the kitchen window, had climbed up on to the dustbins and, being drunk, had fallen heavily and cut his head on the steps, where he now lay moaning. Dorothy at once put on a dressing gown, unlocked the door, and went out to see to him. She washed his head, put something beneath for it to rest on, with a sack to cover him, and went back indoors. All the drunk could do meantime was to mutter '*Harambee! Harambee!*'★ Like most Africans, however, he had great powers of recovery, and when she looked out of the window a couple of hours later he had already staggered off into the night.

I thought this courageous, but much more so – an action of which I would never have been capable – was her tackling of Tom Mboya a day or two later at a crowded independence party which was being held at the Royal College following the presentation of an honorary fellowship to Jomo Kenyatta. Mboya, a man of outstanding ability who could have held his own in the cabinet of any Western country, had become with success increasingly arrogant and cold. 'Tom has political b.o.,' a cabinet colleague of his told me. 'No one, not even former friends and colleagues, can come near him.' And there were many stories circulating of the way he had brushed off old associates attempting to claim recognition. Mboya had been to our house more than once and we had also met him outside. Shortly before this party Dorothy had asked him and his wife Pamela to dinner, saying that Nadine Gordimer, the well-known writer and a friend from South Africa, who was staying with us, would like to meet him. Neither Mboya nor his wife replied, and

★'Unity' or 'all together', the popular cry of Kenyan independence in Swahili.

now, seeing Tom leaving the party, Dorothy went up, stopped him and said she had a bone to pick with him. He looked astonished, but she went on: 'When we asked you and your wife to dinner to meet Nadine Gordimer, who has done so much to fight apartheid and resist the Nationalists inside South Africa, neither of you troubled to reply. All that was needed was a charming note to say how much you would have liked to meet her if you had been able. As it is you gave offence to someone who admires you, a good friend of mine who has worked hard for the same cause as yourself.'

So far from brushing Dorothy off, Mboya looked contrite and upset, said he 'couldn't understand' how this had happened, and undertook to write a note of regret to Nadine Gordimer which Dorothy could send on as consolation.

The weeks of *Uhuru* celebrations were hardly over, however, when a violent storm broke, not only over Kenya but over all the East African countries, threatening to bring down the three governments almost before they had got into the saddle and providing a stern test for the calibre of the new leaders. The first many people in Nairobi knew of it was the sound of firing from Lanet, the barracks just outside the town where the Kenya Rifles were stationed. But for journalists the story had begun ten days earlier when on 12 January the radio announced that there had been a putsch in Zanzibar, the large island just off the coast of Tanganyika.

On the afternoon of that day Dorothy and I were attending the christening of the new son of my cousin Clyde Sanger and his wife Penny. Clyde was on the *Guardian*, so there were many journalists present, both British and American, most of whom were already making plans to get to Zanzibar. Also present was the UN representative, Bernard Chidzero, whom I approached, thinking he might have news which was not yet public. He told me that he had spoken to Julius Nyerere two weeks earlier, when Nyerere had remarked that he 'feared a Cuba off his coasts'. At the time, it seemed, Nyerere had spoken lightly, but the putsch had proved real enough and also 'Cuban', for though the revolution had been carried through in the name of a political party – the Afro-Shirazi Party, which despite being that of the majority had been defeated at the last election – the real power was in the hands of a party of Cuban-trained invaders under a Kenyan roughie, John Okello.

The British, it was known, had instantly offered help to Nyerere to quell the revolt before it got out of hand, but while he hesitated mutiny broke out on his own doorstep. In the barracks outside Dar-es-Salaam the men of the Tanganyika Rifles rounded up their British officers in a dawn raid and packed them off by air to Nairobi. Soon looting and shooting had spread throughout the city, and troops in other parts of the country joined the mutiny.

At the start of this further outbreak of violence Nyerere, for a crucial day and a half, could not be found. It was accepted that his retirement to a 'secret house' was not through fear for his own safety, but because he was shocked by the violence and nationalistic excess, and unwilling to use force against his own people. After long hours of uncertainty he emerged to broadcast . . . . 'What happened yesterday was a disgrace to our nation.' He spoke of 'a day of great shame', and gave the impression that the mutiny was now over. It was not, however, and before long he was obliged to do what he had been most anxious to avoid – appeal to the British government to send in troops. Six hundred marine commandos were flown in, and order rapidly restored.

But the contagion would spread further. Nyerere had made his broadcast on the evening of 22 January, and the same day I flew up to Kampala, capital of Uganda, where I was to give a talk at Makerere University. I asked my Ugandan hosts about the situation and whether there was any fear of an uprising there. Ugandans in those days – well before the time of Idi Amin – were proud of good race relations in their country and assured me that 'It won't happen here.' How could they be sure about the army, I asked, for in general civilians see little of the army and know less about its state of mind.

238

UHURU

'Our army is different from the army in Tanganyika,'*
they replied. 'The army there has got nothing to do and was
simply eating its head off in barracks. But ours is always
active, suppressing tribal revolts and watching our borders
with the Congo and Sudan. It has no time or inclination to
make trouble.'

However that same day two leaders of the new Zanzibar
government, the Vice-President with the Minister for
External Affairs, Abdulrahman Mohammed, known as
'Babu', paid a visit to Prime Minister Obote in Kampala. It
had already been noted that a visit from Babu generally
preceded trouble. They came ostensibly to reassure Obote,
who had expressed concern about the fate of the previous
government in Zanzibar, whose leaders Okello had
threatened 'either to hang or to set fire to'.

This, Babu assured Obote, was 'just the press'. There
would be no hangings or burnings. 'The Zanzibar delega-
tion,' said the statement put out by the Ministry of Information in Kampala, 'gave the Prime Minister a correct picture
of the situation, and assured him that ex-Ministers would
not be hanged or burned.' While they were in Kampala
giving the 'correct picture', Field-Marshal Okello was on the
air in Zanzibar warning 'those who have sold arms to Asians
and Arabs and those who have bought them, that they must
give them up or face the consequences . . . . which could be
hanging, burning, being cut up into little pieces and thrown
in the sea, or being hung up as a target for novice marksmen'.

Around midday Uganda's Minister for Internal Affairs,
Felix Onama, went on the air to declare that the morale of
all the services was high and he had no doubts about their
loyalty. Conditions of service for the Uganda Rifles had
been improved and there were further improvements in the
offing. He condemned 'rumour-mongers and idle specula-
tors'. Shortly after giving this reassurance, Minister Onama
visited the Uganda Rifles' base at Jinja, was seized by them

*Tanganyika did not unite with Zanzibar to become Tanzania until
March 1964.

239

and held prisoner until he signed a paper almost trebling their pay. Prime Minister Obote, who had also just put out a reassuring statement about army loyalty, now appealed to the British government for help, and 400 troops were flown in to take over key points and later to move in on the troublemakers at Jinja.

Next day Babu and his fellow minister flew on to Nairobi where they addressed the parliamentary group of KANU (Kenya African National Union), the ruling party, in Parliament House. I had also flown back on the same day to Nairobi, and on the evening of 24 January the sounds of firing were heard from the barracks of the Kenya Rifles. Kenyatta, however, was fully prepared and where Nyerere had been distressed and Obote had temporized, he acted promptly, calling in the waiting British troops who crushed the mutiny at Lanet and established guards on the airport, at the radio station and at all key points. There was to be no treating with the mutineers, Kenyatta said, and when a member of his cabinet offered to visit them and handle matters on his behalf, he told him bluntly: 'If you move out of Nairobi, you move out of this government.'

All these events roused much anxiety among our students, most of whom came from one or other of the East African territories and with whom at times we had to spend a good part of the day in discussion. One from Tanganyika became so obstreperous and at the same time so idle that I sent him home. It was now near the end of the course and before they left one of the other students – whom even today it will be safest if I call simply Oscar – asked to see me. He had worked hard throughout the six months, securing his diploma without difficulty and I congratulated him, saying I trusted he would be given promotion in the Government Information Office where he was employed.

'That is my trouble, sir,' he replied.

'What is your trouble?'

'I am anxious about what will happen when I go back to my country.'

'What is it that's worrying you, my friend?'

'On this course, sir, I have been learning what it is to be a journalist – that I must try to see things as they really are and write down what I see, not what I am ordered to write by those sitting in an office who have seen nothing for themselves.'

'Yes. And why is this troubling you now?'

'Because my country is a military dictatorship. If I write truly what I see, I shall lose my job and be put in prison. Perhaps worse than that. . . . So what am I to do? Do I forget everything I have learned or do I write what I see and get put in prison?'

'You don't do either of these things, Oscar,' I said. 'As a trained and honest journalist you are an asset to your country, and a country's assets mustn't be thrown away. You are not asked to get yourself put in prison, where you can do nothing for your country or your family. But equally you must not give up what you've learned. If there's one thing we can say for certain about military dictatorships, it is that they won't last for ever. Some of them end very suddenly. When the one in your country ends, they will want honest men in newspapers and to take charge of the radio, men who are trained and know how news must be handled – then you can come forward. In the meantime, keep quiet. Do what the minister orders you to do. But remember all you've learned, because one day you will have the opportunity to use it.'

19

A Student Revolt

The troubles in East Africa did not go away because the army mutineers had been pacified or suppressed. The risings which had originated in Zanzibar were symptoms of a far deeper conflict – the battle between East and West – which, now that so much of the continent had gained independence, was bound to erupt upon the African scene. In part this was a conflict of ideas, Communism versus Capitalism, and in part a battle for 'influence', that is markets and military bases. In Africa south of the Sahara, Western influence during the 1960s was represented not only by the former colonial powers – Britain and France – but also by Portugal which, so long as Salazar lived, clung tenaciously to Angola and Mozambique. On the Eastern side, efforts to direct the course of African events came at this time not so much from the Soviet Union as from the People's Republic of China.

Inevitably the conflict crystallized around local personalities. On the one hand the charismatic figure of Mzee, Jomo Kenyatta, father of his country, hero of the long struggle for independence, and on the other the enigmatic and far less well-known figure of Oginga Odinga. Each champion looked his part. Kenyatta was powerfully built and now heavy with good living, always magnificently dressed and almost weighed down by the amount of gold on his person – rings, a gold bracelet watch and tie ring, the gleam of a gold fountain pen or two in his breast pocket, and a heavy stick, which looked like a combined club and staff of office, also enriched with gold. On his head was a beaded cap in the Kenya colours of black, red and green, and he mopped his brow with flourishes of a huge silk handkerchief.

In the other corner, so to speak, and seemingly only half the champion's weight and stature, Oginga Odinga wore the boiler suit favoured by his Chinese allies, but in dark grey instead of their customary navy blue. Jomo presented himself as the unquestioned ruler, potent, full of confidence; while Odinga's line increasingly was to put himself forward as a man of the people, their friend and representative rather than their boss. These simple images, however, were confused by tribal cross currents since Kenyatta was head of the mighty Kikuyu tribe and Odinga of the Luos, the second largest; and, to complicate the situation still further, Tom Mboya, a leading supporter of Kenyatta with the unconcealed ambition to succeed him, was a Luo, while it was Oginga Odinga who, during the long period of Kenyatta's detention by the British, had led a sustained demand for his release.

There is, however, little gratitude in political life and perhaps little room for it, and at this moment, July 1964, when we were just starting our third training course, Kenyatta was in London for the Commonwealth Prime Ministers' Conference. Before leaving, fully conscious of the opportunity his absence offered his opponents, he had appointed the Foreign Minister, Joe Murumbi, as acting prime minister. Murumbi, son of a Kenyan father and a Goan mother, was a moderate as well as a wealthy man, an intellectual with a renowned collection of Africana. Shortly before this time when Odinga was paying a visit to China, it was Murumbi whom Kenyatta had chosen to accompany him and keep an eye on his activities. Kenyatta, it was understood, had intended to take Odinga with him to London where he would be out of harm's way, and had indeed ordered Odinga to accompany him with the threat that if he did not do so he would be sacked from his post as Minister for Home Affairs. This threat Odinga coolly ignored, calculating that the leader would not risk sacking him and having a political crisis on his hands just as he was leaving the country.

Mzee was not due to be away for long, so Odinga had to seize every chance to take the limelight. Only a short while before this a leading white police officer had been deported from the country; various stories circulated as to the reason for his deportation, but the government had been at pains to minimize the importance of the matter. Now Frank Barton and myself, in common with other journalists and photographers, received a summons marked URGENT to a press conference held by Odinga, at which he declared that the deportation had been 'the first step towards cleansing Kenya of ill-inclined imperialists'. Behind the scenes, it was said, he was making use of the expulsion to strengthen his personal grip on the police force, with the intention of securing control over the Special Branch police who had hitherto been outside his jurisdiction. The importance of this lay in the fact that whoever controlled the Special Branch was uniquely well placed to dig up damaging information about his rivals while covering up any undercover activities of his own.

Meantime Odinga was reported to be using funds supplied by the Chinese to extend throughout the country the influence which had hitherto been confined to his own Luo tribe. Out in the countryside, where there was a strong demand for education and a shortage of schools, he was providing them for tribes other than his own. Here in the capital, Nairobi, funds from the same source enabled him to come to the aid of a number of new MPs who were finding, in Kenya as elsewhere in Africa, that their position was a double-edged blessing. Gratified on election to find themselves for the first time in receipt of a handsome salary, they had lashed out on clothes, a house, entertainment and the recognized status symbol of a Mercedes car, committing themselves up to the financial limit for years to come. But others had noted their new wealth, and the MP soon found himself besieged, not only by relatives he hardly knew but who were entitled under the African 'extended family' system to claim a slice of his prosperity, but by hordes of his constituents, often trekking into Nairobi to pursue their claims. Each demand in itself might be modest but the total mounted to an impossible burden, and under these circumstances a leader with funds at his disposal was a godsend.

Both Frank Barton and I knew a white journalist who was generally reputed to be a Chinese agent. The Chinese system, he explained, though without admitting that he was himself part of it, had been shrewdly calculated to obtain value for money. 'We cannot compete with the West or the Soviet Union in providing huge loans or offering credits for public works. But we can supply cash to a few people in key positions who will use it to buy support from others less highly placed.' A crucial part in the operation was played, according to the same source, by the excellent Chinese restaurants rapidly opened up in the capitals of independent countries. By allowing credit freely to MPs and other influential figures to entertain their friends, the place could quickly be made a centre for information and intrigue. To the objection that this was a slow method of extending Chinese influence, our informant replied that the aim was not to control the policy of the new government but to destabilize it – for which a far smaller leverage would suffice. Six months before this time Chou-en-Lai, while travelling in Africa, had declared the continent 'ripe for revolution'. 'Revolution,' our contact told us, 'is still in 1964 the Chinese policy. And here in East Africa it is a lot nearer than you think.' However revolutionaries, like others, can be too optimistic and a few days later, with Kenyatta away in London, this one organized a march of 'spontaneous protest' about something or other, in which he was misguided enough to take part himself and as a result was sent out of the country.

When Mzee got back he was extremely angry at the turn events had taken while he was away. But he was a shrewd politician who did not allow rage to upset his judgement, and within a day or two he had summoned a public meeting at a spot in the African section of Nairobi where he had made many speeches during his days of struggle. In a talk that hit headlines and was put out repeatedly over the radio, he denounced troublemakers, tribalists, so-called leaders who built up sectional parties to glorify themselves, and politicians who took bribes from other countries in order to stir up trouble in their own. He warned such people that they were being closely watched.

This was, indeed, an obvious line for Kenyatta to take, but far more devious and skilful was the follow-up. This was to go on a tour of Nyanza, Luo country, full of Oginga Odinga's supporters. Wherever he went Mzee made the same speech, stressing Odinga's unswerving loyalty to himself and praising his complete sincerity. Odinga, he said, was a man who would have no part in any intrigue or disloyalty, a man in whom he placed full confidence, and he asked everyone in his audience who knew how devoted Odinga was to himself as leader to raise his hand in testimony. Newspaper readers in Nairobi were mystified when they read the speech, but the explanation was simple. Mzee was putting his rival on the spot in front of his own people and, by stressing his own trust and Odinga's devotion, making it far harder for him to stage a coup in which he must necessarily call on them for support.

These political goings-on formed a principal subject for discussion with the students at our daily news conference, and the sense of upheaval all around made them more than usually argumentative and at times prone to take offence. Halfway through the course an incident of no importance in itself produced a storm of anger. One of our outside lecturers – fortunately it was a fellow African, a Ghanaian – had asked the students to fill in a form for an opinion poll he was organizing. Most either refused, or wrote nonsensical replies, and next day the lecturer became involved in an argument with two or three of them at a bar in town, where he told them their attitude was foolish and backed his opinion by saying I had told him the course was 'the dullest lot of students we had ever had'. At least that was what the students alleged he said, for when I wrote to the lecturer denying having said anything of the kind and asking him to confirm this, he replied at once that of course I had not used the words complained of. Nor had he. The matter was smoothed over, but a tinder-box atmosphere remained.

And now came a real cause for complaint. From the first day I had warned them all that halfway through the course it would be necessary for them to start sharing rooms. Our six-month terms were far longer than the university terms kept by the other students, and while the rest had been on vacation there had been no shortage of accommodation. But now in mid-September the main body of students was returning, the college was under pressure from the government to take in more students, many of them were having to double up and our students were told they must now do the same. To make life easier and give them a quiet place to work we had fitted out a library with easy chairs, reading lamps and carpet, but the change was none the less unwelcome and during the morning murmurings were heard. For lunch our students always went across to the main college, and both Frank and I would go back to our homes. When I returned for the afternoon's work he put a letter into my hand. It was a round robin, signed by all except two of the students, and among other complaints it stated:

1. Being compelled to share rooms with other students is a clear breach of our agreement with the International Press Institute.

2. It is an insult to us all. We are not students, but government officials and responsible senior members of the press.

3. IPI has already separated us from our wives and families by not providing accommodation for our families while we are on this course.

4. It is bad enough that IPI does not provide us with pocket money while here, but it must provide essential comforts.

5. We refuse to accept the doubling up arrangement and demand to be given a room each.

Frank, I could see, was in a towering rage. However he had waited for me to get back before taking any action and in the meantime had looked out the form each student had signed on admission, undertaking to abide by all the rules and regulations of the college. We went in together to the room where they were assembled. One or two did not look up, but most wore a triumphant air as though by sending the letter they had already gained their demands.

Slowly, point by point, I read out their own letter to them, asking first that one of them should go and bring this 'agreement with IPI' guaranteeing them all separate rooms. If anyone had a copy, let him fetch it and read it out. I reminded them that so far from 'guaranteeing' them a room each, we had warned them three months ago that they would be obliged to share. If this was 'a clear breach of agreement', why had none of them objected then?

They were not, I told them, 'senior journalists'. This was a mistake. They were training to become journalists because their countries needed journalists. But they could never expect to become journalists at all if they were incapable of putting up with the minor discomforts every journalist has to contend with. After the last war, when there was a shortage of accommodation, students in the most famous universities in Europe had cheerfully shared rooms so that more of them could receive an education. Was it only in Africa that in difficult times students were too proud, and thought too highly of themselves, to share rooms with one another?

As regards their absence from wives and families, we sympathized with them over this. But it was a choice each of them had made for themselves. It was not IPI which had 'separated them from their wives and families'. It was they who had chosen to be away for a time from their wives and families in order to make progress in their careers, earn better salaries and so benefit their dependants. This had been a proper and courageous decision to make. If now they found they were unable to keep it, they should pack up and go home; explain their decision to their families and their employers; and find themselves some new career. All journalists, however 'senior', had to be away from their homes, sometimes for quite long periods. If this was more than they could take, it was a good thing they had learned it now.

As for the pocket money, I said, the implied demand for this was insulting – not to us, but to themselves. Since when did 'senior journalists' and 'government officials' expect pocket money? They were receiving everything on the course for nothing, including their air fares and their books. We had made it a condition that their governments or newspapers continued to pay full salaries – so that they were better off than if they were still living at home and having to pay their own living expenses. On top of this they now wanted pocket money. . . .

Finally I told them: 'If you refuse to accept the doubling up arrangement you have two alternatives. Those of you who are rich can buy yourselves accommodation in the town so that the rest can have a room each. Or you can go home now. Your air tickets will be ready for you tomorrow morning in the office. But should you, after thinking it over, decide to stay, you must accept the doubling up arrangement which the college is obliged to introduce to meet the wishes of the Kenyan government. And if you *do* wish to stay on, then the letter you have sent must be withdrawn. Meantime all lectures are cancelled until further notice.'

During the afternoon several of the students came to see Frank and invite his help. Two had refused to sign the letter. Others said they were sorry and 'did not really agree with it'. Finally at about four o'clock the oldest student, who came from a missionary journal in Uganda, was sent in to say they all accepted the new arrangement 'under protest', and from that point both sides began to negotiate peace. Next day, as it happened, was a Saturday, and a couple of students came and asked us both to go down to the coffee room. There they said they were sorry about the letter, wanted to take back what had been written and wished to continue with us on the same friendly basis as before. We at once agreed, and readily undertook – when asked – that there should be 'no discrimination' against anyone.

And so our only revolt ended. Three months later the course ended too. By now we had come to dread the final days for the suffering of the one or two students who had failed to gain diplomas; and whereas in Britain such disappointment would usually be borne in silence, here it was the occasion for lamentation and reproaches, in painful contrast to the exultation of those who had done well. James, a student from Zambia who had been a leader in the revolt, had done well and gained distinction. He went around saying, 'I am a man of distinction. I am a distinguished man. I am a man of distinguished intellect.'

'Yes,' said Frank, 'you are a man of distinction – but four other men of distinction came before you.'

'That does not matter. That does not show on my diploma. What shows on my diploma are the words "with distinction".' And he added 'Tomorrow we will be home. We will be away from the white man.'

Another, Ahmed from Tanzania, a good-looking Arab whom Dorothy at the celebration party after the awards was congratulating on his diploma, said that he was happy to have obtained it, adding: 'I was the troublemaker on this course. I am sorry about it. I went this afternoon and told Mr Hopkinson, and he forgave me.'

Our tragedy now was one we had most hoped and struggled to avoid – the failure of our smallest and youngest student, John. We had warned him before he came, and again during the six months, that he was unlikely to pass, but that it was worth his doing the work for the help it would give in his career – advice which later proved true enough. But now when the results were posted and it was seen that he had failed, he was like a man stunned. 'Oh – oh! It is not possible! *How* is it possible? It would be better to die! What will my friends say? What will my editor say? Now I will *never* gain promotion. . . .'

We comforted him as best we could. I showed him the letters I had already written to his editor and his employer, saying how hard he had worked and that he was competing with men much older than himself. Finally John calmed down, went upstairs to the empty library, and wept, but by the evening when we all went out to dinner together he had already begun to smile.

20
Political Currents

In mid-December 1964, following three days of ceaseless ceremonial, processions, performances and presentations, Kenya became a republic. Outwardly all was jubilation, but behind the scenes the knifeplay had been terrific as the factions jockeyed for power. Tom Mboya, whom Kenyatta had now come to trust, had been given the task of drawing up the constitution, which involved considerable reorganization and many cabinet changes. The battle was carried on by the leaders, whose main concern was their own positions and the powers attaching to them; as regards their followers, it was a matter of counting heads and making sure that enough of one's own men had a post of some kind. One minister we knew well told us when we congratulated him on his new appointment, that the first he knew of the switch was when he read about it in the newspaper – and he was far from pleased with what he read.

Oginga Odinga was now Vice-President, which gave him an impressive title but no real political power. All he had got by way of ministry was the consolation prize, justly dreaded by politicians, of being made Minister without Portfolio. His former post of Minister of Home Affairs, through which he was hoping to control the police and eventually acquire power to deport or grant admission to the country, was now split in two. The bulk of the work was taken over by Arup Moi, while the police came under Dr Njeroge Mungai, a Kenyatta supporter and former Minister of

Health, who was now given the Ministry of Internal Security and Defence. Arup Moi who, though coming from one of the smaller tribes now took a big step forward towards ultimate leadership,* was not a member of the ruling Party, KANU (Kenya African National Union) at all, but of the opposition KADU (Kenya African Democratic Union), which advocated a policy of *Majimbo* or government by regionalism. Shortly before Republic Day, however, KADU had decided to dissolve itself so that there could be single-party government, and Arup Moi's new post was a result of that decision. Those who could read the signs noted that while Kenyatta could now command support in the key areas of defence, finance, foreign affairs, economic development, and commerce and industry, Odinga's main success was to have retained a devoted follower, Achieng Oneko, as Minister of Information.

With the introduction of the republic and the accompanying changes in the political scene, the lines were now drawn. It was no longer possible for the Odinga followers to 'hope for the best'; and they began to show their hand more openly. They had always claimed to be socialist, but at a meeting early in February 1965 Odinga, with some of his followers such as Bildad Kaggia – whom Kenyatta had lately thrown out of a minor post for persistently opposing government policies – caused a sensation by accepting the name 'Communist'. They also began to talk openly against Mzee, spreading stories about the amount of land he was buying, the valuable concessions granted to his chief wife and the roads and bridges being built on his estate by government-paid workers. A leading figure in this increasingly vocal group was a Goan, Pio Pinto, who ran a weekly magazine called *Pan-Africa* and was reported to have become wealthy over the last few years by buying up real estate in the centre of Nairobi.

Pinto, one of a small number of MPs of Asian origin, was also thought to be in the pay of the Chinese and indeed to

*On Jomo Kenyatta's death Arup Moi succeeded him as president.

be one of their principal distributors of cash. A journalist who worked for him complained bitterly to me that *Pan-Africa* was not a magazine at all but a propaganda outlet. 'We work hard all week and prepare a magazine readers can enjoy, dealing with matters in our own country – then Pinto comes in with a long speech by Chou-en-Lai or Ben Bella and orders "every word" to be published. I don't know who this makes happy,' he told me, 'but it is certainly not our readers.'

Recently, that is just around the time the republic was declared, Pinto, Bildad Kaggia and others had made a move directly affecting our own work by establishing near the centre of Nairobi what was called the Lumumba Institute. Lumumba, since his murder at the hands of Tshombe early in 1961, had become an African cult hero, and the institute to which his name was now given was described as a training centre for those handling news and information. Its actual activities, however, remained mysterious. In general it was said to be an indoctrination centre, well equipped and supported by both Russian and Chinese funds, aimed particularly at KANU party leaders and trades union officials. The secrecy which surrounded its preparations was blown aside at the official opening, when Bildad Kaggia named with thanks the governments which had contributed so much, praised left-wing politicians who were opposing the new government with, as climax, a resounding tribute to 'our Jaramogi' – the Vice-President, Oginga Odinga.

Chatting shortly after this event to one of Kenyatta's press advisers, I ventured the remark that Pio Pinto's support for the Lumumba Institute, coupled with the articles appearing in *Pan-Africa*, seemed rash under existing conditions when the country badly needed the chance to settle down. The adviser, who was lunching with me at a hotel and had hitherto kept his face buried in his steak as though fearful of uttering anything at all, glanced up for a moment, replied, 'One day he will go too far,' and looked down again at his plate.

Pio Pinto lived not far from us in a house back from the

road which I had to pass several times a day on my way to and from our Centre. It was common to see two or three cars outside his house, but on 24 February, less than three months after the new constitution had been introduced and the Lumumba Institute opened, I could see as I drove home for lunch that something unusual was going on. Cars were parked right on the bend – I recognized the car of the Foreign Minister, Murumbi – and there was the unusual sight of two white police officers on duty at Pinto's gate. After lunch when I drove back the same cars were still there, and an African to whom I was giving a lift remarked, 'Yes. It is trouble!' as we passed.

When I drove home again around five o'clock cars and police were still about, but by now I knew what had happened. Pinto had been shot dead that morning as he walked from his front door to his car, and police were out all over the town looking for his assassin. 'If any Kikuyu is arrested for this,' I was told, 'there will be big trouble.' When I got home Dorothy told me that one or two London papers had been ringing me for stories on the shooting. I was happy to have been out and avoid answering, being more concerned to keep our Centre out of trouble than to supply up-to-the-minute information to the British press.

Over the next few days some scraps of fact could be picked out from the gossip. Gossip said that the car used by the killer or killers had been traced to *Pan-Africa* Press; that Pinto had a number of enemies there, both for personal reasons and as a notoriously mean employer. It was known that for some weeks before the shooting Pinto had been worried and apprehensive; gossip said that on the Friday before the shooting he received a note threatening his life. He went away at once to Mombasa, returned on the Tuesday evening, and was shot on the Wednesday morning at around 9.15. On this morning a policeman in uniform was seen to have been standing near Pinto's gate from around eight a.m. until shortly after nine. The man was traced. He had no business there, ought to have been on duty at another place altogether, and could give no explanation beyond saying that 'the traffic seemed heavy and he thought he ought to watch it'. The suggestion was that he was connected with the car side of the crime, either by giving a signal of some kind or by keeping a space clear for the killers' car to park.

Within a day or two a man had been arrested. He was a member of the Kamba tribe, so neither Kikuyus nor Luos were apparently involved. The pistol which had been used was a Beretta 22, a weapon which requires expert handling and so greatly strengthened the belief that whoever did the killing had received regular training, possibly as a former soldier or police officer.

To account for the murder, two quite different and conflicting theories were soon in circulation. One said this was a Kikuyu killing. The Kikuyus, the argument ran, would never accept that a Luo should be President if 'anything happened' to Kenyatta; they wanted a Kikuyu also as Vice-President. According to this theory, the killing of Pinto was planned as a warning to Oginga Odinga.

The alternative version carried little more conviction. In the speech Odinga had recently made accepting the name of 'Communist', he had also denounced those who kept to themselves money sent into the country for public purposes. Pinto, whose wife was Odinga's secretary, was known to have retained for himself large sums from overseas, and his execution had therefore been a left-wing judicial killing.

In March 1965 a fresh group of twenty students began their six-month training. Some weeks before they assembled I had written to Odinga inviting him, as Vice-President, to address the course. Frank and I held long discussions before deciding to do this, knowing that such a step was likely to be criticized. However we were not willing to accept a situation in which the International Press Institute was regarded as a mouthpiece for Western opinion, as against the Lumumba Institute which was pro-Eastern; we intended, within the limits of what was possible, to expose our students to all points of view, so that we finally resolved to invite Odinga. I was also curious to see this unusual character at close quarters. For six weeks I heard nothing, but in the meantime the political situation continued to evolve.

Just before the middle of April police raided offices which the Vice-President had taken over, carrying off three lorry-loads of arms stored in the basement. Presumably as a result of that raid, the President, Jomo Kenyatta, learned that a Russian arms ship of which he had previously known nothing was arriving at the coast. Those arms too were taken over by the government, which put out a statement that the ship had brought 'a small quantity of arms which the Russian government had presented to the Kenyan government', and that it had been fully aware of the transaction and of the seventeen Russian 'instructors' who had recently arrived in the country. Odinga on his part issued a rather naive explanation for thus using his basement as an armoury, since the raid, though carried out at night, had been much too public to be passed over in silence. The government, his statement explained, 'has only limited storage space. Inevitably it has to move things around from time to time. It is often more convenient to move such things at night because people are working in their offices during the day.' Stories that the Vice-President was 'plotting against the government' were ridiculous because the Vice-President was himself a member of the government, and gossip that the government was intending to imprison him was equally misguided since a government 'would not imprison part of itself'.

It was evident that a coup of some kind *had* been planned, and that Kenyatta kept Odinga where he was because:

1. He was less dangerous in the position of Vice-President where he could be closely watched than he would be at large or in prison where his followers could present him as a martyr.

2. To deprive him of his position would split the government, and still more parliament, where Odinga now had many supporters. Indeed it was doubtful whether, if the matter came before parliament, a majority could be found for his demotion.

My invitation to the Vice-President now looked even

more rash than when I wrote it, but having heard nothing by mid-April we concluded that it had been forgotten – only to be rung up from his office and told that the Vice-President would be with us at ten o'clock one morning in a few days' time. If he were to come at all, it was best to do the thing in style, so we arranged for thorough press coverage.

Oginga Odinga arrived promptly. He was escorted by half a dozen black-coated younger men, an MP or two, secretaries and assistants. There was a burly lieutenant of police as bodyguard. The vice-president was wearing a loose grey Chinese tunic with wing sleeves like a surplice and wrinkled 'elephant's leg' trousers. He had a fair-sized paunch, so that the tunic sloped out in front and hung down at the back. On his head was a beaded cap like Jomo's, mainly in red, green and black but with lines of yellow – 'Chinese influence', Frank suggested in a whisper. He carried a cream-coloured fly whisk and a varnished walking stick.

After I had welcomed him briefly he read out a speech on 'How to Achieve a United Africa' – the subject I had invited him to speak on as being likely to keep us off the East–West conflict. He read the speech – which provided a couple of columns in next day's papers – as though he found it no more interesting than did his audience, and sat down with evident relief to invite questions. If my aim was to keep things quiet, that of the students was to stir things up, and one of them immediately asked: 'Sir, in view of the fact that both the Western and Eastern powers are dangerous to our independence, should we not try to get economic aid only from smaller countries such as Switzerland and Sweden?'

In a moment Odinga was on his feet, looking less like a plump politician than a judo wrestler moving into action: 'I see what has happened to *you*, my friend, you've been listening to tales about bogey men. You know how it is when you have a troublesome child you want to keep indoors.' (He looked confidingly round at us.) 'You say to it "Don't go near the door" ' (shaking the finger of a warning parent). ' "There's a terrible bogey just outside!" So the child is terrified of what lies behind the door' (and he stared with

257

wide-eyed terror at the door leading to the platform). 'So
the child dare not go and play with the others because of
this dreadful bogey' (popping his eyes, tossing his head,
shaking his stick and fly whisk at us) 'which is waiting for
him. This dreadful thing which doesn't exist at all! That's
what propaganda does to you, my friend. They say, "Oh,
the Russians – don't go near them! They're Communists!"
And what do I find when I go to Leningrad? I find the
ships of all those countries which tell us "Don't go near the
Communists" busily trading with these same people! I've
travelled to these countries, my friend, and I can tell you
one thing' (leaning forward as though to impart some secret
information). 'You go to London, you go to Moscow – and
you get the same soup in both places. One isn't Red Soup
and the other Capitalist Soup. It's all just *soup*, and it all
tastes the same!'

What is this man doing as a politician, I kept thinking?
Why isn't he on the films, a famous star? His face was
shapeless and rubbery like that of many actors and comed-
ians, raw material for producing a vast range of expressions.
His face, indeed his whole physique, looked as if it had been
poured out of a jar and not yet fully set. His eyes protruded
naturally, but he seemed able to make them almost pop out
of his head, rolling them up till the pupils vanished, or
switching them from side to side when looking fearfully for
the bogey man. He could even roll them forward till only
half circles showed above the lower lids. . . . .

The Vice-President was now backing towards his chair
and seemed to be sitting down exhausted, but suddenly
sprang forward with outstretched arms and roared at us:
'You talk about education – *this*', striking his forehead
violently with his fist, '*this* is the thing that has to be
educated. This thing inside here,' and amid a burst of
laughter he sat down.

Asked about land policy and Bildad Kaggia's proposal to
divide Kenya up into small parcels of land to be given free
to African claimants, he spoke cautiously. 'Look, my dear,
when we revolted and fought the British, we did not win

our independence by war. In war we were defeated.' I had never heard any leader admit to this before. 'But we got independence by negotiation. So we had to bargain! We could not say' (putting his foot on an imaginary enemy's neck and shaking the fly whisk in his face): "You *have* to accept this! You *must* accept that!" You see, my dear, we had to reach agreement,' and he went on to argue that it was natural for the British government to protect the interests of its settlers, and that when the Kenya government bought them out, it was not – as Kaggia claimed – 'buying back the soil of our country', it was paying for the improvements and developments those settlers had made, and that the money for this purpose had all been received as loans from Britain.

In talking of the settlers he made one revealing remark which I thought some of our settler friends ought to have heard, a remark I had also heard from Congolese talking about the Belgians before independence: 'We know the attitude of Europeans in this country. They may not think it, but we know. You see, my dear, everyone has servants and they all talk in front of them. The Europeans think – "Oh, it's only the boy. He understands nothing." But it all comes back to us, and we know just what these people think and feel.'

When some question set him talking about the past, the vanishing Africa of his childhood, a new tone came into his voice: 'In my own district when I was small there were twelve elders, one of whom was the oldest, most important elder. This was not a small district! No, my dear! It was a district in which ten thousand people lived, and in all that district everything was timed and ordered by that one man. He did not give orders. He did not issue instructions. No! But nobody could start to dig his field until that elder dug his field. And this man was in no hurry. He waited and waited until the weather was right and the season was right. Then one day he got down his *jembe* and his *panga* and went out of his hut.

' "Has he started to dig?" ' (and Odinga became a whole

village buzzing with rumours). ' "Has he started yet? He *has* started to dig!" Then every man in the village took down his tools and went out into the fields. . . .' Carried away now by his memories, the Vice-President went on to describe the relations between the rich man and the poor man. 'The rich man has many, many cattle. But he does not own the land. That is not the African way. So he must send some of his cattle to the poor man to look after. The poor man has to return the calflings, but meantime he enjoys milk and butter from the rich man's cattle. . . . And now one day the poor man wants to get married, so he comes to the rich man and says, "I want to take a wife. *Please* help me to get a wife." ' And Odinga stood humbly there, shoulders bowed, body bent forward, hands facing inwards and folded between his thighs, the very picture of a supplicant.

'Now' (standing up and waving his fly whisk) 'it would be quite wrong for the rich man not to help him. So the rich man says: "I will lend you so many cattle with which to buy your wife, but in return you have to do such and such things for me." A bargain is struck. Sometimes, though, you have to give freely and take nothing. Sometimes the rich man must give freely to the poor. . . .' And, almost as though talking to himself, he added: 'In Africa the land is the mother – *mother earth*! The land is the mother of all people. It is quite wrong to sell part of your mother – to buy and sell her. That is not our way!'

After half a dozen such energetic performances the Vice-President began to look exhausted and sat down, so I brought the meeting to a close. Thanking him afterwards, I said how grateful we were for his visit – 'No one who was present will ever forget your talk.' He looked pleased and said, almost as though surprised by his own words: 'But I have enjoyed being here and talking.'

The morning, so different from what I had expected, had given me – I thought – the clue to a complex, highly emotional nature. Odinga was no mere Chinese stooge, though following a course which might land him in that position. He had a dream of the old Africa which must now, he accepted, be brought out of its timeless village existence into the modern world. But he did not want an Africa of multi-storey blocks and empty Coca-Cola cans, and he believed that if the continent could draw help and inspiration from both East and West, a better balance, retaining more of the old African way of life, might be preserved. Nor did he intend, in plotting his coup, to destroy Kenyatta for whose liberation he had fought so stoutly; rather he intended to turn him into Mzee, a presidential figurehead, leaving himself and other practical politicians to get on with the day-to-day running of the country. . . . But the flaw in this programme was that Odinga, for all his skill as an orator, was far from being what he considered himself to be – a practical politician.

Only a few weeks after the Vice-President's visit, I was summoned to attend the Minister of Information, Achieng Oneko, in his office. A tall, handsome man, seemingly about forty years of age, he was a fellow tribesman and ardent supporter of the Vice-President. The reason for the summons soon appeared – to ask what authority we had for running the journalism training centre. The Lumumba Institute, having become too obviously a Communist indoctrination base, had just been closed down after less than six months, though it had enjoyed at least undercover support from both Odinga and Oneko. Was it our turn now?

'I realize,' the minister concluded a haughty harangue, 'that you are an independent body and finance yourselves. But what government support have you got? What ministry accepts responsibility for your work? What, for instance, is your relation to the Ministry of Education?'

'Extremely cordial – at least until recently. When Mr Otiende was Minister,' (Otiende was one of those whose post had just been changed) 'he called in on us quite often. He knew our work well and had presented our students with their diplomas. I did not want to trouble the new minister so soon after his appointment – but I hope he will come as soon as he can spare time.'

261

'And other ministries . . . do they know anything of what you are doing?'

I could see he was testing the water to see what kind of support there was behind us, and so reeled off the various ministers and MPs who had addressed the students, ending. . . . 'As you know, we had the honour of a visit from the Vice-President only a few weeks ago.'

The minister hesitated. . . 'Well, you see, the fact is that since the Lumumba Institute was taken over, certain MPs are asking, "What about the International Press Institute? Who is supervising that?" '

'I am happy to learn of their interest,' I told him. 'Any MP who would like to attend for a day and see our work, or would like to address the students, will be welcome. Please convey this for us to any who inquire.'

'And what plans have you for the future?' he asked.

'We have one very important plan which I have been anxious to discuss with you. This visit gives me the opportunity I wanted.'

'What plan is that?'

'To take a number of girl students as well as the men. When I was at Nakuru recently to hear a speech by our President Kenyatta, he told his audience of women that the government is determined to raise the status of Kenyan women and open new avenues of employment for them. My colleagues and I decided that our own contribution should be to train half a dozen woman journalists as a beginning.'

'How have you selected these?'

'I invited Miss Margaret Kenyatta, Mrs Mboya and Miss Emma Njonjo to help us in choosing them. But only Miss Njonjo could afford the time'.

The Minister turned to his permanent secretary, Mr Gechathi, and asked: 'What does Emma Njonjo do?'

'She is head of the women's side of education at the Ministry of Education,' he replied.

We were in the clear, it seemed, so I quickly followed up the opening. 'Your own ministry, Mr Oneko, is the one we feel most closely connected with. But you have seen very little of the Centre. We invite you to come whenever you can – but particularly to come when the course ends in August to present the students with their awards.'

And on this agreeable note the meeting ended.

'Odd lot, the Russkies,' Frank said when I told him about the meeting with Oneko.

'What's so odd about them?'

'Taking all that trouble – and then ballsing everything up. You know they came here speaking excellent Swahili. They even made jokes in Swahili at the airport to the customs men. . . . When did you or I last make a Swahili joke? And they brought first-class equipment. No expense spared. But then. . . .'

'Then what?'

'Then they encourage the students to parade round Nairobi carrying slogans that criticize the government. So they all get sent back home. Doesn't make sense.'

'They didn't like it here,' I suggested. 'Missed all that snow and the shortages. Couldn't just pack it in and leave. . . . This way they get home with credit.'

'Wish we could get our hands on their equipment,' Frank remarked. 'I might just ask around here and there in case they forgot to take it all back with them.'

21

The Pot Boils Over

I had spoken to the Minister of Information of our intention to train woman journalists, but had said nothing about our reasons for doing so or of the evident need for them in East Africa. This need was apparent as one went about the country, but it was emphasized for me two or three times each year on my visits to West Africa.

For the past two years we had been running a parallel course to the one in Nairobi over at Lagos in Nigeria for the benefit of English-speaking West Africans, mainly Nigerians and Ghanaians. Being also responsible for the work in Lagos, I had to travel there regularly, a roundabout flight which involved several changes of aircraft and could take fifteen to sixteen hours. I never came back to Nairobi from one of these visits without being sharply aware of how very different was the role of women in West Africa and East.

In Nigeria and Ghana women were the equals of their men. They controlled the household spending; certain forms of trade and commerce and much of transport were in their hands; they took a full part in social life; dressed magnificently; were free and confident in manner, proud and often beautiful. In Kenya women in general were little more than household servants and beasts of burden. Driving in and out of Nairobi every day I would often have to swing the car into the middle of the road to avoid the ends of logs being carried home for the fire, and always by the woman. A thong would be passed round the log and across her forehead

264

and her whole body strained forward painfully to support the weight, her arms being bent awkwardly behind her to take some of it off her back. She trudged along barefoot, while the man walked some paces behind her carrying nothing. In parts of the country, it was said, no young Kikuyu man would marry a girl who had not a deep indentation in her forehead from log-carrying, since he did not wish to find himself burdened with a lazy wife.

Dorothy had once ventured on the subject to Tom Mboya, remarking that what Kenya really needed was not large loans for dams or the recent introduction of television, but twenty thousand donkeys.

'What do we need donkeys for?'

'To take the place of wives in carrying loads, and allow them to have *Uhuru* (independence) as well as the men.'

Mboya was not pleased.

Frank and I had also discussed what it might be possible to do, and concluded that the most practical step we could take would be to train a few woman journalists, who might one day take up the cause of East African women much more effectively than we could.

With the assistance of Emma Njonjo and Margaret Kenyatta we interviewed a number of girls from Kenyan schools, out of whom we finally chose six. Since none of them had any experience of journalism, and since all would be in reach of their homes, we decided to extend their course from six months to almost a year, timing it so that they would start in the middle of one course and finish at the end of the next. A student from our second course, Timothy Nyahunzvi from Zambia, who by now had experience as a lecturer as well as practical journalism, was taken on to our staff to be specially responsible for the girls. James Gichuru, the Minister of Finance, opened their course with a friendly, welcoming speech, but it was noticeable that, though a number of highly placed Kenyan women had been invited, not one of them was present.

Our men students, on learning of our intention, were

openly indignant: 'Why are you training women to become journalists? There *are* no women journalists in our country.'

'That's exactly it,' I said. 'It's *because* there are no woman journalists that IPI is going to train some. You need not be afraid for your future jobs. We shall only train six to start with. And we are not taking on fewer men – there will be twenty men students on the next course, just as there are twenty of you here today.'

'But if you can take on six girls, you can afford to take six more men! Why do you not take six more men instead?'

And though Mr Oneko, the Minister of Information, had given his approval to our plan, some of his officials did not approve at all, and I had to send a letter stating that the decision to train women as journalists was entirely our own, and that we should not expect the Information Ministry to offer employment to any of them after the course ended.

When they first arrived most of the girls were painfully shy and withdrawn. One of them, Birgitta, did not speak a word for nearly two weeks. But once they had become accustomed to us and to the work they studied hard and made rapid progress. By the time the course ended not only had their prospects been transformed, but they had become lively and vivacious. Despite what it had said, the Ministry of Information took on three of them, one of whom, Charity Mumbi, had soon become a senior information officer, broadcasting regularly on radio and television, and the author of two books. It was Charity who, when we were interviewing the girls beforehand and asked how many brothers and sisters she had, replied, 'Forty-two.'

'Forty-two?' I asked incredulously.

Charity explained that they came 'from five wombs', meaning that her father, a petty chief in an up-country village, had five wives.*

For the next two or three months all went harmoniously, but when the course ended in August our usual upheavals broke out. Our troublemaker throughout the six months

---

African Assignment, by Frank Barton, p. 70.

had been a student from Uganda whom I will call Batman. Batman arrived some days late, having had difficulty in escaping from his creditors, and from then on he cut lectures, borrowed money from fellow students and occasionally disappeared. When I told him off for being out all night, he denied it flatly, and when I told him I'd been to his room first thing in the morning and seen that his bed had not been slept in, he objected. 'But someone has been watching me!'

'Yes,' I said. 'I've been watching you, and I mean to go on watching you. When the course started I thought you could be the best student in it, but I don't think so now. You miss so many classes, you're behind even the slowest.'

'I can see,' said Batman, 'you have already decided I am to do badly at examinations.'

'No,' I told him, 'it's *you* who have decided not to work hard enough to do well. You could still be the best student if you made up your mind to be, or at least one of the best.'

'My health is not good. I have had a lot of pain. . . . The only times I missed classes was when I had to see the doctor. . . .'

When the exams finally came round, Batman had secured a diploma but came almost at the bottom of the list.

'I am leaving early. I shall not come to the party with the others. I said you intended to make me do badly in examinations, and I know now I was right. *I shall remember this*. . . .'

It was not until months later that the meaning of Batman's threat would become clear; meantime there were both tears and rejoicings from the rest. Henry, sent by an East African Ministry of Information, was the only one who had failed to gain a Diploma. He came into my office, sat down and burst into tears. 'For nine years I am nothing but a clerk . . . no promotion. . . . I am allowed to write only little bits of news . . . my pay is pitiful. . . . Then I hear of this course, I want to go. . . . I keep asking and begging to be sent. . . . At last my boss says to me, "Very well, you can go. We will see what you are made of. We will see if there is anything inside your head, or not." And now they will know there is nothing in my head . . . I shall *never* be promoted . . . *never*!'

I tried to comfort him, assuring him that I knew his director personally and would write on his behalf.

'I know you will do all for me you can,' Henry cried. 'I know you will Mr Hop . . . Mr Hopski . . . Mr Hospisson. But I know the people in my Ministry – it will do no good.'

Sadly, I thought that the ministry's judgement on Henry might well be right. It was a measure of his ability that after six months of talking to me, seeing my name and hearing it spoken by the other students, he had only the haziest idea of what to call me.

In contrast to poor Henry, Mack from Malawi was overcome with joy. 'I cannot tell you what this means,' he said at our supper party. 'Far more than any person in this room I have reason to be grateful, to you, to Mr Barton and to IPI. You *chose* me! You could have rejected me, but you chose me out. When I came here to Nairobi you looked after me. You asked me to your homes. You taught me everything. This is the turning point of my life! I must tell you that back at home I am nobody. My father divorced my mother. My mother is a very poor woman. There was nothing in our house at all. When I wanted to come on this course my editor did not want to recommend me. But I kept asking, and at last persuaded him. Now I will go back home and I will be somebody! This is the turning point of my life. Far more than anybody here I have reason to be grateful. . . .'

I tried to stop him, taking him on one side and saying, 'Mack, be grateful to yourself! If you gained a lot from these six months, it's because you earned it. Few of our students work as hard as you did. You gained your diploma, and you won the prize for shorthand though you had never done a shorthand note before this in your life. . . . It's *yourself* you have to thank.'

But he still kept on. 'Nobody has such reason as I have to be grateful. I was *nothing* – and you could have rejected me! Instead you chose me out!'

★   ★   ★

In August one group went home. Early in November a new group, the fifth and – though I did not know it – almost the last with which I should be associated, arrived. We had arranged for the girls, who had worked through the inter-vening months, to lay on a 'welcome party' for the men. IPI would provide food, drink and music, but the girls were to arrange it as they wished. They had livened up remarkably at the arrival of twenty men, and the men, delighted with their welcome, showed no sign of wishing that the girls had been six more of themselves.

'This is the best lot we've had,' Frank told me. 'More of an age, and more on the same level. No one outstanding that I can see, but no one really backward like poor Henry.'

'Good,' I said, 'at last we're going to have an easy run.'

Within a week, on 11 November 1965, Ian Smith had declared UDI in Rhodesia and the students were in an uproar. It was nine o'clock on a Friday morning when I reached the Centre and Frank had been having a rough time with them already. I suggested that we cancel all regular work and give them a bellyful of Rhodesia. Frank, who had worked in that country for years, would cover the historical background. Our law lecturer would give them the constitu-tional position and all that was involved in a unilateral declar-ation of independence. I would try and get Mwai Kibaki, one of Kenya's finance ministers, to come in on Saturday to explain what was meant by 'sanctions' and what might be their consequences. I would sit in on all the talks so as to know, when the inevitable arguments arose later on, just what each speaker had actually said. For the moment the students were pacified, and the plan might have worked out but for something I had overlooked. Friday afternoon was spent mainly on current affairs with a Welsh lecturer, who – when asked over the phone to prepare a talk on the Rhodesian situation – readily agreed. I knew him as an able speaker who kept up to date with what was happening: what I did not know was that he was a Welsh nationalist and a strong critic of Harold Wilson.

He started off by telling the students that Wilson's going

to Salisbury would be like Neville Chamberlain's pre-war visit to Munich. Britain's policy towards the Rhodesian whites had been throughout one of 'sickening appeasement'. The only course now was for Britain to send an army, invade Rhodesia and throw Smith out. This was just what the students wanted to hear and, when he finished his talk and asked for questions, mine was the only voice raised in objection. In fact I was far from thinking that the issue of Rhodesia had been handled wisely by the British government; Wilson, I thought, had been double-crossed and made a fool of by the wily Smith. However, I had enough sense of reality to know that an invading army could not be got together in a few days; that it could not operate without bases; and that the lecturer's suggestion of 'dropping a few hundred para-troops to take over the country in a couple of days' was absurd.

The students were excited and eager to take action publ-icly. But parading their opinions in public was what had caused the Lumumba Institute to be closed, and we had enemies, I knew, in high places who could with justice demand the same treatment for ourselves. Before going home I managed to persuade the students to take no action that night, but everything would depend on how Mwai Kibaki spoke to them in the morning.

Fortunately for us the line he took was sober and impartial. He assessed Britain's difficulties and confused loyalties towards its own settlers. He said the course the government was now taking – declaring the Smith government illegal and organizing sanctions – was correct, though belated. When he asked for questions, one of the students at once wanted to know whether it was true that Rhodesia was so strong it could not be directly attacked. This was because I had told them that it would be impossible for Britain to mount a direct invasion at such a distance from home bases and so Kibaki's reply would be crucial for my credibility. To my relief he said that direct invasion would be 'completely stupid'; what was needed was a coordinated uprising supported from outside, and he made two good points:

1. This was a test case for Rhodesian whites who claimed to be liberals. Would they support an illegal Smith regime, or not?

2. That the so called 'freedom fighters' who had hung around Nairobi, Dar-es-Salaam, Accra and elsewhere in Africa for years, living in hotels, should now go to Rhodesia and do some freedom fighting. 'It's the best chance they will get' – and the governments in East and West Africa should order them to get cracking.

In the afternoon students from University College paraded through the town carrying placards calling on the whites to fight Rhodesia – 'Hang Smith and Skin Him Alive', 'Release John Okello* to Conquer Rhodesia'. They booed any whites they met but did not harm them, and a friendly African policeman escorted Dorothy through the middle of the procession when she wanted to cross the road. The demonstrators marched on the British High Commission and presented a petition to Lawrence Pumphrey, the Acting High Commissioner, demanding that Britain declare war on Rhodesia. Pumphrey handled the situation well, listened courteously to their arguments, expressed the British point of view, shook hands – and all ended amicably. But in Dar, despite an appeal for calm by Nyerere, demonstrators half wrecked the High Commission, hauled down and burned the Union Jack, burned the High Commissioner's car and sacked the British Information Services' office. Nyerere ordered the police to round up the demonstrators and bring them to Government House in police vans. There he gave them a sharp telling off and ordered them to go back and apologize to the High Commissioner.

For two months after this peace reigned, but in January 1966 the fire broke out more violently, not this time on our side of the continent but over in Lagos where our other Centre was based. A distinguished visitor from Lagos was with us at the time, Peter Enahoro, ex-editor of the Nigerian

*The 'wild man' who had overthrown the Zanzibar government two years previously and was now in prison.

Daily Times. He had been to Salisbury to interview Ian Smith; was visiting our President, Kenyatta, in Nairobi; then travelling up to Addis Ababa to meet the Emperor of Ethiopia. On frequent visits to Lagos I had got to know Peter well. During the afternoon he gave a talk to our students on West Africa, and in the evening came to dinner at our home where we had a number of guests to meet him. Though still a young man, he was a tall, impressive figure in his Nigerian robes and very much the centre of attention. Our talk was of the situation in Nigeria where, following a disputed election in October, there had been increasing riots and killing throughout the Western Region. Though everyone knew of such incidents, it was government policy to play down the troubles and induce the newspapers and radio to ignore them.

When we asked Peter how the situation would develop, he spoke reassuringly: 'Nigerians often talk wildly and sometimes behave wildly. But underneath we are a commonsense people. Our Federation is not going to break up. We are not going to have civil war. A few cars will get burned and a few heads "chopped", but the government will come through all right.'

Next morning Peter rang me from his hotel to ask if I had heard the news – the military had taken power in Nigeria. The federal Prime Minister, Sir Abubakar Tafawa Balewa, had been seized together with his Finance Minister, Okotie-Eboh, and two regional Prime Ministers had been shot. We offered to put Peter up if he thought it wiser to stay on for a while, but he had a wife and young family to look after and wanted to return.

As soon as I could arrange matters with Frank, I also went over to Lagos to discuss with our two men on the spot, Bill Crampton and Stanley Bonnett, what action to take and, once we had agreed what to do, I applied myself to finding out just what had happened on the night of Saturday 15 January, the very one on which Peter Enahoro had been dining with us in Nairobi and talking over the situation in Nigeria.

272

The coup had been planned by a group of young army officers, and for it to succeed they needed to kill a number of their superiors who were likely to stay loyal to the federal government. On the chosen night they invited them to a party in Lagos, telling them not to worry about accommodation since 'all this will be provided for you'. When the party ended, the invitees went back to the particular rooms reserved for them in hotels, where at three o'clock in the morning their hosts of the previous evening came to visit them. In the Ikoyi Hotel, Lieutenant-Colonel Segana had retired for the night. In the next room was a missionary. Shortly after three o'clock the missionary was woken by the sound of shots. He looked out and saw Segana's body being dragged away by soldiers armed with automatic weapons. 'I shut my door quickly,' he reported.★

Over at the Bristol Hotel a room had been reserved for Lieutenant-Colonel Pam. He was the man who had commanded the Nigerian forces in Tanzania after Nyerere asked the British troops, which had put down the military revolt of two years earlier, to get out. The colonel happened not to like the room reserved for him and insisted on another. Normally the hotel was full, but on 15 January there happened to be another room vacant and, though it was late, the management obligingly made the change. Shortly before three o'clock Pam was awakened by the sound of men battering on the door of his former room. He looked out, realized what was happening, and also shut his door quickly.

It had been arranged by the revolutionaries that all lights and telephones in Lagos should be cut off precisely at three o'clock. In the few moments before this happened Pam was able to ring the army commander, Major-General Aguiyi-Ironsi, warning him of the coup. Ironsi went not to the army but to the police headquarters. This saved his life. He instructed Pam to join him there, but Pam, making his way through the darkened streets, was recognized and killed by

★Cf. article by T.H. 'Grim Humour of a Revolution', *London Magazine*, May 1966.

the young officers he had previously avoided. His inspired change of room had lengthened his own life by two hours, that of Ironsi by a good deal longer. Ironsi – given the choice of joining the coup or being shot – sensibly chose the first alternative. Or rather, as soon appeared, the coup joined him, appointing him head of state.

Meantime up in Ibadan the Prime Minister of the Western Region, Akintola, also heard noises at around three a.m. Supposing that these were thugs from the opposition he resolved to teach them a lesson and came out, cowboy-style, carrying two six-shooters – to be almost cut in half by fire from the automatic weapons of the soldiers come to arrest him.

Much further to the north in Kaduna, the powerful and haughty Sardauna of Sokoto was aware there was danger in the air, but he had a strong bodyguard and had been importing arms from Arab countries to the north. He was so confident that he had lately taken to threatening the south; he intended, he said, 'to lead his armies to the sea' as his grandfathers had done. He was prepared – but against assassination, not against military attack and when the army surrounded his house, bringing up armoured vehicles and opening fire with bazookas and grenades, the game was up. The leader of the attack was Major Chukuma Nzeogwu. Having flung a hand grenade, he followed up too closely and got a piece of his own grenade in the neck. And when, after a hot argument over the telephone, Nzeogwu came down from Kaduna to Lagos for discussion, he was put into Kirikiri prison just outside the city 'for his own protection'.

Shortly before the coup, at almost the last interview he ever gave, Sir Abubakar Tafawa Balewa had been asked if he knew that ministers in his government were corrupt. He replied: 'I am the headmaster. I know that some of the pupils in my school are unruly. But I do not like to use the cane.' This reluctance – combined with an excessive unruliness among his pupils – cost him his life. Though the manner of his death is uncertain, it is believed to have been accidental. No one particularly wished to kill Balewa, but they just did not know what to do with him. He was taken aboard the *Nigeria*, a frigate lying in the port, for questioning, after which he was gagged and bound too tightly and so strangled accidentally. His body was kept in a Lagos mortuary until it was decided to dump it by a roadside some thirty miles outside Lagos. As for Finance Minister Okotie-Eboh, whose fortune after a few years in office was estimated at from thirteen to fifty million pounds stowed away in Swiss banks, no one felt any compunction towards him, and he was battered to death with gun butts in Congo style. 'You know my regular fee is £50,000,' had been his customary phrase in dealing with firms or businessmen from overseas.

The coup had been carried out by Ibos – the people of Eastern Nigeria. However, it was felt to have been in the national interest and for a time Ibo popularity rose. Some Ibos saw the new government as the chance to heal old splits, others as a unique opportunity to establish supremacy once and for all. Many saw it as both at once. An Ibo newspaperman, thumping the Bible from which he had just compiled his editorial, told me: 'It was God who carried out the coup, not us. God was sick of the corruption – and God wanted to bring peace throughout Nigeria. We Ibos *all* want peace. And if those devils from the north attack us, let them know that every Ibo is a warrior! We will *eat* them. Eat the men – and eat their horses too!' It would not be long after this before the Ibos were at war with both the other regions.

Before going back to Nairobi I copied into my notebook a final word from the *West African Pilot*, angry because British newspapers were still voicing misgivings about the new military regime: 'There should be an immediate stop to the insults which Nigeria can put up with. He that is against us is not for us.' And with this I noted down an extract from the memorandum submitted by the Association of Contractors to the new Military Government, submitted before the rifle barrels cooled or the blood dried, requesting their support and ending: 'Please remember that the Contractors like the Army "move on their stomachs. . . ." '

★ ★ ★

The upheaval in Nigeria, however, was not the end of trouble in the territories we served, for in the next month, February 1966, came the downfall of Nkrumah. Through his vanity and extravagant lifestyle Kwame Nkrumah, once the idol of black Africa, had increasingly lost touch with his own people and indeed with reality. Disaster came to him in the grand manner. He had left Ghana on a state visit to Hanoi with an entourage of sixty, those who might be useful and those he dare not leave behind. On arriving at Hanoi he was accorded the full treatment, Ho Chi Minh and a top-level turnout at the airport, a ceremonial drive with Ghanaian flags everywhere, slogans of welcome, dancers, singing. The professed purpose of the visit was for Nkrumah to present proposals for the ending of the Vietnam war.

But at around nine on the morning of 25 February a group of young army officers seized power in Accra and throughout Ghana. They at once started rounding up all ministers, party officials and the whole crowd of Nkrumah hangers on. In Hanoi Nkrumah now found himself faced with the painful problem of whether to go through with a programme of conferences, discussions and ceremonial banquets – and, if not, what to do and where to go. Unable to return to Ghana, he took refuge with Sékou Touré in Guinea, where he remained until dying of cancer in Paris some years later.

Nkrumah's fall made it even clearer that the decision Stanley Bonnett, Bill Crampton and I had already taken was the only one possible. This was to close down the Lagos Centre as soon as its course ended, after which any West African trainees would be brought over to Nairobi to work with those from East and Central Africa.

22

A Kind of Message

Early in March 1966 we had a visitor, Don Rowlands, who was in charge of the training of overseas journalists being done by the Thomson Foundation in Cardiff.* I had first met Don when he visited Johannesburg some years earlier as one of a group of editors from British provincial newspapers; he had also come over with me on a visit to Lagos in June 1965. Don was now on his way to Malawi, and I brought him out from Nairobi to lunch with us one Sunday. Afterwards, as I drove him back to his hotel, he said: 'I have a kind of message for you,' and went on to explain that the recently founded University of Sussex were thinking of launching a Department of Mass Communications. They had been hoping the newspaper industry would guarantee the costs of running a small department for seven years, after which it would be taken over by the university on a permanent basis. Hard times for newspapers, however, had already begun; the money had not been raised, and the university was falling back on a smaller project. They now proposed to appoint some journalist of standing to work out over a two-year period a scheme for journalism training within the university setting, which might be acceptable both to academics and the media. The project had been

---

*In recent years the work has been transferred to London. Don Rowlands is now Director of the Thomson Foundation, and his place as Director of Training has been taken by Norman Cattanach.

discussed between Asa Briggs – at that time Professor of History, but due to take over before long as Vice-Chancellor – Don Rowlands, and John Dodge, the able and energetic director of the National Council for the Training of Journalists. My name had come up, and Don was now saying that, if Dorothy and I were willing to leave Africa, the position was likely to be available. It might prove only temporary, but the pay was reasonable and I would be free to do my own writing.

I expressed interest, but said I was committed until the end of the year and would need to talk the idea over with Dorothy, which I did as soon as I got home. Rather to my surprise, for we had talked very little about leaving Africa, she accepted straightaway that we would be going back to England at the year's end, and that Brighton was to be our future home.

'I shall be quite happy to go back now. But what about you? Won't you miss all the excitement and the travel?'

I said that I would indeed miss these, and miss Africa and Africans still more . . . 'but every white man here is working himself out of a job. He has to hand over whatever he's doing to an African successor before long. IPI can't expect to run their operation more than two or three years longer; nor do I think the Ford Foundation would want to fund it after that. Frank has put everything into the work and ought to have a couple of years as director before the set-up folds. And if you and I *did* want to stay on in this continent, I really don't know how I would earn a living – so this looks like the solution.'

Our sixth course, which was to be my last, began in June and proved to be what we had always wanted and never previously enjoyed – a quiet and peaceable six months. As regards numbers it was our biggest yet, since we brought over eight Nigerians and a Liberian to add to our twenty-one from East and Central Africa. We warned them all at the outset that this was a Pan-African experiment. Outsiders often said that those from East and West Africa could never work harmoniously together, so it was up to them to prove

278

the opposite. But though on the whole everything went smoothly, our life was not without surprises.

Part way through the term one student, Robert K.,* asked to see me privately. He was a heavily built man, who studied hard, but both Frank and I had found him unusually silent and reserved. At coffee time in the mornings, when we all met and chatted, we would joke with him and try to draw him out, but with little success. He now told me solemnly that what he was going to say had to be kept secret, to which I agreed, and he then went on: 'I must inform you, sir, that I am not what I seem.'

'How do you mean, Robert?'

'I am here on this course as a student, but really I am from my country's Special Branch police. I am here to observe what you are teaching, and report to the authorities back home.'

'Why do the authorities want a report on what we teach? Anyone who wishes, any MP or person in authority, can come and sit here all day and listen for himself.'

'Sir, on your previous course there was a certain student from my country. I believe this man failed in the examinations, or perhaps failed to do as well as he expected. When he got home he wrote a letter to the authorities saying that this place is nothing but an indoctrination centre for imperialism.'

'Was that *all* he said?'

'He said that Mr Barton is a Rhodesian who lived and worked under Ian Smith, and that you are a South African who served under Dr Verwoerd. He said both of you are enemies of African socialism and that you try to turn students against African socialism.'

'Was there anything else?'

'Yes. He said you are "selling Africa to America through the Ford Foundation". Also that both of you invite students

---

*His name, of course, was not Robert, and one or two other details have been altered. It is also nearly twenty years ago since our talk took place, so that no confidence is broken.

into your own homes for the purpose of indoctrinating them.'

'Well,' I said, 'on all that about indoctrination you've seen for yourself, so there's no need for me to say anything. What you may not know is that in Rhodesia Mr Barton twice had newspapers he was in charge of closed down for being too pro-African. It's true that I lived in South Africa when Dr Verwoerd was prime minister, but it's also true that his newspaper called me "a bastard", and that I sued for libel and got damages from his newspaper.'

'You need not tell me about your opinions, sir. I know that both you and Mr Barton are here to help us become good journalists and learn to manage our own newspapers. It is because I have seen and understood this that I am telling you I am from the Special Branch.'

'Thank you for telling me, Robert. I appreciate your openness.'

'But what am I to do?'

'Do exactly what your superiors asked. Write the report they want and send it to them. Write it exactly as you would if you had never spoken to me.'

'And what about the course? Am I to stay on after this?'

'Certainly you are, if they allow you to. You won't be any worse as a Special Branch man for being able to think and write clearly. And if one day you stop working for the police, you'll have another job you can take up. You can become a journalist.'

Two days Robert K. came back asking me to look at his report, and I glanced quickly over the first page. It said that the IPI Centre was engaged in teaching journalism and not in propaganda. I read no further, but it was evident from the manner in which the typing had been done, with a string of letters and reference numbers at the head, that the writer was following formal police procedure. He would be sending the report in shortly, he said, and 'I know this will be all right.' We never referred to the matter again; Robert completed the course, took his diploma and went home.

The second incident was a tragic one. A couple of years

before this, on our second course, we had a student called John Menya sent to us by *Baraza*, a Swahili newspaper based in Nairobi. Tall and well-built, but gentle and considerate, he was liked by everyone and did notably well. Now he had just been appointed assistant editor of *Baraza* and seemed destined for a successful career – when he was suddenly murdered in what seemed a pointless quarrel.

'Was he married?' Frank asked our informant.

'No. But he had just bought a young girl,' was the very African reply, which we took to mean that John had just paid *lobola* or bride price to the family of some girl he wished to marry. Strangely, it appeared that it was his gentleness which brought about his death. He had been in a bar in the town with a girl, either the one he had just 'bought' or another. Some fellow in the bar started to shout and become abusive, and instead of throwing him out of the door – which John could very well have done and probably to the general satisfaction – he got up with his girl and started to leave. To do this he had to turn his back on the trouble-maker, who seized the opportunity to draw a knife and stab John, killing him instantly. So far as our informant knew, the two men had not seen each other before that evening.

On hearing this account I felt as I did later when one of our most promising girl students took her own life on account of some love trouble. It was not just a human life that had been lost, not just family and friends who had been deprived. A trained man or woman in Africa is equivalent to a costly piece of machinery which his or her country desperately needs. To produce it great sacrifices have been made by the person concerned and by his or her relations – often a whole family will have gone short of food and clothing so that just one member of it can be given the blessing and benefit of education. When such a life is lost, or sometimes seemingly thrown away, the loss is not only personal; it is the destruction of a national asset. I could have wept for both of them.

And now as the weeks and months went by, as we made preparations to sell our home and to try and find jobs for our two house men and gardeners, I began to feel more and more what we were leaving. I also started to ask myself, in a way I could not do while engaged in the day-to-day running of our centre, what, if anything, it had achieved.

The numbers involved were all too small. During the six years IPI's Africa scheme lasted – the four just ending and the two more still to come – just over three hundred students from eighteen different countries had received some sort of training. The vast majority arrived knowing little or nothing about journalism, remained for six months, and left competent for the work they would be required to do and the conditions under which they would operate. Frank Barton in *African Assignment* has recorded:

We tried to keep tabs on the students who passed through the courses, and it was sometimes alarming to see the progress they made. So short is Africa of trained media people that it was commonplace for a man to leave us and double, treble or even quadruple his salary. To go from, perhaps, an information assistant in a fairly remote bush station of his country to Press Attaché of the United Nations in New York, was typical of the sort of progress that was made. Another man left us and was immediately appointed Director of Broadcasting in Tanzania. . . .'*

A student from Lesotho whom Frank helped to redesign his newspaper while on the course put up the sale when he got back from 4000 to 25,000 copies.

But if the individual successes could be dramatic, they were dwarfed by the scale of the problem. A survey made by the UN in 1964 showed that, for the total African population of around 250 million, there were only 220 newspapers. The sale of all put together amounted to no more than three million – far fewer copies than the *Sun* or the *Daily Mirror* sell in Britain every day. In Africa's central tropical belt fifteen countries possessed not a single daily paper for a combined population of twelve million, and in seven others there existed nothing but a duplicated sheet put out by governments mainly for their own officials. All we were doing therefore was to plant a few seeds where the climate

*Op. cit., p. 72.

was as arid as the need was desperate. And in radio, which is much more important in Africa as a means of communication since it bypasses the problem of illiteracy,★ the need for trained men and women was equally great and we were attempting to meet the needs of both media.

A further difficulty arose from the fact that journalism was by no means an honoured calling, and over most of Africa there was no tradition of the press as either a national institution or a liberating force. In Britain, but far more in America, the press enjoys prestige from the part it played during the long struggle for freedom and democracy. But this was far from being the case in most African countries.

'Don't talk to me about "freedom of the press",' Tom Mboya said to me once. 'When we were fighting for our independence, none of our meetings, none of our speeches, would be reported in East African papers. Now it's our turn – and we don't feel obliged to give space to the views of opponents who gave none to ours.'

As regards Kenya, Mboya was right. The biggest daily paper in Nairobi had been a 'settlers' newspaper', supporting the British government whole-heartedly and printing the British royal coat of arms at its masthead right up to the day independence was declared, when it became an equally unquestioning supporter of the new regime. Challenged on the ethics of this policy switch, the editor of the time explained, 'But we are a *government-supporting* newspaper. We supported the colonial government then. Now we support the African government. It's all perfectly consistent.'

Where the press is little esteemed, the status of journalists is inevitably low. After our first Lagos course had been opened with typical geniality by the president of Nigeria, Dr Nnamdi Azikiwe, the renowned and venerable 'Zik', I walked back with one of our new students. In a truly Nigerian blend of appreciation and cynicism, he remarked: 'I see what you are trying to do for us, Mr Hopkinson. You try to make us feel that being a journalist is something

★The figure for illiteracy in Africa at this time was 85 per cent.

important and worthwhile. What you do not realize is that in our country a man becomes a journalist only because he has failed or been thrown out of something else. I myself was thrown out of the civil service. That man in front was sacked from being a schoolmaster. . . .'

One could sum up our six years' work by saying that the IPI operation, with the backing of the Ford Foundation, had tided Africa's slender network of communications over the immediate crisis caused by the departure of whites and the fact that the black press workers, for all their eagerness to learn, had seldom been allowed to become anything except teaboys, messengers and leg-men. But what would become of the media now was out of our hands.

Apart from the work itself, Dorothy and I had enjoyed enormous benefits from our stay. We had spent four years in a beautiful country with a near-perfect climate. We had made many friends. I had travelled more during the past four years than in the whole of my life before and since. It was not only the repeated journeys across and up and down the continent of Africa, plus visits to New York for discussions with the Ford Foundation. Because the International Press Institute held its annual conference in a different place each year, I had enjoyed spells in Oslo, Istanbul, London and Zurich, and would shortly be paying my second visit to India. As a result of all this travel I had seen more of my daughter Lyndall – who lived in Rome, a convenient stopping-off place on whatever journey I was making – than I had seen since she was a child. My youngest daughter, Amanda, had been out to stay with us for a long holiday. Only of Nicolette had I seen little, and she by now had taken degrees at Cambridge, studied at the College of Europe in Bruges, become a qualified interpreter, married and settled down in Munich. Though living far away, I had in the past years come closer to all three.

Despite the time-consuming nature of the work, I had also managed to write. Almost as soon as we settled in Nairobi I was asked by the editors of *Time-Life* Books to write the volume on South Africa for their *Life World Library*. The task was exacting and in a way tedious, since each volume was constructed to a precise formula – so many chapters of exactly so many words, starting with the climate and physical conditions and ending with the outlook for the future. The formula had been carefully thought out but allowed little scope for variation and none for imaginative flights. As soon as it was completed I started – almost from relief – to write a long novel centred in Nigeria which, more than twenty years later, I am still writing. One other benefit our four years had brought us deserves the next chapter to itself. . . .

And now all too soon for me, in November 1966, my last course ended. At a final ceremony James Gichuru, Kenya's Minister of Finance, presented the students with their diplomas, and thanked me on behalf of his government for the work IPI had done. This work would be carried on with complete success over the next two years by Frank Barton, before being handed over as the basis for a new Department of Communications in University College.

Our home in Spring Valley Road had already been sold. Our staff had left, their handcarts loaded with the belongings Dorothy had given them. Dorothy herself would soon be going back to Brighton where her daughter and her husband had lent us a flat until we could find one of our own. I would be leaving shortly with Frank for New Delhi and the IPI Conference at which he would take over from me. Meantime Dorothy and I were spending our last few weeks in Africa as guests of two good friends, Walter and Tattie Bell of the British High Commission.

My feelings about the continent in which we had spent the last nine years can be simply expressed. I loved it. I had come out to Africa only because Dorothy said to me when we were asked to go, 'I will, if you will.' Now I looked on it as my home. I should be happy if one day we should be drawn back here again to live, but had no wish at all to come back as visitor or tourist. . . . All or nothing.

E.o.s.

23

On the Wild Side

Though our life in Kenya was mainly concerned with journalism and politics, there ran through it a different thread – an intense enjoyment of the countryside, nature and wildlife. In Johannesburg we had been living in the suburbs of a great city, and the roaring we used to hear from our balcony at night came from caged lions. Here we were five miles out of a country town, in a part of Central Africa hardly visited by white men before the beginning of this century and whose black inhabitants, far from stamping out the wildlife, lived on and with it in an equitable balance. There had then been room enough for all.

Here, so close to the Equator, days and nights were roughly equal and we had neither winter nor summer, no outburst of spring, no general harvest, no shedding of autumn leaves. Each crop – maize, tea, coffee – had its own separate harvest time; and because Nairobi had been built on an upland plateau at a height of 5000 feet, the days, though hot, were never sweltering as they were down on the coast, at Mombasa or Dar-es-Salaam, and, being blessed with two rainy seasons, we were seldom seriously short of water. From the point of view of climate the Kenya uplands offer as near to an earthly paradise as can be found, though there was a certain tedium in the fact that the daylight hours scarcely change throughout the year, so that one sometimes hankered for the drawn out evenings of an English summer.

The day began with a natural routine. Soon after six the

286

weaver birds, thousands of whom made their nests in a tall
bamboo clump close to the house, started to wake. Weaver
birds live in colonies with their domed nests packed tight
together. Being seed eaters they do not peck about the garden
but go off like businessmen at a regular hour each morning,
and come home when it is beginning to get dark. Our
bedroom window was about the same height as the
bamboos, and as the sky lightened a noisy rustling would
break out as though a hailstorm was sweeping through the
garden – the birds were waking up, coming out of their
nests, shaking themselves as they clung in thousands to the
feathery heads and stalks of the bamboos. There would be
a pause and then a particular group would begin to chatter,
their noise rising in a crescendo after which they fell silent
for some seconds, and then, as if at some invisible signal,
the group took off together for the feeding grounds.
Immediately they had gone a second group began its
communal chattering, before it too fell silent and then whir-
ringly set off in a slightly different direction. Their noise,
morning and evening, would attract the skinny cats from
neighbouring houses to prowl round looking hopefully up
at the chattering crowd, but the bamboo stalks were too
close set and their sides too razor-sharp for cats, a mongoose
or even rats to penetrate.

While the weaver birds were organizing themselves, the
insect eaters – flycatchers, thrushes, white-eyes and sunbirds
– were working over the bushes and plants still wet with
dew and the previous evening's watering, for the garden had
to be watered for an hour morning and evening. Diligently
the birds hoovered off the caterpillars, grubs and insects
from rosebushes, oleanders, hibiscus and poinsettias. They
did not so much search for insects as go directly to the spots
where they were to be found. Above our porch a security
light, kept on all night, would be visited by three bulbuls
to pick off the fat moths from the bracket itself, the surface
of the wall and the ground below. Immediately they left an
elegant black sunbird hovered up, darting its slender beak
into crevices they could not reach, paying particular attention

to window corners, delicately abstracting out of spiders' webs any prey they had not yet devoured.

In our Nairobi house, as everywhere we lived, Dorothy had organized for me a study where it was a pleasure to work or sit. One whole side consisted of windows looking out over the steep hillside which was our back garden. To the right were coffee plantations with a fringe of forest; down below ran a tropical stream; and to the left were our neighbours' hillside slopes, a tangle of blue gums and mimosa. It was my routine to get up around six and write for a while in my notebooks. While doing this I would watch the swallows. In Kenya, besides the European swallows, there was a smaller one with tawny head and rump and a striped breast like a footman's waistcoat. These nested all around the house, building long sleeves of mud with a pocket at the end where their eggs could be protected. The birds and their young would sit along the gutters, a few inches from my head, chattering to one another and turning rapidly round so that one moment I was looking at their heads and the next at their crossed tails and rumps, until with a squeak they would fling themselves off and start to cut arcs in the sky after high-flying insects.

The stone of which the house was built had many projections. Leaning out of the window before going to bed one night, I noticed a black patch on one of the stones which I thought must be an enormous bat or perhaps a rat, for I had seen a black rat run straight up the wall the night before. I fetched a torch and saw it was two of the striped swallows sleeping flat against the stone with wings outspread and claws hooked into crannies. Early next morning I watched them wake, shake themselves, hop on to another stone and fly off – but after a couple of minutes they came back and settled down again, evidently thinking it was too early and there was not enough insect life around.

Only when there was full daylight would the convoy of green pigeons arrive. I would be half writing, half waiting for them, and suddenly they had come flashing out of the fringe of forest, about a dozen birds in tight formation. They swung round the corner of the house, swooped over the banana clump and headed at full speed for a tall tree with heavy foliage standing directly in their way. Always following the same route, they must have known exactly where it stood but would fly straight at it as though expecting it to open up. Only at the last second, when no opening appeared, did the leader veer sharply to the side and the flight closed ranks, compressing itself into a column which threaded its way with astonishing virtuosity between mimosa trees whose tops were almost touching. An intense enjoyment of their own skill and daring seemed to radiate from them. Nothing more of the green pigeons – short, thickset birds with apple-green bodies and red legs and feet – would be seen during the day, which they spent lurking in upper branches uttering a harsh croak better suited to tree frogs than to doves or pigeons.

Just as they followed a routine for feeding, so most birds had their time for singing, usually around sunrise or sunset before settling down. But there was another group, mainly cuckoos, which skulked all day in the trees, and some of them had calls which sounded surprisingly like words. 'Hello, Georgie!' the emerald cuckoo would repeat in a tone of surprise. 'Did he do it?' asked another, known as the didric cuckoo, to be answered by its mate repeating '*Did* he do it?' in a tone which seemed to imply, 'Why ask? Of course he did it!' The red-chested cuckoo, known as the rainbird because its call was heard just before the rainy season, cried, 'It will rain!' and a bird I could not identify living close to the bamboos would call 'Okey dokey!' for ten minutes each morning, and another squeaked continuously for hours like a cart with ungreased wheels. Many of these birds, it was evident, preferred gardens, where there was always something happening – worms and grubs being turned up, butterflies attracted by the flowers, and insects to the fruit and refuse – to life in the wild places; and the proximity of humans seemed to reassure rather than intimidate them.

For them all the great feast of the year came with the rainy season. For days clouds had been massing more and more heavily until the sky seemed to close down upon our heads. Then one morning we would wake up to silent birds and the patter of heavy rain. At the time when the sun should be rising we were still in twilight, and I looked out of the window into thick cool mist. Columns of what looked like smoke were pouring out of the soaked ground as though a volcano were starting to open up. Millions of flying ants, stimulated to life by the coming of the rains, were emerging from their nests, separating as they rose higher into a horde of insects which filled the sky for as far as one could see. Each ant resembled a dragonfly in shape, but whereas dragonflies hover gracefully, the ants threshed around with effort. They had two pairs of wings beating in turn so that they moved like tiny helicopters, but though their flight looked clumsy I watched many duels with hawking birds in which the bird had to give up baffled as the insect, rising and falling as though on an invisible thread, deftly evaded each attack. The ant's life, however, lasted a mere three hours, and before long the gutters and window ledges were lined with birds too gorged even to peck at the insects dropping exhausted down beside them. Among the puddles on the path hopped toads of twice their normal size, mouths fringed with wings from the ants they had devoured. Out in the villages African children would be putting bags or sacks over the nests, then pulling off the wings and roasting the ants to supply much-needed protein.

But birds and insects were only small change in the rich East African wildlife. We were within a few miles of the Nairobi Game Park to which I sometimes retired for a couple of hours after work to calm my mind with the sight of giraffes and gazelles. Wildlife from the reserves spilled out over the countryside, wildebeest wandered at times down the road leading to the airport, gazelles darted across it and even in Nairobi dustbins were raided by hyenas. With us the most daring were the jackals. Driving to the office I had to go over a stretch of waste land leading to the crossroads where Pio Pinto had been shot. One morning there darted from a garden a long, low creature, grey flecked with brownish red, and I slowed the car down to keep pace. The jackal came at full gallop down a slope, cleared the stream at a bound, turned sharp across the road in front of me and raced on towards the bushes and cover. It had a look about it as though it had been plundering a hen run, not a guilty look such as a dog might wear, but defiant and alert. Another time, coming home in the dark along the Loresho Ridge just across town from our own valley, the headlights caught a jackal which appeared to be dancing in the road. Absorbed in its activity, it ignored the car and we slid closer. A large toad was crossing the road and the jackal, fascinated but fearful, was dancing round it, uncertain how to attack and dabbing at the creature with its paws.

My abiding impression of wildlife, however, came from visits to Nick Carter, whose base of operations was at a place called Kiboko between the Amboseli Reserve and the Tsavo National Park, within sight of Mount Kilimanjaro. It was some hundred miles down the road to Mombasa, a road which in those days was not yet tarred so that the car swerved alarmingly in the dust which came steaming through the floorboards. Nick Carter was a game warden, a Viking in appearance, tall, powerfully built with a massive chest and a gold beard. It was his task in life to round up a rhinoceros or two each week and convey it from an area where poachers were active into another of comparative safety. To this task he brought persistence, ingenuity and a natural sympathy with these powerful but persecuted creatures. Soon after we met and I showed interest in his activities, he asked me down for two or three days to Kiboko where he had a small cement bungalow out in the wilds, an enclosure for keeping rhinos in transit, a specially reconstructed lorry for conveying them, plus half a dozen Turkana scouts and a baby rhinoceros the size of a sofa which supposed Nick to be its mother and would gallop after him squealing if he got out of its sight.

The system for rescuing a rhinoceros when Nick took on the job had been to drive after it in a Land-Rover until it was exhausted, lassoo and rope it up, winch it into the back of a lorry and then bump it along for several hours before turning it loose into a strange environment. Those rhinos which survived the chase were so bewildered by the journey and their new surroundings that a high proportion of them died within a few days.

'Everybody thinks,' Nick Carter told me angrily, 'that because a rhinoceros is a powerful creature it can have no feelings. Just the opposite! It's an extremely sensitive animal. Its nature's not at all aggressive and it only attacks when it feels threatened.' We were standing outside the enclosure and he was feeding a captured rhino with leaves and small branches from a favourite bush. 'Treat the beasts kindly, behave sensibly to them, and they give no trouble.'

'I see they don't give much trouble to you,' I remarked. 'But how d'you start making friends with an animal that size – and with a horn like that?'

But he did not explain. 'Damn any man who can't get on terms with a wild animal after he's had it around the place for a few days,' was all he said.

When appointed to his job Nick had worked out a scheme for 'darting' the rhinoceros instead of chasing it to exhaustion. Using a crossbow and darts carrying a measured dose of drug, he either crept up to within forty or fifty yards of the creature and fired the dart into its backside where the skin was thinnest, or else darted it more safely from a Land-Rover or jeep. As soon as the drug took effect, the scouts roped and winched the rhino up into the lorry, whose sides were lined with steel rollers so that it would not hurt itself if it threshed around. Then it was carried back to an enclosure, where Nick would soothe and feed it personally for a few days before coaxing it into a metal container, conveying it to a place of release and allowing it to wander down the ramp and find its way out into the bush.*

I had been down several times to Koboko and gone out

*Nick Carter has told his own story in an excellent book, *The Arm'd Rhinoceros*, André Deutsch, London, 1965.

with Nick on rhino hunts. It was interesting, often exciting; but it was a day when we did not even see a rhino which seems, looking back, to have given me what I had been looking for ever since we came out to the continent.

We had risen at five, drunk a cup of tea and gone out into the cool air. Nick and three of the scouts were in the jeep which had a hole in the roof, well padded all round, through which he stood up to fire the darts. All four were wearing white crash helmets. I climbed into the front of a lorry of which I could see nothing except dashboard lights and a thicker darkness for the driver, but whispers from the back showed that the other scouts were huddled there for warmth. We headed eastwards down the Mombasa road and after about an hour's hard driving there was a fiery glow ahead as though furnace doors were opening, against which low hills covered with trees showed a faint outline.

After a while we turned off into a rutted track where we travelled slowly in low gear and the forest closed in on us. No rain was falling, yet the whole forest dripped. The grass and foliage were grey with it. Long sprays of a shrub which looked like lilac or buddleia lashed the windscreen, and there were spiders' webs everywhere so full of dew that they looked like handkerchiefs spread out to dry; webs in pockets like weaver birds' nests dangled from twigs; long, ropelike webs linked tree to tree. It was daylight now, but still grey and misty, and I could see the driver's tense face as he braked and swerved to avoid guineafowl with their families of fluffy chicks, sand grouse and yellownecks which scampered along the track ahead of us, swerving wildly from side to side to find an opening but never taking off into the air. When for some distance the track ran straight a grey troop came bounding along which I took to be prowling jackals or hyenas, until as they vanished into the undergrowth I realized they were vervet monkeys whose dark, peering faces gave them the look of creatures wearing masks.

When we stopped in a clearing to stretch our legs and eat the few biscuits we had brought, Nick explained that he would now go ahead with the jeep and its crew to the spot

293

where rhino had been seen, and the rest were to stay near the lorry till he called for us on the radio telephone. Once the jeep had gone the scouts scattered to pick berries, leaving one listener in the lorry, and I drifted off, keeping the direction clear in my mind. Guineafowl, quails and yellow-necks – looking like partridges crossed with a small breed of hen – scurried about. Under a baobab tree two hornbills were wrestling with their enormous red beaks interlocked while a third looked on squealing with excitement, and as I came over the edge of a slope a bustard the size of a turkey shot straight up into the air as though ejected from a gun. Up it went to treetop height, turned a somersault and came down with dangling legs and drooping wings.

I looked back to be sure of my direction, and pushed on. A snake five or six feet long, the largest I had yet seen, slid across in front of me. Darkish green in colour, it moved with a swimming, sliding motion, its head a few inches above the grass. I have no special aversion to snakes, so just stood still and it swam on. And now, emerging from a belt of trees, I came on what seemed to me the heart of Africa. It was a stretch of plain in which giraffes and many gazelles and wildebeest were feeding. The nearest giraffe lifted its head and stared in my direction, but I stood stock still behind a tree and it soon resumed its feeding. It was browsing from the top of an acacia, bending its long neck down and scything the foliage into its mouth with a blue tongue. Out of the plain, no more than a hundred yards away, rose a spine or dorsal fin of reddish rock over which a troop of baboons, some with young clinging round their necks, were playing and scampering. The herds must have caught my scent for they started to move off, and I too caught a scent, or rather a stench from somewhere close at hand.

Against a rock, in deep shade where I had not noticed it, lay a zebra disembowelled, over, around and inside which hopped and crawled more than a dozen dark shapes. As I approached, the vultures raised their bloodstained heads and dripping beaks to gaze malevolently. When I flung a stone they flew slowly, heavily, up on to the dead bough of a tree where they ranged like a row of evil spirits – except one which refused to move even when I came within six feet of it. Looking for another stone I found only a lump of dried dung. Struck squarely with it on the back, the vulture at last began to move; with long padding strides as if approaching the high jump it ran a dozen paces, sprang clumsily into the air and soared away.

When I got back the scouts were already in the lorry. A call had come for help; the jeep had fallen into a poachers' pit and we were needed to pull it out – but how to find the spot? Directions were useless in the forest. 'Under some baobab trees' – but baobab trees were everywhere. At last one of the scouts saw a light soar up into the sky, marked its direction and in time we found the spot. It turned out that the jeep, which carried a Very pistol, had been down to its last flare. Six flares, old army stock, had failed to ignite, and only the seventh went off.

The scouts were accustomed to their work and soon had the jeep out of the pit, but by now the morning had gone and it was far too late to search for rhino. For the others it had been a wasted day, but for me a memorable one. Years earlier, living in London and not imagining I should ever visit Africa, I had dreamed one night of a vast rocky pinnacle down which crawled crocodiles at war with hosts of vultures. In the five years we had lived down south and in the four we had now spent in East Africa, I had seen crocodiles and innumerable vultures – besides lions, leopards, cheetahs, elephants, and deer of every kind from those no bigger than hares to waterbuck the size of ponies. Lately I had been at close quarters with rhino, young and old.

But the wasted morning had given me something I had never experienced till now – the sense of being for a while outside our familiar world, in the heart of ancient Africa.

24

The View from the Summit

It was the end of 1966 when Dorothy and I got back from Africa, and in the new year I began my job with the University of Sussex at which I had been given the imposing title of Senior Fellow in Press Studies. My task was to draw up a plan under which that university – and others that might later wish to do so – could be brought into journalism training. When the plan took shape it had to be acceptable to the universities, whose values were academic, and to the newspapers and other media, whose values were practical and down-to-earth, and I started by going around the country to examine the various ways in which journalists were already being trained. Some six to seven hundred young men and women were coming into newspapers every year, and it was soon evident that, though there was good provision for 'school-leavers' in their teens who formed the great majority of entrants, similar provision for the 150 or so who had been to universities scarcely existed.

School-leavers could benefit from professional training organized by the National Council for the Training of Journalists in a number of centres up and down the country, usually in polytechnics. It was not difficult to obtain a place, and the students, provided they did the necessary work, had little difficulty in securing jobs. Men and women from universities, however, had either to find some editor willing to employ and train them, or compete for a place on one of the few training courses run by large groups such as the Thomson Organization and the Westminster Press – or, in the case of radio and television, by the Independent Broadcasting Authority and the BBC. None of these organizations took on more than a handful of entrants in a year, and I talked to many graduates, seemingly well qualified, who were going through my own experience of forty years earlier, writing dozens of letters to editors asking for an interview, but getting few replies and no one willing to offer them a start. National newspapers would only employ those with experience in the provinces, but not many provincial editors were interested in training or considered that they and their senior staff had time to spend in this way. There was also some prejudice against graduates who, I was several times assured, are 'conceited, unwilling to learn, and within a few weeks start telling me how to run my own paper'. In those days there existed a further prejudice, now happily fast disappearing, against employing women.

By mid-1967 I had a clear picture of the British situation, but before drawing up a plan I had to see what could be learned from the experience of other countries. By far the most varied and interesting work was being done in the United States, where well over a hundred universities and colleges ran schools of journalism or mass communications, and since there were no funds available for me to pay the necessary long visit to the US I wrote to the Ford Foundation, which had financed our training work in Africa, asking if they would provide a grant so that I could travel round a selection of American journalism schools. Their answer was generous and immediate, so I approached an organization of newspaper editors in New York and asked them to provide the addresses of a dozen university schools of journalism. What I required, I said, was a list to include four where training was first-rate, four where it was noticeably bad, and four where it was average; but without telling me which was which.

In autumn 1967, having made the necessary arrangements,

297

I travelled across the USA from New York to Minneapolis, over to California and down to Texas, before coming home in time for Christmas. A month or two later I had completed and handed in my report – but there proved to be some conflict of opinion within the university as to whether they wished to go ahead with their project or not. Summer came and the academic year ended; no decision had been reached, and at the end of 1968 my appointment would run out. At this moment came a letter from the University of Minnesota, one of those I had recently visited, inviting me to become their visiting Professor of Journalism for the academic year 1968–9.

Being committed to Sussex, where they might still establish their own course, I asked whether we might take on the work for two terms instead of three. They agreed and we went, much enjoyed our stay, and were back in March 1969. I then found that Sussex were accepting my proposals, but had no finance to implement them. This could only be done if I – or someone – raised a sum estimated then at £75,000, to construct a centre where the new course could be set up. I replied that I had no experience in raising funds and no inclination to acquire it, and we parted amicably enough, but leaving Dorothy and myself with the problem of how we were to make our living.

We had spent nine years in Africa, enjoyable and perhaps useful years, but they had left us no better off financially than when we first went out. Indeed, had it not been for Dorothy's wise advice to buy the house in Spring Valley Road which, with the return of white confidence under Jomo Kenyatta, we had sold at several thousand pounds' profit, we should have been worse off than when we left London back in 1958. A further two years at Sussex had been spent marking time, so that we were back at the beginning, except that we were now eleven years older.

Neither of us had ever lived with one eye on the future, Dorothy because of her faith and I because I imagined I could go on working as long as I remained alive and that, by reducing our demands to whatever I was capable of

298

earning, we should arrive at the grave in good condition and unburdened by heavy debts. At sixty-three, however, the future was fast becoming the present and I could hardly expect to go on finding full-time jobs. We decided therefore, after much discussion, to look for a small place in the country where we could live cheaply and look after ourselves. During our two years at Sussex I had managed to pick up some freelance journalistic work, and on this and the books I meant to write we thought we should survive. In the summer of 1969, after spending a few days driving around, we found the place we meant to make our home – a cottage in Wales at the foot of the Brecon Beacons. It was semi-derelict, but the owners were friendly and willing to put it in order for us.

Before I could begin my new life as author I had, however, one final chore. A letter had arrived from University College, Cardiff, saying they were considering setting up a department of journalistic studies some time in the future; they understood I had done some work in this field and would be glad of my advice. So we arranged to spend one night in Cardiff on our way to complete arrangements for the cottage. But those arrangements were destined never to be completed, and the plans I had worked out were not after all to be wasted. University College adopted them; we settled down nearby in Penarth; our overnight stay has already extended over fourteen years and looks likely to last for as long as we shall.

It was May 1970 when I joined the college and I had already reached the normal retirement age of sixty-five, but with the help of first one and later two talented lecturers, Val Williams and Norman Cattanach – plus assistance from the principal and other colleagues – a Centre for Journalism Studies was duly set up, with myself as director, and opened at the beginning of October. The basis of our plans, a one-year postgraduate course leading to work on newspapers, radio or television, proved to have been well laid.★ Before long twenty to thirty students were applying for every vacancy, most of whom on completing the course had little difficulty in finding jobs. For me contact with the students was exhilarating; I felt I was lucky indeed to have found such an enjoyable task so late in life – doubly lucky, I soon realized, because, in the depression which hit Fleet Street, very little of the freelance work I had been counting on would prove to be available.

Though my new life was interesting and active, imperceptibly the whole pattern of existence now began to change. Whereas formerly I had lived a life of almost continuous action – interrupted by occasional, not very frequent, spells of thought – I now began to spend time reading and thinking, even just looking out of the window at the sea, an inactivity I would once have found intolerable. Later this change would be accentuated when in 1975, after having been director of the journalism centre for five years, my contract ended and was not renewed. As a result of this changed pattern in our life Dorothy and I were brought into much more continuous contact and the basic differences in our natures began strongly to emerge.

Such differences showed themselves through incidents which were trivial, but whose effect was cumulative. We both received a good deal of correspondence, and when a letter arrived requiring an answer I would answer it rapidly and briefly. Dorothy would set it aside for a week or more, and then take all morning or all day over framing a reply. But the reply went to the heart of the situation, answering rather what the writer implied or wished to ask than what he or she had written. Meantime I would become exasperated as she searched, first for the original letter which had buried itself somewhere on her desk, and then for the right words in which to answer.

★Anyone interested in the launching of this course will find it fully described in 'Journalism Today: The Proceedings of the Institute of Journalists', Vol. 2, No. 4, Autumn 1971.

I was a thrower away. If printed matter arrived that had no immediate appeal; if I had looked briefly through a magazine or paper; if I found myself with something I no longer used or liked, I threw it out. Quite often, after I had thrown it out, one or other of us would want it back. Dorothy on the other hand was a hoarder. She kept books, magazines, catalogues which had interested her once and possibly might do so again. It was true that I kept notebooks, scantily filled, in which I often failed to put down events or thoughts I intended to record. But Dorothy not only kept notebooks, she kept books or boxes filled with recipes, book reviews, fashion notes – hoards of print that might one day come in handy.

But though she treasured and preserved much ephemeral matter, her thoughts, her concentration were turned inwards, and even when she was cutting up magazines or knitting something for herself or me, her mind was seldom on what she was doing. Her values, her concentration were inward and spiritual, whereas mine were material and practical. She judged all situations by her sense of what was right; I by my idea of what was convenient or advantageous. I was living in space–time, and she outside or beyond it. If she had been asked her ultimate aim in life, she would probably have replied, 'to reach a state of inner peace and calm'. Had I been asked mine I might, even now in my seventies, have answered, 'to see as much of the world as possible and spend my life as interestingly as I can'.

Besides being a keeper and preserver, Dorothy was also a sharer. She had always refused to be content with a surface relationship – newspapers at breakfast, separate daytime routines, a couple of hours watching television or reading, followed by bed at night. Now she was constantly seeking to prise me out of my shell and bring me into closer contact. 'We never really talk,' she would complain. 'We just live side by side without properly meeting. I don't know what you think and feel. I appreciate how much work you do and all you manage to get through. But can't we have at least *some* time – if only an hour each day – when I can tell you

301

what's going on in my mind, and you aren't in a hurry to be doing something else?'

'Yes, indeed. A good idea – we must try to work something out,' I would reply, as I edged towards the door or slid off into my study.

Evasion which had been easy, however, over the twenty years during which action predominated – when there was always somewhere else I 'ought' to be, or some other person I 'had' to meet – had become more difficult now that I spent nearly all my time at home. Long since, at one of our first meetings, Dorothy had concluded a long talk by asking me what was my attitude to truth, and I had replied: 'In the last resort I will accept the truth.' Now in the final years of life, it was evident I had reached the last resort – but what was this truth I had undertaken to accept?

As I looked back over the past I found my thoughts returning again and again to the few meetings I had had with Meher Baba on his visits to England in the 1950s. Baba had impressed me more than any other being I ever met, impressed me as living on a different plane of understanding and as seeing into the heart of everyone who came to him. I recalled how, the first time I had been in his presence, I was sitting as a journalist does, on the edge of every situation, an outsider looking in, personally uninvolved. Baba had concentrated his attention on Dorothy, his devoted follower for many years, and then, after some exchange of words and thoughts with her, had looked at me and asked, by means of signs to an attendant since he never spoke, why I had come. I replied, with the first words that came into my head, that I only wanted to see him. That would, I had no doubt, be the finish of the matter. We would shake hands, and leave Baba to continue with his silence while we went back into the world of telephones and buses.

But he had focused his dark eyes on mine and asked, 'And do you like me?' I had then found myself struggling to bring out the extraordinary declaration – which I yet knew to be the truth – 'I love you.' Finally, overcome by inhibition, I had to be content with a halting, conventional, 'Yes, I like you' . . . and we left.

We had seen Meher Baba again some four years later, on and off over a period of three days when he was once more visiting London, but never since that time, although twice when in India for press conferences, I had tried to contact him, only to learn that he was in seclusion, seeing no one. Baba did not himself write letters, but occasionally we and others had been allowed to write him a short letter. We also received from his sister Mani, who often acted as his secretary, a monthly newsletter reporting his activities. In this way we had maintained contact until, in January 1969 while Dorothy and I were in Minneapolis, we learned that, having told those about him that his work was now completed, Baba had died, or as Indians more accurately express it, he had 'laid down his body'.

It was too late to visit Meher Baba in the flesh, but there was a mass of literature about as well as by him, and this I now set myself to read, in search of that truth I had long since promised one day to accept. Much of it I had already glanced at, a little I had read carefully, but I now resolved to tackle the books in the way I had been accustomed to read when I was a student, memorizing and making notes. Baba, I was already aware, had not been one of those masters who build up fortunes in real estate or encourage their followers to give them Rolls-Royces for birthday presents. He had lived a life of extreme hardship and simplicity, travelling vast distances on foot or by the cheapest possible means, accepting whatever accommodation offered or, when in India, sleeping under trees or in the open.

Baba had founded no new religion: 'I have come,' he said, 'not to teach but to awaken.' The great religions of the world already contain everything man needs to know concerning his purpose here on earth and his relationship to God, and he called on all his followers to live in accordance with the principles of whatever religion they already held, but discarding meaningless ritual which serves only to obscure the truth while fostering spiritual pride. At the age of thirty-one Baba had started to observe silence, a silence which would remain unbroken for forty-four years. 'Because man has been deaf to the principles and precepts laid down by God in the past, in this present Avataric form I observe silence. You have asked for and been given enough words – it is now time to live them.'

The further and deeper I read into Meher Baba's writings, the further I was impelled to go; and the deeper I went, the harder the going became, but the wider the picture of life expanded. Dorothy had been reading Baba for many years and we would talk over together what I had lately read. One day as we were doing so I remarked: 'Of all the books about Meher Baba, there isn't one which gives a simple record of his life and an impression of his teachings which an ordinary man or woman can understand.' A day or two later Dorothy woke up with the idea that we should write a book ourselves and offer it to the firm of Gollancz which had published one or two books of mine in the past. Victor Gollancz was now dead, and his daughter Livia was in charge of the firm. Not expecting her to be familiar with the name of Meher Baba, I had prepared newspaper cuttings and leaflets – unnecessarily as it happened, since she knew of his life and work and was quite ready to commission the book we had in mind. When asked if we had a title in mind, Dorothy proposed 'Much Silence', from a Swahili proverb 'Much silence makes a mighty noise.'

We left the Gollancz office elated but apprehensive. 'All we have to do now,' I remarked as we got outside, 'is to write it' – a task which would prove far longer and more exacting than either of us imagined. To Livia's inquiry as to how long our book would take to write, I had answered easily 'about six months'. In fact it took us two years and came out only late in 1974.* In this country and in America it aroused little interest and virtually no reviews, but in India it became popular and several paperback editions sold out –

*Much Silence: The Life and Work of Meher Baba, Gollancz, London, 1974.

much to our surprise, since the book was intended as a simplified version for Westerners of ideas and beliefs already accepted in the East.*

But if the effect of *Much Silence* on readers appeared slight, its effect on the two writers was dramatic. Authors and married couples can set themselves few more frightening tasks than the joint production of a book. To minimize areas of disagreement, we had divided the work into halves: I was to write Baba's life story and Dorothy the section on his teachings, but each had to approve what the other produced, and in the effort to reach agreement the conflict between our two natures reached its climax, a climax which extended over many months. Battles would break out over a sentence or a phrase but in essence they were all over the same issue, one which summed up our contrasting attitudes to life: I was all for getting the book done, and Dorothy was determined to get it right. When she raised objections to some passage I had looked on as complete, I would object angrily: 'At this rate we shall still be writing *Much Silence* in ten years' time.' To this Dorothy, equally angrily, would retort: 'And if we aren't going to get it right, it won't be worth writing anyway.' When I still continued arguing, she would be driven back on a last defence: 'Well, it's *your* book, anyway. Write it whatever way you please. Only don't put my name on it. It's all yours.'

After sulking for a while, I would seek her out with apologies, coax her back into partnership, and we would set to work once more.

By the time we finished our task something unexpected had happened to us both. An underlying tension due to the difference in our natures had vanished from our lives. This was partly because we had come to understand and accept

*Of approximately 400 books and pamphlets about Meher Baba, perhaps the most important are the three volumes of his dictated *Discourses*, published in paperback by Sufism Reoriented Inc., 1290 Sutter Street, San Francisco, California 94109, 1967, and frequently reprinted; also *God Speaks: The Theme of Creation and its Purpose*, by Meher Baba, Dodd, Mead and Co., New York, 1955, reprinted 1973.

each other's different natures, and partly because we had grown more alike. Back in 1952 when we first settled down together we had been 'complements', opposite halves of the same coin, each to some extent making good deficiencies in the other. But now, after more than thirty years of life together, we had become 'affinities'; I had absorbed some of Dorothy's insistence on trying to reach the truth on any issue; she had acquired my determination to press on with whatever one undertakes until it is complete. When we differed now, we differed amicably, neither of us feeling any need to win arguments or justify mistakes. It had become easy to say 'I was wrong about this and you were right.'

The acceptance of another's right to be different, to stand for different values from one's own, in effect to challenge much that one takes for granted, faces every man or woman who enters upon marriage and it presents each one of us with the alternatives – to push all differences under the carpet, pretending they do not exist, or to live with and through them and eventually come out the other side. It is my belief that the increase of consciousness about oneself and one's own motives, with the widening out of life which results from wholehearted acceptance of a partner's different nature, constitutes one of the great rewards of married life. But it is a reward not easily secured.

The accepted symbol of married love consists of two inter-secting hearts, and twice at different stages of our life together I have given Dorothy pieces of jewellery carrying this poetic symbol. But the experience of married life is, I believe, for very few an experience of easy harmony and bliss. For most of those who choose to face reality rather than practise self-deception, married life might be symbolized not by delicately interlacing hearts but by two grindstones. Grindstones, however, wear themselves and one another smooth in course of time; and similarly in the course of time the partners in a marriage soften down the harshness and obstinacy in each other's characters until in the end they are no longer two individuals. They have become a pair, which is to say two in one.

* * *

Finally a man who is almost eighty years of age, who has tried to live in the flow of human existence and not take shelter from it, may be allowed to say in a few sentences what he feels he has learned from it all.

As I sit at my study window in the attics of an old Victorian house, I look out across the Bristol Channel to the coast of Somerset. It is the view Coleridge looked out on as he wrote 'The Ancient Mariner', and it is strangely similar to the view which enthralled me as a child when I gazed from the window of our little house at Aber, counting the flashes from the lighthouse on the point between Anglesey and Puffin Island. I shall be content if this is the last earthly view I look at, and neither Dorothy nor I can expect to look at views much longer.

In our case, being convinced believers in reincarnation, we expect to come back in another body and another age and to look at other views. But whether one accepts reincarnation or does not should make little difference to one's attitude to death. All the great religions, all great religious teachers, have declared with our own Meher Baba that the only part of man which dies is the physical body, to which, the older one grows, the more willing one becomes to say goodbye. The inner nature of each of us lives on. Neither Dorothy nor I therefore has any fear of death since in death, as the end to life, we do not believe.

But if one does not fear death, equally one need not fear the future to which, in our way of thinking, we must before very long return, for the future of the universe does not lie in the hands of man alone. There are beings and forces more powerful than man which guide his destiny as he stumbles towards a better, more loving, more understanding way of life. It is in man's nature to make mistakes and invite catastrophes, but the only final disaster would be to despair.

The thoughts and writings of Mother Julian, whose shrine at Norwich Dorothy once took me to visit, were forgotten or ignored for centuries, but have lately drawn much attention. Mother Julian left as her statement about the future of

307

mankind the words: 'All shall be well and all shall be well and all manner of thing shall be well.'

It was, of course, a long-term view. But Mother Julian was not hazarding a guess. She was speaking of what she saw and knew.

ALSO BY THE SAME AUTHOR
Of This Our Time   4370